SEX, CELIBACY, AND DEVIANCE

LITERATURE, RELIGION, AND POSTSECULAR STUDIES
Lori Branch, Series Editor

SEX, CELIBACY, AND DEVIANCE

THE VICTORIANS AND THE SONG OF SONGS

Duc Dau

THE OHIO STATE UNIVERSITY PRESS
COLUMBUS

Copyright © 2024 by The Ohio State University.
All rights reserved.

Library of Congress Cataloging-in-Publication Data
Names: Dau, Duc, author.
Title: Sex, celibacy, and deviance : the Victorians and the Song of songs / Duc Dau.
Other titles: Literature, religion, and postsecular studies.
Description: Columbus : The Ohio State University Press, [2024] | Series: Literature, religion, and postsecular studies | Includes bibliographical references and index. | Summary: "Illuminates the interplay of Victorian literature, religion, and culture via an analysis of how writers and artists employed and interpreted the Song of Songs to explore and challenge gender, romantic, and marital norms"—Provided by publisher.
Identifiers: LCCN 2023048043 | ISBN 9780814215036 (hardback) | ISBN 0814215033 (hardback) | ISBN 9780814283363 (ebook) | ISBN 0814283365 (ebook)
Subjects: LCSH: Brontë, Charlotte, 1816–1855—Criticism and interpretation. | Hardy, Thomas, 1840–1928—Criticism and interpretation. | Burne-Jones, Edward Coley, 1833–1898—Criticism and interpretation. | Traquair, Phoebe Anna—Criticism and interpretation. | Drane, Augusta Theodosia, 1823–1894—Criticism and interpretation. | Rossetti, Christina Georgina, 1830–1894—Criticism and interpretation. | Solomon, Simeon, 1840–1905—Criticism and interpretation. | Gray, John, 1866–1934—Criticism and interpretation. | Field, Michael—Criticism and interpretation. | Bible. Song of Solomon—In literature. | Bible. Song of Solomon—In art. | English literature—19th century—History and criticism. | Sex in literature. | Religion in literature. | Queer theology. | Feminist theology.
Classification: LCC PR468.S48 D38 2024 | DDC 820.9353809034—dc23/eng/20231226
LC record available at https://lccn.loc.gov/2023048043

Cover design by Melissa Dias-Mandoly
Text composition by Stuart Rodriguez
Type set in Minion Pro

♾ The paper used in this publication meets the minimum requirements of the American National Standard for Information Sciences—Permanence of Paper for Printed Library Materials. ANSI Z39.48-1992.

CONTENTS

Acknowledgments		vii
INTRODUCTION		1
CHAPTER 1	"Love Is God": Charlotte Brontë and Thomas Hardy	21
CHAPTER 2	Violence, Eroticism, and Art: Edward Burne-Jones and Phoebe Anna Traquair	42
CHAPTER 3	Celibacy, Sisterhoods, and Women's Poetry: Augusta Theodosia Drane and Christina Rossetti	64
CHAPTER 4	Queer Hands, Bodies, and Masculinities: Simeon Solomon and John Gray	92
CHAPTER 5	"Stronger than Death": Michael Field and the Culture of Death	118
CODA		141
Bibliography		147
Index		161

ACKNOWLEDGMENTS

I have discovered that erotic topics can take a surprising amount of work, time, money, and therapy to reach their climax. In other words, this project was not all fun and games. But funding bodies, colleagues, and friends made the journey worthwhile (I think). In the end, I experienced almost as much pleasure as suffering.

This project was funded by an Australian Research Council Discovery Early Career Researcher Award (DECRA) and the University of Western Australia Early Career Research Fellowship Support Program Award. The first award paid for my salary and travel allowance, while the second paid for my research assistant, Marina Gerzic, with whom I have become friends and coauthor of an article about queer and interspecies relationships in *Doctor Who*.

During my fellowship, I received the University of Western Australia Vice-Chancellor's Research Award for Early Career Investigators and a Baylor University Armstrong Browning Library Visiting Fellowship. Both awards provided additional research funding, for which I am appreciative.

For keeping me employed as a researcher for a period of time, I thank Rob Cover, Katie Ellis, and Mike Kent. These scholars guided me toward exciting areas of social research. The University of Western Australia Alumni Fund Grants enabled me to conduct mixed-methods research about the LGBTQ+ student experience at the university, breaking new ground for me in areas of service and research. I employed Penelope Strauss as a coresearcher on the project. This study and the opportunity to develop UWA's Transgender Policy are the two things of which I am most proud from my time at the university. For these opportunities, I thank Kent Anderson and Malcolm Fialho, respectively. I am also grateful to members of the UWA LGBTIQA+ Working Group, which I cochaired with Kent for a period of time. I thank my manager and colleagues at my current workplace for their continued understanding and support.

I am fortunate to have benefited from the wisdom, assistance, and generosity of academic colleagues and a few mentors. These people include: David Barrie, Nicholas Birns, Kirstie Blair, Megan Brown, Elizabeth Cumming, Louise D'Arcens, Dennis Denisoff, David Ellison, Misty Farquhar, Ann Gagné ("You're a wanker, number 9!"), Pamela Gilbert, Helen Groth, Zoë Hyde, Mark Jennings, Jongwoo Jeremy Kim, Mark Knight, Carolyn Lake, Lizzie Ludlow, Deborah Lutz, Andrew Lynch, Emma Mason, Simone Murray, Shale Preston, Christopher Reed, Jason Rudy, Talia Schaffer, Lesa Scholl, Madeleine Seys, Michelle Smith, Summer J. Star, Meg Tasker, Andrew Tate, Mandy Treagus, Jessica White, Tess Williams, and respondents to my queries on the VICTORIA online discussion forum. And, of course, Kieran Dolin and Fred Roden.

I am indebted to staff and librarians who assisted me at the British Library, British Museum, Brontë Parsonage Museum, Huntington Library, New York Public Library, Morgan Library and Museum, National Library of Congress, Scottish National Library, and at the various special collections of Columbia, Harvard, Princeton, Toronto, and Yale. I also wish to thank staff I had contact with at the Birmingham Museum and Art Gallery, Hugh Lane Gallery, Jewish Museum, Leamington Spa Art Gallery and Museum, and Scottish National Gallery. I have also benefited from the online resources of the Simeon Solomon Research Archive. Whoever set up archive.org is a lifesaver, to exaggerate only slightly. Many thanks to those who assisted me at UWA's Library (especially the interlibrary loan staff), the Office of Research, and the Humanities Office; a special mention goes out to Richard Small.

I cannot speak highly enough of the staff, faculty, and students attached to Baylor University's Armstrong Browning Library. I was a lucky recipient of their generosity and southern hospitality during my time as a visiting fellow. Christi Klempnauer ensured that I felt at home, and she went above and beyond when I was suddenly overcome by an awful bout of hay fever for the first time in my life. Joshua King hosted me at the library and at his house for dinner. Elizabeth Travers Parker lent me a bike for the month and drove to me to Austin for a day trip—I still remember our conversations in the car. I would also like to thank Cynthia Burgess, Melvin Schuetz, Jennifer Borderud, and Melinda Creech for their assistance.

The sisters at St. Dominic's Convent in Stone kindly allowed me to stay over for a few nights while I pored over Augusta Theodosia Drane's archives during the day. They also provided meals, for which I am grateful. Ashleigh Lin and Kelly Somers hosted me when I was in Birmingham and drove me to St. Helen's in Darley Dale to view Edward Burne-Jones's stained-glass windows.

I would like to thank colleagues at the following associations and gatherings for their feedback and guidance on portions of the project. These include the North American Victorian Studies Association; the Australasian Victorian Studies Association; the Arts and Feeling in Nineteenth-Century Literature and Culture conference at Birkbeck College; the Feeling (for) the Premodern Symposium hosted by the ARC Centre of Excellence for the History of Emotions at UWA; the Nineteenth-Century Studies Seminar Series at Anglia Ruskin University; the Monash Nineteenth-Century Studies Research Unit Seminars at Monash University; and the Friday Talk at the Lawrence Wilson Art Gallery at UWA.

An earlier version of chapter 5 was published as "'Stronger than death': The Song of Songs in Michael Field's Poetry and Life-Writing," *Religion and Literature* 50 (2018): 17–38. Many thanks to Editor in Chief Romana Huk for permission to reuse a version in this book.

At The Ohio State University Press, I thank Editor Ana Maria Jimenez-Moreno for her patience (she's used to my thanking her for this). I'd like to thank her predecessor, Lindsay Martin, as well as Kristen Elias Rowley, Lori Branch, Elizabeth Zaleski, Chloe Phillips, and Stuart Rodriguez. The talented Melissa Dias-Mandoly designed the cover. I also appreciate the generous feedback and kind words from the anonymous reviewers of my book proposal and completed manuscript. OSUP was my first choice of press because of its excellent publication record in nineteenth-century literature as well as literature and theology. I am so glad that this book has found a home with them.

I am grateful to family members and friends who checked in on me, listened with kindness, and nodded in sympathy over a project that consumed my life for far longer than I had hoped. In the ironic words of one of my friends, Claire Bowen, "definitely getting some writing done." Finally, I thank my chosen family: you are my lilies among thorns.

INTRODUCTION

> "Jude," she said brightly, when he had finished and come
> back to her; "will you let me make you a *new* New Testa-
> ment—like the one I made for myself at Christminster?"
> "O yes. How was that made?"
> "I altered my old one by cutting up all the Epistles and Gospels
> into separate *brochures,* and re-arranging them in chronologi-
> cal order as written, beginning the book with Thessalonians, fol-
> lowing on with the Epistles, and putting the Gospels much
> further on. Then I had the volume rebound. My University friend
> Mr. —— —but never mind his name, poor boy—said it was an
> excellent idea. I know that reading it afterwards made it twice
> as interesting as before, and twice as understandable."
> "H'm," said Jude, with a sense of sacrilege.
> —Thomas Hardy, *Jude the Obscure,* 157

> Our modern sense of the Bible is so limited, so closed, so pious, that
> it will inevitably be blasphemed against from within the Bible itself.
> —Yvonne Sherwood, *Biblical Blaspheming,* 3

HIGHER CRITICISM AND THE SONG OF SONGS

In Thomas Hardy's *Jude the Obscure* (1895), Sue Bridehead tells her cousin Jude Fawley that she is able to improve the Bible, making it "twice as interesting as before, and twice as understandable." Jude, who has designs on being a church minister, is shocked and distressed by her revisionary, or even blasphemous, stance toward not only the Bible but also the city of Christminster, where he had long hoped to study though without success. Earlier he had exclaimed "How modern you are!" when she had maintained that she would rather sit in the railway than the Cathedral because, in her words, the railway is "the centre of the town life now; the Cathedral has had its day!"[1] Likewise, Christminster, filled with cathedrals, and to which Jude still holds an attachment, is "in the middle ages."[2] Christminster stands in not simply for Oxford but, of course, Christianity. Sue calls for something radical: "The

---

1. Hardy, *Jude the Obscure,* 139.
2. Hardy, *Jude the Obscure,* 139.

2 • INTRODUCTION

mediaevalism at Christminster must go, be sloughed off, or Christminster itself will have to go."[3] For Sue, Victorian medievalism represents outmoded ways of thinking and of reading the Bible. Earlier in the novel, Jude encounters a specter in Christminster who apostrophizes the city as one "so unravaged by the fierce intellectual life of our century."[4] The biblical book that Sue uses to demonstrate the outmoded nature of Christian hermeneutics is the Song of Songs (or Song of Solomon).[5]

The "medievalism" of Christminster, and that which it represents, is a reminder of the medieval practice of chaining Bibles in English churches, ostensibly to protect them from theft, mishandling, and vandalism. And yet, as Hugh S. Pyper argues in *The Unchained Bible: Cultural Appropriations of Biblical Texts*, "the subversive misreading of this enchainment as a symbol of a book in captivity to the established church is hard to suppress."[6] Once released from its chains, "the Bible proves to be a text that gets everywhere and which undergoes surprising and sometimes contradictory metamorphoses."[7] Indeed, the history of biblical reception demonstrates that reception—which, like Ika Willis, I conceive in a broad sense as including how audiences both interpret and use a text[8]—is not a passive act. Nor is it always reverential. We can see that there is more than one kind of Bible, and it is undoubtedly the unchained Bible to which Sue refers when she asks Jude if she can make him "a *new* New Testament." As something cut up and rearranged, her new text is literally and intellectually untethered from orthodox reception. Like Sue's New Testament, the unchained Bible is both recognizable and unrecognizable. While familiar in many aspects, its unconventional interpretation and reordering render it "*new.*" Its blasphemy comes from the text itself, to cite Yvonne Sherwood from the second epigraph of this introduction. In some instances, particularly in relation to queer artists, the unchained Bible allows for messages to be transmitted in familiar if not licensed guises.

Sue rails against the chained Bible by attacking allegorical, typological, and desexualized readings of the Song of Songs. She raises the topic of the chapter headings of the Song of Songs, which are found in the King James Version. Accompanying these headings are expositions, such as, for Chapter 1, "The church's love unto Christ" (verse 1), "She confesseth her deformity" (verse 5), "Christ directeth her to the shepherds' tents" (verse 8), and "The church and

---

3. Hardy, *Jude the Obscure*, 155.
4. Hardy, *Jude the Obscure*, 82.
5. Hardy, *Jude the Obscure*, 157.
6. Pyper, *Unchained Bible*, 2.
7. Pyper, *Unchained Bible*, 2.
8. Willis, *Reception*, 1.

Christ congratulate one another" (verse 12). Sue values a historicized understanding of the Song of Songs, making her similar to the character of Alfred Hardie in Charles Reade's *Hard Cash* (1863). In a canceled passage from the novel (running over several paragraphs), Alfred savagely upbraids his sister, who upholds the allegorical interpretation of the Song of Songs. Instead, he offers a historical context for its authorship and purpose:

> This story, faintly told and overloaded with fulsome expressions and similes, as inapt and hyperbolical as the similes in Solomon's genuine works are just and sober, was sung at Jewish bridals in this sense for centuries and was written eleven hundred years before Christ was born; yet you think to please the God of truth by pretending that it is all about Christ and the Christian church and that Solomon is the writer.[9]

Alfred critiques typological interpretation, in which the Old Testament is believed to foreshadow and be fulfilled by the New Testament. This form of reading remained an influential mode of interpretation in Victorian theology and literature.[10]

The examples above demonstrate that some British novelists were reading the Bible through newer methods of exegesis, notably, higher criticism. Also known as historical criticism, higher criticism came into prominence in the late eighteenth and early nineteenth centuries in Germany, was brought into England by Samuel Taylor Coleridge, and became more widespread through the publication of George Eliot's translations of David Friedrich Strauss's *The Life of Jesus, Critically Examined* (1846) and Ludwig Feuerbach's *Essence of Christianity* (1854). Hardy's library contained Eliot's translation of *The Life of Jesus*, which aims to uncover the historical Jesus.[11] Though the edition dates from 1898, four years after *Jude the Obscure* was first serialized, it is almost certain that Hardy was familiar with Strauss's work before that date. Indeed, his library contains Strauss's two-volume *A New Life of Jesus*, which was written for the layperson, whereas *The Life of Jesus* was intended for theologians; and yet, as Strauss declares, "So greatly have things changed in the interval! The general public can no longer be considered unprepared for inquiries of this nature."[12] It was a volume called *Essays and Reviews*, however, that caused widespread controversy among the Victorians. Written by a group of liberal Anglican theologians and published in 1860, three years before *Hard Cash*,

---

9. Bowers, "Canceled 'Song of Solomon' Passage," 230.
10. See Landow, *Victorian Types, Victorian Shadows*.
11. Millgate, "Thomas Hardy's Library at Max Gate," 247.
12. Strauss, *New Life of Jesus*, vol. 1, vii.

Essays and Reviews incorporated higher criticism and nineteenth-century science. *Essays and Reviews* outsold Charles Darwin's *The Origin of Species*, published a year earlier, which had sold all 1,250 copies on the day of publication, with 1,200 new copies printed three months later.[13] In contrast, nine editions of *Essays and Reviews* sold no fewer than 17,000 copies in the first year of publication.[14] Hardy read *Essays and Reviews* when it was newly published and made claims of being "impress[ed]" by it.[15] Charles LaPorte argues of the "hermeneutic revolution" that "British Anglo-Catholics, Roman Catholics, and Jews felt the force of the higher criticism, yet Protestant believers felt it especially keenly in this context because of their theoretical commitment to the Bible's independence from (or self-sufficient sovereignty over) subsequent traditions of interpretation."[16] In his essay for *Essays and Reviews*, Rowland Williams says, "Devotion raises time present into the sacredness of the past; while Criticism reduces the strangeness of the past into harmony with the present."[17] This mode of interpretation brings clarity to, that is, it demystifies "the strangeness" of, a text composed in a different time.

Higher criticism exerted an undeniable influence on the reception of the Song of Songs. In other words, for a number of nineteenth-century theologians, though of course not all, the Song of Songs was no longer chained to centuries-old exegesis. Like Sue Bridehead and Alfred Hardie, these theologians no longer held onto the authority of allegorical or typological interpretation. Hardy satirizes this *volte-face* in his poem "The Respectable Burgher on the Higher Criticism" (1901), whereby "Reverend Doctors now declare," among other things, "That Solomon sang the fleshly Fair, / And gave the Church no thought whate'er" (lines 1, 13–14).[18] Nineteenth-century French Protestant theologian Albert Réville writes in a summary of the reception history of the Song of Songs,

> [Hugo] Grotius contributed, to a great extent, to confirm the reasoning which so long maintained the allegorical interpretation. . . . The Canticle interpreted literally is immoral. If so, there is then an immoral book in the Bible. Such a conclusion is impious. It is therefore necessary, if its literal interpretation be immoral, to interpret it allegorically. The Voltairian [*sic*]

---

13. Nixon, "Kill[ing] Our Souls," 34.
14. Nixon, "Kill[ing] Our Souls," 34.
15. Hardy, *Life of Thomas Hardy*, vol. 1, 43.
16. LaPorte, *Victorian Poets*, 16–17.
17. Williams, "Bunsen's Biblical Researches," 50.
18. Hardy, *Complete Poetical Works*, vol. 2.

unbelief was enchanted at coming into contact with such a delightful confu-
sion of reasoning.[19]

Réville rejects the allegorical interpretation of the Song of Songs and the
long-held belief that it was written by Solomon. He does not, however, declare
it impious: "It is very far from constituting an immoral book in its general
conception."[20] Though there be passages that to modern sensibilities might
seem "indelicate," he claims that "the fundamental intention of the poem is
profoundly moral and beautiful."[21]

Higher criticism did not always lead to the same evaluation of the Song
of Songs. While Réville considered the Song of Songs to have moral and aesthetic worth, Unitarian minister William Maccall denounced it in a lecture as
"the chief stench in the Bible."[22] Like Réville, Maccall did not believe Solomon
to be the author of the Songs of Songs. Citing the work of scholarly analysis,
he argues that, since its Hebrew is that of the Exile, a few hundred years after
Solomon, the text could not have been written by the legendary king. Maccall
goes on to explain what genre the Song of Songs might be and how a book
of "hot amatory breathings"[23] might have made its way into the canon. (He
argues that it made its way into the Hebrew Bible before the individual books
became canon.) Dismissing the possibility that it might be a drama—"the
orientals, and especially the Hebrews, have never succeeded in, and seldom
attempted dramatic poetry"—he concludes that "the tendency at present is, to
admit that the Song of Songs is a cluster of amatory poems and fragments of
poems. One German critic has found in the Song of Songs as many as fourteen distinct poems and six fragments."[24] Influenced by higher criticism, Maccall's reading demystifies the Song of Songs, but his attitude toward the text is
not as favorable as that held by either Réville or Sue Bridehead.

For Sue, and no doubt her author, the Song of Songs is a book about erotic
love and desire—of "hot amatory breathings," as it were. Jude comes to a similar interpretation of the text as a result of his love for Sue and because of her
influence on his thinking. While Jude's initial shock is a foil for Sue's approach
to scripture, Sue in fact represents Strauss's intended reader for *A New Life*

---

19. Réville, *Song of Songs*, 10. Jude declares Sue "Voltairean" shortly after she offers to make
him "a *new* New Testament." Hardy, *Jude the Obscure*, 157.

20. Réville, *Song of Songs*, 19.

21. Réville, *Song of Songs*, 19.

22. Maccall, *Song of Songs*, 3.

23. Maccall, *Song of Songs*, 5.

24. Maccall, *Song of Songs*, 5.

of Jesus: an "educated or thoughtful person."[25] Thus, when Jude decides that Christminster is no longer what he seeks—saying, "I care for something higher"—Sue responds, "And I for something broader, truer."[26] Her reading of the Song of Songs captures this "broader, truer" perspective. After Jude declares her Voltairean, she proclaims, "People have no right to falsify the Bible! I *hate* such humbug as could attempt to plaster over with ecclesiastical abstractions such ecstatic, natural, human love as lies in that great and passionate song!"[27] The Song of Songs is for her a paean to love, sex, and women's agency, yet its reputation has become distorted by "humbug" interpretations. Sue adds, "What I insist on is, that to explain such verses as this: 'Whither is thy beloved gone, O thou fairest among women?' by the note: '*The Church professeth her faith*' is supremely ridiculous!"[28] Sue unveils the mystique that centuries of Judeo-Christian allegory has placed over the text. Smitten, Jude declares, "I am—too inclined just now to apply the words profanely," and suddenly quotes from Song of Songs 1:8: "You know *you* are fairest among women to me, come to that!"[29] While Sue's profanity derives from her interrogation of the church's traditional interpretation of the text, Jude's is driven by a desire for Sue that dislodges from his heart his first love, Christminster, "that ecclesiastical romance in stone."[30]

UNCHAINING THE SONG OF SONGS: QUEER AND FEMINIST THEOLOGIES

What interests me in *Sex, Celibacy, and Deviance: The Victorians and the Song of Songs* is the unchained Bible. In particular, I am interested in one biblical book, the Song of Songs, and how it has been received in feminist, queer, and often materialist ways in Victorian literature and art. In considering the unchained Bible, I use Richard Terdiman's concept of the "counter-discourse" as a starting point for thinking about how, through complex modes of translation and transformation, alternative styles of reading and reinscription spring from the dominant discourses they contest.[31] New modes of reading the Bible led to new ways of writing about it in Victorian literature. While

---

25. Strauss, *New Life of Jesus*, vol. 1, vii.
26. Hardy, *Jude the Obscure*, 156.
27. Hardy, *Jude the Obscure*, 157.
28. Hardy, *Jude the Obscure*, 158.
29. Hardy, *Jude the Obscure*, 158.
30. Hardy, *Jude the Obscure*, 31.
31. Terdiman, *Discourse/Counter-Discourse*, 67–70.

writers such as Charlotte Brontë and Christina Rossetti considered themselves religious and therefore not questioning the authority of the Bible, their feminist reception of the Song of Songs was not always conventional, as we shall see. Indeed, the Song of Songs is a prime candidate for unchained, and more specifically, counter-readings by women, same-sex attracted authors and artists, celibates, effeminate men, and those outside the established church. The Song of Songs was, and continues to be, a different book to different people, and no other book from the Bible has been so variously interpreted.[32]

This book contributes to the field of reception studies and its intersection with gender and queer studies. The reception of the Song of Songs is inseparable from issues of power relations and their interrogation. Given that I am influenced by liberation theologies, particularly contemporary queer and feminist interpretations, I turn most of my focus on those whose gender, gender expression, sexuality, or depictions of sexuality situated them outside the political center.[33] For one reason or another, these artists or the characters they depicted existed on what Gayle Rubin calls "the outer limits," which is beyond the "charmed circle" of acceptable sexual behavior.[34] I claim a goal of queer theology, which is to investigate "what forms of non-normative love, touch, marriage and sex effectively challenge patriarchal power, and how such non-normative forms can assist in the remodeling of 'normative' relationships."[35] Similarly, I am enamored of Marcella Althaus-Reid and Lisa Isherwood's proclamation that queer theology is "a radical form of the 'love-talk of theology,' that is, a theology which introduces a profound questioning into the ways of love in our lives as individuals and as society, and the things love can do in our world."[36] Queer theology is thus "from the margins which wants to remain at the margins."[37] One's relationship to power determines both one's interpretation of the Bible and the biblical books to which one is drawn. For instance, Jeff Nunokawa and Amy Sickels recount a story of Oscar Wilde's rebellion at Magdalen chapel, Oxford. Wilde was to read the weekly lesson, from Deuteronomy 16, but to the assembled congregation, including Queen Victoria's youngest son, he chose to read from Song of Songs 1:1–2: "The song of songs which is Solomon's. Let him kiss me with the kisses of his mouth: for

---

32. Pope, *Anchor Bible*, 17.

33. For more on queer and feminist theologies as liberation theologies, see Dau, "Reception," 113–23.

34. Rubin, "Thinking Sex," 281.

35. Dickinson and Toomey, "Continuing Relevance of 'Queer' Theology," 4.

36. Althaus-Reid and Isherwood, "Thinking Theology and Queer Theory," 303.

37. Althaus-Reid and Isherwood, "Thinking Theology and Queer Theory," 304.

thy love is better than wine."[38] First, I must acknowledge that Wilde's social status enabled him to perform this kind of literary subversion. Second, it is possible to see why he used the Song of Songs in an act of rebellion, given the text's uneasy status in the biblical canon.[39] The Song of Songs is canonical, but its erotic language invites a level of unease.

"There is a long-standing difficulty for critics in knowing what to make of Wilde's interest in Christianity," argues Mark Knight.[40] The same could be said of the "difficulty" for some commentators in knowing what to make of the Song of Songs' place in the Bible. Yet, I argue that it is in the text's equivocal reception throughout history that queer authors could find purchase. Queers like Wilde turned to an ostensibly heterosexual text such as the Song of Songs to describe and affirm queer desires because they saw the vilified status of their desires in the strangeness (or queerness) of the Song of Songs within the biblical canon. Wilde's one-act play *Salomé* (1893), which featured provocative illustrations by the queer artist Aubrey Beardsley, uses the Song of Songs to subversive and queer effect. Upon meeting with the prophet Jokanaan, Salomé alludes to the biblical passage that Wilde read out at Magdalen chapel by boldly declaring, "I will kiss thy mouth, Jokanaan. I will kiss thy mouth," and "Let me kiss thy mouth, Jokanaan."[41] Moreover, a series of long speeches, "in which she alternately adores and reviles the different aspects of his body, his hair, and his mouth," are "plainly evocative of the descriptions of the lovers in the Song of Songs."[42] Helen Tookey points to the radical act of Wilde ascribing to Jokanaan *"female* signifiers":

If we look closely at Salomé's speeches we find that, through correspondences of images and wording, she connects Jokanaan not to the man of the Song but to the woman. Jokanaan's hair is black—'there is nothing in the world so black as thy hair.' The male lover of the Song has hair of 'finest gold' (5:11); but the woman's hair is 'lustrous black' (7:5). Even more explicitly, Salomé describes Jokanaan's mouth as 'a band of scarlet on a tower of ivory. It is like a pomegranate cut with a knife of ivory.' Similarly, the man in the Song describes his lover's neck as 'a tower of ivory' (7:4). Twice repeated are the lines 'Your parted lips behind your veil are like a pomegranate cut open' (4:3; 6:7).[43]

---

38. Nunokawa and Sickels, *Oscar Wilde*, 25–26.
39. Meyers, *Discovering Eve*, 177.
40. Knight, "Wilde's Uses of Religion," 206.
41. Wilde, *Salomé*, 23, 24.
42. Tookey, "Fiend That Smites," 34–35.
43. Tookey, "Fiend That Smites," 35.

Tookey believes that when Salomé's desire reaches its climax, the play hints at both the menstrual and homoerotic nature of the kiss: "The taste of love, for Salomé, is the taste of blood."[44] I would argue that the description of Jokanaan's body might equally be that of a feminized or queer man, with the bitter taste of blood on his mouth precipitating the kiss of death (at least in the eyes of the law) to any man who desires him. Two years later, Wilde would justify male-male attraction in his trial for indecency by appealing to the cultural authority of Plato, Michelangelo, and Shakespeare. Yet, he and other queer authors and artists also turned to the canonical Song of Songs to describe and affirm queer desires. After all, might a text that espoused the ascendancy of love over death also espouse all forms of love?[45]

In addition to queer theology, the exploration of Song of Songs reception is an ideal enterprise for feminist theology. The main speaker of the text is a woman, making it a superlative feminist text. One of the endeavors of feminist theology is to recover female perspectives in the Bible, wresting it from male-centric perspectives and ensuring the Bible's relevance to women. This endeavor includes the rehabilitation of Eve's reputation, the location of female communities, and the recovery of women's stories. The final aim explains the place of the Song of Songs in feminist theology. Athalya Brenner states,

> The text promotes opportunities for discussing female culture, its reclamation, and the affinities of the [Song of Songs] with other female poems in the Bible (such as the so-called Song of Miriam, Exod. 15; and the Song of Deborah, Judg. 5). In short, it is relevant to quite a few of the issues that have stayed in the foreground of feminist biblical criticism for decades.[46]

In relation to the Victorian period, the centrality of the lover's voice and perspective in the Song of Songs aligns with what Kerry McSweeney observes to be the era's increased emphasis on the female point of view in textual representations of romantic relationships.[47] Moreover, F. Elizabeth Gray argues that Victorian women poets appealed to the biblical authority of the Song of Songs to suggest female agency in relationships between men and women.[48] Women's devotional poetry was also one of the most widely produced and

---

44. Tookey, "Fiend That Smites," 35.

45. For a discussion on allegorical interpretations of the Song of Songs as being acts of queer reading, see Moore, *God's Beauty Parlor*, 27–28.

46. Brenner, "Reading the Hebrew Bible," 28.

47. McSweeney, *Supreme Attachments*, 8.

48. Gray, *Christian and Lyric Tradition*, 149–50.

read genres at the time.[49] Even so, few critics have discussed their use of the Song of Songs at length. For example, unlike most sonnet sequences, Elizabeth Barrett Browning's *Sonnets from the Portuguese* (1850) is written from the perspective of a female speaker. Like the woman in the Song of Songs, Barrett Browning's speaker calls the object of her affection "Beloved."[50] This kind of address also moves against the grain of the traditional sonnet sequence in which the male speaker, the lover, addresses the woman as his beloved.

SEX, CELIBACY, AND DEVIANCE; OR, WHY THE SONG OF SONGS?

The title of this book signals the unique relationship between sex, celibacy, and deviance in the nineteenth century. It is obvious why aspects of sexual behavior could be considered socially deviant, yet few readers are likely to know why celibacy might be regarded as such. The controversy over celibacy revolved around denominational antagonism. Catholic sisterhoods, for instance, were a fixture of anti-Catholic discourse in England throughout much of the nineteenth century, but especially so during the 1850s, following the reestablishment of the Catholic hierarchy in 1850. Anti-Catholicism was endemic in the popular imagination, where it was used to establish and maintain national, religious, and sexual norms. "In the multi-voiced religious culture of Victorian Britain," notes Maureen Moran, "anti-Catholic mockery was a popular activity for politicians, historians and sages as well as churchmen."[51] Given the intertwining of church and state, engaging in anti-Catholicism was a popular method of asserting Protestantism and preserving religious and national norms, especially if these norms were deemed to be under threat.[52] Furthermore, anti-Catholic discourse was another way of establishing the boundaries of nationalism, respectability, and sexuality. George Mosse reminds us of the relationship between nationalism and respectability in the nineteenth century. In their mutually supportive roles, "both have condemned the unconventional as threatening to the state and to society: normal and abnormal behaviour must be clearly defined and distinguished from one another in order to guarantee a happy and healthy world."[53] The eighteenth-century confluence of revolution, nationalism, and religious revival, along with the emerging influence

---

49. Gray, *Christian and Lyric Tradition,* 180.

50. Barrett Browning, *Works of Elizabeth Barrett Browning,* vol. 1.

51. Moran, *Catholic Sensationalism,* 2.

52. Moran, *Catholic Sensationalism,* 2.

53. Mosse, "Nationalism and Respectability," 221.

of the middle class, matured in the nineteenth century with the drive toward respectability, particularly in the realm of sex.[54]

Many English Protestants considered Catholicism a foreign force, something wholly other.[55] Geographically speaking, it was synonymous with Rome, in particular, and the Mediterranean, in general. Britons and northern Europeans of various sexual attractions traveled to the Mediterranean to loosen their sexual inhibitions.[56] Concepts of sexual deviance often have commonly established national borders, as exemplified by the stigmatizing association of sexually transmissible illnesses such as syphilis with foreign countries and therefore with subsequent invasion.[57] Likewise, a great deal of anti-Catholic literature was of a lurid and sexualized nature in order to emphasize the uprightness of Protestantism and the otherness of Catholicism. John Henry Newman declared in 1851,

> The popular demand is for the prodigious, the enormous, the abominable, the diabolical, the impossible. It must be shown that all priests are monsters of hypocrisy, that all nunneries are dens of infamy, that all bishops are the embodied plenitude of savageness and perfidy.[58]

The anti-Catholic sensationalism of which Newman speaks here draws on the sexual excesses of the gothic tradition and its depiction of Catholic religious orders.[59]

Yet religious celibacy was as admonished and feared as much as syphilis or a foreign invader. Thus, for years after his conversion in 1845, Newman continued to be treated with suspicion by "the majority of his countrymen, and public attacks on his 'treachery' were not uncommon."[60] Newman had betrayed his country through his conversion. Commentators, chiefly the Anglican clergyman and novelist Charles Kingsley, defined Newman's conversion as a "perversion."[61] Not only did he pervert to Rome and therefore deviate from the true faith of England, but his celibacy, sexual ambiguity, and effeminacy spoke to the traditionally gendered use of perversion to signify a religiously wayward woman such as a heretic.[62] Coincidentally, Newman's

---

54. Mosse, "Nationalism and Respectability," 221–22.
55. Buckton, "Unnatural State," 360.
56. Aldrich, *Seduction of the Mediterranean,* xi, 69.
57. See Gilman, "AIDS and Syphilis," 91–92.
58. Newman, *Present Position of Catholics,* 140.
59. Moran, *Catholic Sensationalism,* 14; Wheeler, *Old Enemies,* 214.
60. Buckton, "Unnatural State," 359.
61. Buckton, "Unnatural State," 360–61.
62. Buckton, "Unnatural State," 361.

confirmation name was Mary. Likewise, Catholic nuns, or daughters of Mary, moved against the ideals of respectable English femininity by repudiating the country's Protestant norms of marriage and motherhood.[63] The popular imagination envisioned secretive religious spaces devoted to celibacy and sisterhood, where women were overseen not by men but by other women. Through a lens of gendered anti-Catholicism, the public could not help but imagine other perversions such as sexual extravagance. In fact, a refusal to differentiate between perversions, and the belief that one inevitably led to another, can serve to emphasize the contrast between abnormal and normal sexuality.[64] By this thinking, the nun could be the virgin and the whore, the Virgin Mary and Mary Magdalene in one.

This book is the first to explore the influence of the Song of Songs in Victorian literature and culture. More than 350 hermeneutical readings of the Song of Songs were published in Great Britain and America in the nineteenth century.[65] The biblical text was also translated into a range of British dialects such as North Yorkshire, Lancashire, Northumberland, Newcastle, Durham, and Lowland Scotch, among others. Despite its presence "everywhere in English literature,"[66] there has hitherto been no major study of the literary and cultural impact of the Song of Songs in the nineteenth century. While a number of essays and book chapters have explored the influence of the Song of Songs on Victorian literature and art, no extended study has been produced on the topic. This lack is striking, given that the century is known for its religious debates and concerns, its increased production and popularity of romantic verse and novels, and, moreover, its propagation of the modern concept of "romance." It is also surprising, given the text's widespread cultural presence. Indeed, the Song of Songs appears in surprising places, including sixty-three sermons by Baptist minister Charles Haddon Spurgeon as well as Havelock Ellis's translation of Ernest Renan's French-language dramatization.[67] As the Bible's only love poem, the Song of Songs is undoubtedly the canonical Judeo-Christian book on love. The Song of Songs therefore provided the Victorians with an authoritative and literary language for love, marriage, mourning, sex, and religious celibacy. Despite what I have outlined, the

---

63. Peschier, *Nineteenth-Century Anti-Catholic Discourses,* 78–79.

64. See Mosse, "Nationalism and Respectability," 223–24.

65. Paxton, *Willful Submission,* 5.

66. Exum, "Song of Songs," 272.

67. Larsen, *People of One Book,* 257; Renan, *Song of Songs as a Drama.* The original date of Ellis's translation of the Renan text is 1878, that is, from Ellis's early days in Australia, before he returned to England to train as a doctor.

extent of the text's influence on nineteenth-century literature and culture has not been adequately detailed in a study until now.

Studies about Victorian romantic relationships tend to focus on secular themes,[68] whereas I aim to redress the imbalance by turning my attention to religious concepts upon which Victorian depictions of love, sex, celibacy, and marriage rest. By exploring the importance of the Song of Songs, I demonstrate how people saw themselves and their experiences reflected in a biblical text. Exploring the various ways by which Victorians of different religious, social, and sexual backgrounds used the Song of Songs in their work, I look at the fashioning of, and challenges to, norms of romantic love, marriage, and gender roles. Moreover, by addressing the social relevance of the Song of Songs in relation to shifting and conflicting religious, gender, marital, and sexual contexts, my study provides a fresh perspective on Victorian literature and culture. Spanning the early decades of the era to the first two decades of the twentieth century, this book explores poetry, novels, and visual culture. Key authors and artists in the study include Charlotte Brontë, Thomas Hardy, Christina Rossetti, Edward Burne-Jones, Simeon Solomon, John Gray, and Michael Field. In the process, I break new ground with in-depth explorations of two accomplished Victorians who have received little critical attention from a literary perspective: the Irish-born Scottish artist Phoebe Anna Traquair and the Catholic religious leader Augusta Theodosia Drane.

The book is part of a broader movement to address what Frederick Roden calls the "secularization of Victorian studies."[69] The Bible remained an influential book throughout the Victorian era. Sue Bridehead's own attempts to create a *new* New Testament attest to the Bible's enduring cultural and religious power. And while, as we shall see, Jane Eyre recognizes undesirable qualities in St. John Rivers's brand of evangelical Christianity, she remains firmly Christian. Indeed, the common understanding of Victorian literature as a contest between faith and doubt is both reductive and clichéd. The "well-trodden histories of secularization [in the nineteenth century] . . . tend to lean heavily upon an idea that religion was actually dying in mid-century Britain," argues LaPorte.[70] In speaking of poetry, he notes that academic trends have dictated our understanding of religion in the Victorian era, for poems about religious doubt seem a more attractive prospect for study, both in content and in form, than religious poetry. Similarly, Gray asserts that literary scholars over the past fifty years "have tended overwhelmingly to focus on and privilege the

---

68. See Corbett, *Family Likeness*; Michie, *Vulgar Question of Money*; Schaffer, *Romance's Rival*; Shanley, *Feminism, Marriage, and the Law*.

69. Roden, *Same-Sex Desire*, 7.

70. LaPorte, *Victorian Poets*, 2.

poetry of questioning and of doubt, which . . . has skewed our understanding of the significance of religious devotion in the century's creative work."[71] Both LaPorte and Gray argue convincingly that religion remained a vital part of Victorian culture, just as historians of religion have recently provided evidence that, instead of being a postreligious era, there was "tremendous vitality throughout the century."[72] Indeed, Timothy Larsen notes that,

> although the Victorians were awash in texts, . . . the Bible loomed uniquely large in Victorian culture in fascinating and underexplored ways. The extent of the Bible's dominance, presence, and reach has to be encountered in the specifics of Victorian lives to be grasped fully."[73]

In short, the Bible was "a dominant presence in Victorian thought and culture."[74] It was "the foundational textbook in schools and the main volume through which people gained basic literacy skills."[75] For much of the nineteenth century, children learned to read at Sunday schools, church-sponsored schools or religious organizations, and independent, working-class schools.[76] Both within and beyond the universities, biblical scholarship had a wider circulation than ever before, culminating in the creation of the New Revised Version (NRV) of 1881 and 1885—the first authorized translation since the time of King James.[77]

The Church of England continued to exert an influence on literature and culture, with Kirstie Blair arguing that poets who were Dissenters and Catholics "were at least in part forced to define themselves in relation to Anglican norms, including poetic norms."[78] Mark Knight and Emma Mason also recognize that

> expressions of faith outside the Church of England remained highly contingent on the Established Church. In many respects, the so-called secularization of religion in the latter part of the nineteenth century is best understood as a diminution of the power and reach of the Established Church rather than the decline of Christian ideas and culture.[79]

---

71. Gray, *Christian and Lyric Tradition*, 3.
72. LaPorte, *Victorian Poets*, 2.
73. Larsen, *People of One Book*, 1.
74. Larsen, *People of One Book*, 1.
75. Larsen, *People of One Book*, 2.
76. Larsen, *People of One Book*, 2.
77. LaPorte, *Victorian Poets*, 6.
78. Blair, *Form and Faith*, 18.
79. Knight and Mason, *Nineteenth-Century Religion and Literature*, 7.

Of course, the churches did not have the sole word on religion. Literature also had its part to play. For instance, literature provided an outlet for women to engage with, and contribute to, religious discussion within a cultural context. Rebecca Styler argues that Victorian women "used literature as a means to engage in theological discourse, through which they reinterpreted Christianity to meet deeply felt personal and political needs."[80] In fiction, poetry, essays, and so on, these authors contributed to the articulation and circulation of religious ideas.[81] Elizabeth Barrett Browning is one such author.

Barrett Browning deployed the Song of Songs in work that is personal, religious, and political. Her religious poetry has begun to attract significant attention from literary critics.[82] Blair argues that Robert Browning and Barrett Browning "perceived religion as the *sine qua non* of poetry, and saw poetry as vital for the understanding and practice of religion."[83] Indeed, in the preface to the first edition of her volume *The Seraphim and Other Poems* (1838), Barrett Browning (writing as Elizabeth B. Barrett) declares: "'An irreligious poet,' said Burns, meaning an undevotional one, 'is a monster.' An irreligious poet, he might have said, is no poet at all. The gravitation of poetry is upwards. The poetic wing, if it move, ascends."[84] A Congregationalist, she sought to reclaim a religious role for poetry, asserting in a letter to her friend Mary Russell Mitford, "Whatever degree of faculty I have, lies in poetry—still more of my personal happiness lies in it—still more of my love. . . . Christ's religion is essentially poetry—poetry glorified."[85] Love is central to Barrett Browning's faith as a Dissenter, thereby reminding us of the etymological link between the word "belief" and love.[86] Most dissenting writers emphasized love as the central principle of faith, and Barrett Browning was familiar with such dissenting ideologies and several of its leading writers.[87] Her poetry continually returns to the theme of love.[88] On his deathbed, Aurora Leigh's father exhorts her to "Love, my child, love, love!" (*Aurora Leigh*, 1. 212).[89]

Barret Browning's verse novel, *Aurora Leigh* (1856), tells the story of a woman's development into an independent woman and a successful poet. In her influential study, *Women Victorian Poets: Writing against the Heart*,

---

80. Styler, *Literary Theology by Women Writers*, 1.
81. Styler, *Literary Theology by Women Writers*, 1.
82. Blair, *Form and Faith*, 124.
83. Blair, *Form and Faith*, 122.
84. Barrett, *Seraphim and Other Poems*, xv.
85. Cited in LaPorte, *Victorian Poets*, 39–40.
86. I thank Matthew Fenwick for drawing my attention to the etymology.
87. Blair, *Form and Faith*, 132–33.
88. Blair, *Form and Faith*, 134.
89. Barrett Browning, *Aurora Leigh*. All references to the poem are from this volume.

16 • INTRODUCTION

Angela Leighton expresses, as her subtitle suggests, a certain amount of anxiety about locating Victorian women's poetry in the realm of the domestic (the hearth) and the sentimental (the heart). Leighton's study chooses instead to focus on the sociopolitical reality of women's lives. For instance, she argues that *Aurora Leigh* "is the epic of the woman poet who finds love, not in unique and tragic isolation on a cliff, but in the dust of the real world where it is rarely clean of double standards, power, crime and suffering."[90] Yet I argue that in reevaluating the place of love, in particular that which is located in the sentimental, that is, the heart, one is able to explore its potential to empower the role of women in romantic relationships with men. Thus, in Barrett Browning's poetry, love is not simply a confessional display of emotion, as many Victorian reviewers appear to have thought; it is also a considered exploration of interdependent relationships, like petals on a flower. Romance is not neglected or brushed aside, but its broader and more complex design is evident through Barrett Browning's use of the image of a flower from the Song of Songs. Linda H. Peterson rightly notes that one of the final sections of *Aurora Leigh* draws on the Song of Songs.[91] Finally united in love with her cousin Romney, Aurora mentions, "First, God's love." Romney responds:

And next, . . . the love of wedded souls,
Which still presents that mystery's counterpart.
Sweet shadow-rose, upon the water of life,
Of such a mystic substance, Sharon gave
A name to! human, vital, fructuous rose,
Whose calyx holds the multitude of leaves,
Loves filial, loves fraternal, neighbour-loves
And civic—all fair petals, all good scents,
All reddened, sweetened from one central Heart! (9.881–90)

The flower here is the rose of Sharon, made famous by Song of Songs 2:1, in which the bride says, "I am a rose of Sharon, a lily of the valleys." Barrett Browning uses the image of the petals of the Rose of Sharon as an emblem of love in a network of romantic, familial, and social relations. This love begins with God, the calyx holding the petals together. Next, it moves to "the love of wedded souls," that which the love story in Song of Songs so clearly illustrates. Finally, it expands to encompass other forms of human love. Each of these loves is necessary for the flower to fully bloom; there cannot be one missing.

---

90. Leighton, *Victorian Woman Poets,* 108.
91. Peterson, *Traditions of Victorian Women's Autobiography,* 140.

Hence, the rose of Sharon encapsulates a complete picture of love divine, romantic, familial, and social. In this way, the Song of Songs has a combined romantic, theological, and social application in the poem.

THE CHAPTERS

Chapter 1 of *Sex, Celibacy, and Deviance: The Victorians and the Song of Songs* is devoted to the experience of lovers in Charlotte Brontë's *Jane Eyre* and Thomas Hardy's *Far from the Madding Crowd* and *Jude the Obscure*. Like Barrett Browning, Brontë emphasizes a particular aspect of Christian discourse, notably the centrality of love in human relationships. For her, the foundation of all forms of love is God, and literature is a means of articulating the interlocking ideals of harmonious marriage and divine-human relations. To this end, Brontë uses the authority of the Song of Songs to reinforce the role of middle-class women as equals in their romantic partnerships. The discussion of Hardy looks at two novels published roughly twenty years apart, *Far from the Madding Crowd* and *Jude the Obscure*. Like Brontë, Hardy is originally drawn to the model of companionate marriage and a union of like minds, which was becoming increasingly popular in the nineteenth century. Over time, however, he begins to show a strong ambivalence toward both marriage and the Song of Songs. Even so, he demonstrates that the Bible, in general, and the Song of Songs, in particular, remained relevant in the nineteenth century, whether it be by outlining an ideal relationship or the perils of chaining oneself to an incompatible union.

Chapter 2 turns to visual culture by exploring works by the Pre-Raphaelite artist Edward Burne-Jones and the Edinburgh-based Arts and Crafts exponent Phoebe Anna Traquair. With Burne-Jones, I focus on unhappy marriages, specifically violent marriages. I discuss the nature of marital violence in the Victorian era and the "rape culture" of the Bible by looking closely at Burne-Jones's rendering of the violent scene from Song of Songs 5:7. The scene is part of the artist's series of church stained-glass window depictions of mostly unpoetic and unromantic scenes from the Song of Songs. By examining the stained-glass window alongside Burne-Jones's unpublished drawings of the Song of Songs, we can see that, like Hardy by the time he wrote *Jude the Obscure,* the Pre-Raphaelite artist reveals an ambivalence toward marriage and the Song of Songs. I focus on happier visions of romantic unions and the Song of Songs in Traquair's commissioned decorations of a grand piano. In depicting the biblical text, Traquair opts for a narrative about a love triangle and the triumph of love. She transposes the eroticism of the Song of Songs onto the function of the piano as an instrument of sympathetic vibration, flirtation, and courtship. As a common presence in middle-class households, the piano is an ideal instrument of love and seduction because it marries touch and harmony and allows for the haptic dimension of both perception and emotional experience. For the pianist, the instrument makes possible a romance of touch through a multisensory experience, and for the listener it attunes the ear to love and the body to sensory vibrations. Traquair also shifts the eroticism of the Song of Songs onto the figure of the earthy and musician goat-god Pan, who appears on the lid of the piano. He entrances Psyche and, indeed, all of nature with his music, thereby creating harmony between the Christian, classical, and scientific elements of Traquair's worldview.

In chapter 3, I discuss Augusta Theodosia Drane and Christina Rossetti, two women poets who extolled divine love and the possibility of agency within chastity and sisterhood. Little has been written about Drane, who was a convert and prioress, later becoming Mother Provincial. She was also an intellectual and a prolific author of histories, essays, and biographies. In this chapter, I look at some of her unpublished writings at length. Drane also authored a popular volume of religious poetry, which included interpretive translations of John of the Cross. She is the first of four converts in this book who found inspiration from the Spanish mystic whose verse bears the influence of the Song of Songs. Her most poignant engagement with John of the Cross is through his concept of the dark night of the soul, whereby the soul senses God's withdrawal before it is finally united with him. For Drane, loving God is not an easy task, and it is in fact demanding and difficult. In some of her poems, she employs military images from the Song of Songs and those of the nun as warrior to describe the sacrificial and hardening nature of her vocation and to indicate that her closely guarded virginity is for Christ alone. In my discussion of Rossetti and chastity, I interpret "Goblin Market" as a poem that empowers women to reserve the right to remain unmarried and to prioritize relationships with either direct family members or a community of women. A number of Rossetti's religious poems contain a spiritual eroticism linked to the Song of Songs, and "Goblin Market" is no different. The ostensibly secular and fairy tale qualities of Rossetti's poem, however, result in biblical references that are echoes rather than direct quotations. Focusing on two elements from the Song of Songs in "Goblin Market," sweetness and the aspect of invitation, I compare and contrast the poem to pornographic ditties from the erotic periodical *The Pearl* so as to demonstrate Rossetti's suspicion of the sweet seductions of the material world that lead one away from sisterhood and Christ.

In chapter 4, I explore queer touch, bodies, and masculinities in the art of Simeon Solomon, a Jewish Pre-Raphaelite, and the ekphrastic poetry of Catholic convert and priest John Gray. With Solomon, I begin with a lengthy exploration of same-sex handholding in his illustrations and paintings alluding to the Song of Songs. Some of these depictions combine Sappho with the Song of Songs, and they exemplify Solomon's penchant for combining the homoerotic with the Hebraic and Hellenistic. Seeing the combined queer and erotic potential of hands, he subverts the interpretation of the Song of Songs as a heterosexual love triangle; in his renderings, the beloved daringly expresses bisexual or same-sex attraction through the placement of his hands. Through their limp wrists, the male lovers exude a certain kind of effeminacy that draws a link between concepts of Jewishness, the *effeminatus,* and Hellenism. I then turn my attention to Gray who, like Solomon, was same-sex attracted and had a highly attuned aesthetic sensibility. In fact, Gray's decadent Catholicism was a kind of aestheticized faith that thrived in an intensely homosocial, literary, and artistic world. I place a spotlight on Gray's ekphrastic poetry about the quintessential Catholic object of devotional gaze and desire: the crucifix. These works are reminiscent of waṣf poetry, an ancient Arabic style of poetry found in the Song of Songs to describe and celebrate the lovers' bodies. Gray, however, uses the waṣf style to highlight Christ's moment of greatest ugliness, humiliation, and suffering. In so doing, he maintains a queer devotional gaze on Christ's broken and vulnerable body, the feminization of which places it into closer alignment with that of a dandy priest than a muscular Christian ideal. I conclude with an exploration of the influence of John of the Cross's poems, which depict the vulva-like wounds of Christ's eternally crucified body as the entrance to the seat of love, the Sacred Heart.

In the final and fifth chapter, I explore how love and death are intimately interwoven in the Song of Songs, just as it was to the Victorians. While scholars of Song of Songs reception have quite understandably chosen to focus on love and the erotic, I ensure that death has not been forgotten. Again and again in Victorian literature and culture, we encounter the phrase "love is strong as death" (Song of Songs 8:6) and its variation, "love is stronger than death." I look at this phrase in depth, especially in relation to death in the writings of Michael Field, the pen name of the aunt-niece couple Edith Cooper and Katharine Bradley. I draw extensively on Cooper and Bradley's unpublished journals and letters, introducing readers to the importance of the Song of Songs to the women's understanding of the intertwinement of love and death. The first section looks at the deaths of Emma Cooper (Cooper's mother and Bradley's sister) and Robert Browning. Cooper and Bradley used the Song of Songs to blur the division between the discourses associated with romantic and familial intimacy. In the section on the death of their beloved dog, Whym Chow, I follow Cooper and Bradley's conversion and suffering for Christ—acts of love signaled by the image of fire—as means of reuniting with the beloved in heaven. I also posit that, despite the women's interest in John of the Cross, the provenance of Whym Chow's designation, "Flame of Love," is not from the saint's *The Living Flame of Love* but from the Song of Songs. Finally, I explore Cooper's impending death by focusing on the use of flower imagery from the Song of Songs. Flowers are reminders of life's brevity and of Cooper and Bradley's desire to become "spouses in Paradise": that is, spouses of each other and of Christ.

CHAPTER 1

"Love Is God"

Charlotte Brontë and Thomas Hardy

Art is much, but Love is more!
O Art, my Art, thou'rt much, but Love is more!
Art symbolizes heaven, but Love is God
And makes heaven.
—Elizabeth Barrett Browning, *Aurora Leigh*, 9.656–59

The Song of Songs is the only book in the Bible written predominantly from the first-person perspective of a female speaker. Indeed, it is the only biblical book in which a woman uses her own words to speak about herself as well as her relationship with her beloved. The Song of Songs therefore provides a model for depicting female characters possessing an independent voice in their relationships. In *Jane Eyre* (1847), Charlotte Brontë combines the emerging first-person perspective of the literary heroine with the newly ascendant genre of the novel. Brontë's titular character alludes to the Song of Songs and other biblical images of marriage to describe a union in which both partners are equal before God, regardless of class differences. The novel offers a story about "the necessity of human love"[1] and of parity through love. In *Jane Eyre*, as with the Song of Songs, it is love rather than family name or property that becomes the primary consideration of union. Like Brontë, Thomas Hardy was drawn to the ideal of companionate marriage and a union of like minds, which was becoming increasingly popular in the nineteenth century. Over time, however, he began to show a strong ambivalence toward marriage and the Song of Songs, as exemplified by Sue Bridehead's youthful defiance in the early chapters of *Jude the Obscure* (1895). Ultimately, my aim in this chapter is to contribute to a feminist analysis of relations between men and women by

---

1. Peschier, *Nineteenth-Century Anti-Catholic Discourses*, 109.

22 • CHAPTER 1

focusing on romantic narratives told from the perspective of female characters. These love stories take place in large part within rural and pastoral landscapes, not unlike the drama that unfolds in the Song of Songs. The landscape and the animals within them play a role in articulating the relationship of harmony or disharmony between humans.

BRONTË, HARDY, AND RELIGION

Like many of her contemporaries, Brontë was deeply religious and knowledgeable about the Bible and theological matters. In the words of Marianne Thormählen, "The Christian life is a foreign country to most people today, and I believe it serves some purpose to be reminded that to the Brontës it was home, with the occasional irritations as well as the manifold blessings of the domestic sphere."[2] The novelist's father, Patrick Brontë, was a priest of the Church of England, and most of the books owned by the family were of a theological nature.[3] According to Elizabeth's Gaskell's biography of Brontë, Patrick Brontë relayed the following of his daughter as a child: "I . . . asked Charlotte what was the best book in the world; she answered 'The Bible.'"[4] Brontë's friend Ellen Nussey wrote the following about Brontë as a schoolgirl: "No girl in the school was equal to Charlotte in Sunday lessons. Her acquaintance with Holy Writ surpassed others in this as in everything else."[5] Indeed, Lisa Wang argues that there are over 450 direct allusions to the Bible in Brontë's novels.[6] The novelist was devoted to the Church of England, though not uncritically, for, as she writes in a letter shortly after the release of *Jane Eyre,* "I love the Church of England. Her Ministers, indeed I do not regard as infallible personages, I have seen too much of them for that—but to the Establishment, with all her faults—the profane Athanasian Creed excluded—I am sincerely attached."[7]

Brontë's first and most famous novel, *Jane Eyre,* offers a fictionalized account of her childhood in its first half, with a marriage plot in its second. A number of Victorian reviewers criticized the novel for its apparent attack on Christianity.[8] Yet for other readers, and to Brontë herself, the novel offers a sharp rebuke of religious hypocrisy. Thus, in addressing the "timorous or

---

2. Thormählen, *Brontës and Religion,* 9.

3. Peschier, *Nineteenth-Century Anti-Catholic Discourses,* 110.

4. Gaskell, *Life of Charlotte Brontë,* 46.

5. Nussey, "School Days at Roe Head," 104.

6. Wang, "Uses of Theological Discourse," 31.

7. Letter to W. S. Williams, 23 December 1847, in Brontë, *Letters of Charlotte Brontë,* 581.

8. Thormählen, *Brontës and Religion,* 7.

carping few . . . whose ear detect in each protest against bigotry—that parent of crime—an insult to piety," she asserts in the second preface to her novel,

> Conventionality is not morality. Self-righteousness is not religion. To attack the first is not to assail the last. To pluck the mask from the face of the Pharisee, is not to lift an impious hand to the Crown of Thorns. . . . Appearance should not be mistaken for truth; narrow human doctrines, that only tend to elate and magnify a few, should not be substituted for the world-redeeming creed of Christ.[9]

Both halves of the novel are deeply infused with pious religious content, forms, and interpretations. Linda H. Peterson notes that *Jane Eyre* "use[s] spiritual autobiography in the first half . . . to raise questions about modes of self-interpretation, about women's authority in biblical and other hermeneutics," while the second half shows the influence of missionary journals and memoirs.[10] I argue that Brontë's writing engages with a Christian discourse that promotes the centrality of love in human relationships and of love as a guide for mutual respect and equality between men and women. The Song of Songs plays a role in this discourse.

Harold Bloom calls Hardy an heir to the Brontë sisters and their largely Byronic- and Gothic-inspired brand of "Northern Romance."[11] I would add that Hardy uses the Song of Songs to articulate an ideal kind of romance. This argument is in keeping with Timothy Hands's observation that Hardy associates love with religion, which his use of biblical allusion makes plain.[12] Yet Hardy divests the Song of Songs of its centuries-old religious discourse in order to reveal it as essentially a text about human relations that makes no mention of God. As I have explored in the introduction, Hardy's later position on Christianity and the Bible was likely nurtured by higher criticism, which aimed to read the Bible through the lens of history and linguistics rather than that of divine inspiration.

Hardy observed that marriage stripped of its traditional religious mystique is a partnership that rests upon human dimensions and liable to human failings. After all, whereas Jane Eyre experiences a successful marriage to her first love, Hardy's fourth novel, *Far from the Madding Crowd* (1874), includes Hardy's first major portrayal of a failed marriage,[13] while *Jude the Obscure* contains two disastrous marriages (or three if one includes the delayed marriage of

---

9. Brontë, *Jane Eyre*, 3–4.
10. Peterson, *Traditions of Victorian Women's Autobiography*, 81.
11. Bloom, *Charlotte Brontë's Jane Eyre*, 1.
12. Hands, *Distracted Preacher?*, 48.
13. Daleski, *Paradoxes of Love*, 57.

Sue and Jude). "Love, in Hardy, means pain," holds one scholar.[14] We witness this pain not simply in the novels but also in the poems inspired by the marriage to his first wife, Emma. In the poem "Had you Wept" (1914), the speaker holds, "You felt too much, so gained no balm for all your torrid sorrow, / And hence our deep division, and our dark undying pain" (lines 15–16).[15] After Emma's death, Hardy discovered a bitter diary entitled, "What I think of my Husband," which served to deepen his grief and remorse.[16] Though originally governed by love, their union was the cause of considerable emotional pain.

It is probable that Hardy's complex relationship with Christianity and marriage played a role in his changing reception of the Song of Songs. Hardy was not an orthodox Christian believer for the majority of his adult life, yet the influence of Christianity stayed with him throughout, as one might expect of a man who had considered a career as an Anglican clergyman—an aspiration he finally rejected in 1866.[17] An orthodox evangelical sermon he wrote in 1858 at the age of eighteen, the Bible he acquired in 1861 and annotated for nearly forty years, and church attendance at both evangelical and High Church services suggest that "Hardy as a young man had a personal faith of a distinctly Evangelical cast," argues Pamela Dalziel.[18] While intellectual integrity prevented him from remaining within the church, he was "throughout his life profoundly Christian, not only culturally and emotionally, but also ethically and even to some extent theologically."[19] Norman Vance argues that Hardy was "post-Christian rather than anti-Christian," responsive to radical challenges of the Bible and retaining some "Christian-humanist baggage."[20] Despite the changes in his adherence to the church, Hardy "retained an Evangelical penchant for scriptural allusion," with his fourteen novels containing over 600 biblical allusions, notes Hands.[21] Indeed, the first page of *Far from the Madding Crowd* tells us—through biblical allusion no less—that the character Gabriel Oak is not religious.[22] The "shiftiness" of Hardy's allusions is

---

14. Daleski, *Paradoxes of Love*, 15.

15. Hardy, *Complete Poetical Works of Thomas Hardy*, vol. 1.

16. Jane, "In Defence of Emma Hardy," 40.

17. Millgate, *Thomas Hardy*, 92.

18. Dalziel, "Gospel According to Hardy," 11.

19. Dalziel, "Gospel According to Hardy," 14.

20. Vance, "Thomas Hardy," 116.

21. Hands, *Distracted Preacher?*, 38.

22. Gabriel "felt himself to occupy morally that vast middle space of Laodicean neutrality which lay between the Communion people of the parish and the drunken section,—that is, he went to church, but yawned privately by the time the congregation reached the Nicene creed and thought of what there would be for dinner when he meant to be listening to the sermon." Hardy, *Far from the Madding Crowd*, 9.

what sets them apart from that of other authors: as Mary Rimmer argues, "the sacred and secular mix freely in them, and they can be moving, ironic, playful and irreverently mocking, sometimes almost instantaneously."[23] In the words of Hands, Hardy "uses Scriptural allusion like an Evangelical and agnostic combined, referring to the Bible frequently, yet wondering what its importance may be; seeing that it may have great meaning, and yet doubting whether it has any meaning at all."[24]

ONE BONE, ONE FLESH

Toward the end of *Jane Eyre*, the titular character tells the reader the following:

> I have now been married ten years. I know what it is to live entirely for and with what I love best on earth. I hold myself supremely blest—blest beyond what language can express; because I am my husband's life as fully as he is mine. No woman was ever nearer to her mate than I am: ever more absolutely bone of his bone, and flesh of his flesh. I know no weariness of my Edward's society: he knows none of mine, any more than we each do of the pulsation of the heart that beats in our separate bosoms; consequently, we are ever together. To be together is for us to be at once as free as in solitude, as gay as in company. We talk, I believe, all day long: to talk to each other is but a more animated and an audible thinking. All my confidence is bestowed on him; all his confidence is devoted to me: we are precisely suited in character; perfect concord is the result.[25]

This paragraph stands as one of the highpoints of the novel, illustrating what we today would regard as an ideal of romantic and sexual compatibility. The former governess and her former employer have overcome the mighty obstacles in their path on the road to marriage, such that now each is able to live with "what I love best on earth," to exist in complete accord with the beloved, and to never tire of each other's company. Compare Jane's account of her marriage above, and thus her own position as a wife, to her cousin St. John Rivers's description of his ideal spouse. Following his unsuccessful proposal to her, he says, "I want a wife: the sole helpmeet I can influence efficiently in life, and retain absolutely till death,"[26] to which Jane declares unequivocally sometime

---

23. Rimmer, "My Scripture Manner," 20–21.
24. Hands, *Distracted Preacher?*, 122.
25. Brontë, *Jane Eyre*, 450–51.
26. Brontë, *Jane Eyre*, 406.

later, "I scorn your idea of love."[27] She continues: "You have introduced a topic on which our natures are at variance—a topic we should never discuss: the very name of love is an apple of discord between us."[28] But like St. John, Jane will also become a missionary of sorts by the novel's end. She foreshadows this fate as she says to herself, "In a few more hours I shall succeed you on that track, cousin."[29] But her mission will be of another kind. Articulating the type of missionary that Jane will turn out to be, J. Jeffrey Franklin notes, "Jane is off to Rochester—whose conversion in her hands is beyond doubt—as a missionary of spiritual love."[30]

Catherine Brown Tkacz argues that *Jane Eyre* "contains 176 scriptural allusions."[31] I believe that this number is the bare minimum and that these allusions join together with other allusions to justify Jane's unconventional marriage to Rochester. As Jane states in the first quoted passage, her marriage to Rochester leads to lives entwined in mutual respect, and to a veritable union of minds, bodies, and souls. In style and wording, the most powerful and romantic moments in the passage clearly exhibit the influence of the Bible. The frequent use of chiasmi imbues the passage with both poetic resonance and biblical authority. One in particular has echoes of the Song of Songs. Jane's assertion, "because I am my husband's life as fully as he is mine," evokes the following passages from that biblical text: "My beloved is mine and I am his" and "I am my beloved's, and my beloved is mine" (2:16; 6:13). Her assertion precedes an allusion to Genesis, in which Adam says of Eve, "This is now bone of my bones, and flesh of my flesh"; and it is for this reason a husband and wife "shall be one flesh" (2:23; 2:24). These two verses from Genesis are reiterated in Ephesians 5:30–31 to describe the marriage-like union between Christ and the church: "This is a great mystery; but I speak concerning Christ and the Church" (5:32). Victorian Anglican commentators such as Henry Sulivan, Rector of Yoxall, associated these verses from Ephesians both typologically and allegorically with the Song of Songs.[32] Others would see connections with additional biblical books. One such person is B. S. Clarke, a vicar of Christ Church, Southport, whose translation of the Song of Songs later in the century includes as epigraphs bridal imagery from Ephesians 5:32 and Revelation 21:9 ("I will show thee the Bride, the Lamb's wife").[33] Furthermore, in

---

27. Brontë, *Jane Eyre*, 408.

28. Brontë, *Jane Eyre*, 409.

29. Brontë, *Jane Eyre*, 421.

30. Franklin, "Merging of Spiritualities," 482.

31. Tkacz, "Bible in *Jane Eyre*," 3.

32. Sulivan, *Sermon Preached on Sunday*, 7.

33. Clarke, *Song of Song*, inside cover page.

his introduction to Clarke's book, Horatius Bonar, a poet and minister of the Church of Scotland, draws a connection between Ephesians 5:31–32 and the nuptial imagery from Genesis and Revelation, that is, from the first and final books of the Bible.[34] As he says,

> if we would understand aright what is written here concerning the Bridegroom and the Bride, we must go back to the Book of Genesis, and read there the symbol as given us on the formation of the first man and woman,— a symbol whose root is in creation, but whose development is in redemption; a symbol whose outline is given us in the first Book of Scripture, whose filling up is reserved for the last.[35]

Most importantly for the present study, he argues for a direct link between the Song of Songs and Revelation 22:20 through their images of marriage:

> [The bride of the Song of Songs] says, "Make haste, my Beloved, and be Thou like to a roe or to a young hart upon the mountains of spices" (viii.14). These last words strikingly link this Song with the Book of the Revelation, uttering the same deep-drawn sigh, the same eager anticipation, the same heart-felt prayer as that with which the Apocalypse concludes: "Even so, come, Lord Jesus." The resemblance between the two passages is too vivid to be overlooked. "The Spirit and the *Bride* say, Come."[36]

While *Jane Eyre* predates these interpretations by Sulivan, Clarke, and Bonar, it is possible that Brontë was familiar with similar ideas as a result of her wide reading of religious works or through her father and his networks. Certainly, linking Genesis with the Song of Songs, Ephesians, and Revelation through the trope of marriage helps to elucidate the novel's puzzled-over ending, which concludes with a letter from St. John to Jane. At the very end of this letter and thus at the very end of the novel, St. John quotes from the previously mentioned passage from Revelation 22:20: "'My Master,' he says, 'has forewarned me. Daily he announces more distinctly,—'Surely I come quickly;' and hourly I more eagerly respond,—'Amen; even so come, Lord Jesus!'"[37] While Jane and St. John could be viewed, as I have shown, as opposites in love, they should also be regarded as theological types, particularly if we associate Jane's marriage with Rochester to that in Genesis and St. John's marriage with

---

34. Bonar, introduction to *The Song of Songs,* 12.
35. Bonar, introduction to *The Song of Songs,* 11.
36. Bonar, introduction to *The Song of Songs,* 14.
37. Brontë, *Jane Eyre,* 452.

Christ to that in Revelation. After all, the name "Jane" is a female variant of "John," the name also given to the author of Revelation; not only are the two cousins both missionaries (in a sense), they are also brides. Jane is the bride on earth, St. John in heaven. Typological interpretation regards the brides of Genesis, the Song of Songs, Ephesians, and Revelation as types or versions of each other, with the New Testament brides being the fulfilment of their Old Testament counterparts, just as Christ would become the Second Adam, the perfect version of his predecessor. As such, we can interpret St. John's marriage to Christ as the typological fulfilment of Jane Eyre's marriage to Rochester. Hence, an awareness of typological interpretations of bridal imagery in the Bible, including that around the Song of Songs, enlightens us as to the novel's enigmatic ending and its relation to Jane's ideal marriage to Rochester: Jane and Rochester's marriage foreshadows the heavenly marriage between the soul and Christ and is thus blessed by Christ.

It might appear that I have downplayed the significance of Jane and Rochester's relationship as merely a foreshadowing of a future spiritual marriage with Christ. But at the same time, the novel's final words about St. John, drawn from the penultimate verse of Revelation and calling on Christ to come, have already been enacted by Jane and Rochester, rendering the latter reunion extraordinary in itself. Shortly after she rejects St. John's marriage proposal, Jane experiences a vision of Rochester calling out her name. Her response is, "I am coming! . . . Wait for me! Oh, I will come,"[38] making her like Christ returning to earth. As we shall see, her return to Rochester sets in motion a new heaven and earth, as seen in Revelation. This reading of Jane's return through the events of Revelation makes the reunion of Jane and Rochester even more remarkable than at first glance. Yet, as we shall see, it is the Song of Songs rather than Revelation that draws a link between romantic reunion and nature's regeneration in *Jane Eyre.* Though severely wounded, Rochester survives his own apocalypse, as it were, by literally coming out of the burnt ruins of his home, Thornfield Hall. What remains, or rather, replaces the old, is a new realm of possibilities for Jane and Rochester. The lovers are now able to rekindle their romance, following the tragic death of Rochester's wife Bertha.

The reunion between Jane and Rochester is not simply reminiscent of the new heaven and earth of Revelation 21 but also reminds us of the lovers in the natural world of the Song of Songs. Just as Hardy was to use pastoral images either from or reminiscent of the Song of Songs, so, too, does Brontë. An admirer of John Ruskin's *Modern Painters,* in which Ruskin speaks of having the "gift of taking pleasure in landscape,"[39] Brontë was repeatedly drawn to

---

38. Brontë, *Jane Eyre,* 420.
39. Cited in Henson, *Landscape and Gender,* 11.

the sensuous, pleasure-giving sights of the natural world. Indeed, her poem "Pleasure" (1830) is about the delights of nature. Several of her poems describe the wonder of spring, summer, flowers, and sunshine. In the undated poem "Winter Stores," she says, "the sun shone kindly o'er us, / And flowers bloomed round our feet,— / While many a bud of joy before us / Unclosed its petals sweet" (lines 33–36).[40] "Winter" (1830) includes the following:

> Dismal and death-like is the scene;
> But soon, arrayed in robes of green,
> Spring will come,—the budding hour!
> And the snow-drop, humble flower,
>
> Heralding her coming step,
> From the verdant earth will peep;
> While the little birds will sing
> At the approach of gentle spring. (lines 33–40)

In "[I thought in my childhood how pleasant would be]," another undated poem, she speaks of "My native woods . . . / Sacred to calm and rest" and of "Wild fruits and flowers and flocks of birds, / And green grass through the year, / And deer in the park in graceful herds" (lines 12–13; 16–18). Nature's verdant and fecund beauty is to be celebrated, and the capacity to appreciate and, indeed, delight in it, is a desirable quality in a lover. Rochester recognizes that Jane has "an eye for natural beauties."[41] In contrast, St. John cannot find pleasure in such beauty, his senses subdued by religion. Says Jane:

> Nature was not to him that treasury of delight it was to his sisters. He expressed once, and but once in my hearing, a strong sense of the rugged charm of the hills, and an inborn affection for the dark and hoary walls he calls his home: but there was more of gloom than pleasure in the tone and words in which the sentiment was manifested.[42]

These images from Brontë's poems reverberate in *Jane Eyre*. The novel, however, offers explicit allusion to the Song of Songs, conferring a sacredness to the romantic qualities of nature in the novel. The morning after their reunion, Jane coaxes Rochester outdoors by quoting, in part, from the Song of Songs: "'It is a bright, sunny morning, sir,' I said. 'The rain is over and gone

---

40. Brontë, *Poems of Charlotte Bronte*. All references to Brontë's poems are from this volume.

41. Brontë, *Jane Eyre*, 249.

42. Brontë, *Jane Eyre*, 351.

and there is a tender shining after it: you shall have a walk soon.'"[43] In Song of Songs 2:11, the lover says, "For, lo, the winter is past, the rain is over and gone." This line might be fruitfully juxtaposed with Revelation 21:4, in which we are told there will be no more tears, pain, or death, "for the former things are passed away." Rochester responds to Jane with his own images of nature: the skylark, the skylark's singing, and the sunshine, all of which he associates with her.

Jane then leads Rochester both literally and figuratively "out of the wet and wild wood into some cheerful fields: I described to him how brilliantly green they were; how the flowers and hedges looked refreshed; how sparklingly blue was the sky."[44] This pastoral scene, complete with hedges, is nature tamed or "cheerful" rather than "wet and wild." It is more pleasure-giving and vital than the reader's first impression of a drab and enclosed garden at Jane's grim childhood school, Lowood. Jane's introduction to that garden occurs at the end of January, when "all was wintry blight and brown decay," and on a day when "all underfoot was still soaking wet with the floods of yesterday."[45] A *hortus conclusus,* this garden is sealed off from the world, "surrounded with walls so high as to exclude every glimpse of prospect."[46] While it is reminiscent of the (virginal) bride as an enclosed garden of Song of Songs 4:12, it is far from romantic. Nonetheless, winter makes way for spring, and the garden becomes a paradise in which "a greenness grew over those brown beds."[47] This garden might be compared to that of Madame Beck's house in Brontë's novel *Villette* (1853), which, while said to have conventual origins, affords opportunities—at least on summer evenings—for protagonist Lucy Snowe to "keep tryst with the rising moon, or taste one kiss of the evening breeze, or fancy rather than feel the freshness of dew descending."[48] Such a garden invites sensory gratification and a communion with the outer world. In similar fashion, Jane and Rochester's lush field is the fitting setting for Rochester's second—and legitimate—proposal to Jane, in readiness for their happy marriage. With Rochester's earlier account of the singing skylark ringing in the reader's ear, we can see how Jane (in concert with Rochester) reinscribes the words from the Song of Songs through both action and description: "For, lo, the winter is past, the rain is over and gone. The flowers appear on the earth; the time of the singing of birds is come" (Song of Songs 2:11–12).

---

43. Brontë, *Jane Eyre,* 439.
44. Brontë, *Jane Eyre,* 439.
45. Brontë, *Jane Eyre,* 48.
46. Brontë, *Jane Eyre,* 114.
47. Brontë, *Jane Eyre,* 75.
48. Brontë, *Villette,* 106–7.

Despite the novel's weighty immersion in biblical hermeneutics and discourse, several reviewers of Brontë's time believed her novel to be shocking because it appeared to undermine Christianity and support gender and class equality.[49] I agree to a large extent with John G. Peters, who argues that the novel "is not subversive because it rejects Christianity or because it advocates gender or class equality"; it is subversive "because it advocates a Christianity in which all are equal before God, regardless of gender, class, or any other differentiations."[50] The exception is the character of Bertha, who is depicted problematically as bestial and mad. But building on Peters's argument, I believe that the novel is remarkable from the position of class and gender, by advocating a Christianity in which the Song of Songs plays a part in describing this most unusual of Victorian marriages. In the Song of Songs, the beloved tells his lover that she is "a lily among thorns" (2:12), and he says to her, "Behold, thou art fair, my love; behold, thou art fair" (1:15). Brontë conflates these two descriptions in Rochester's pronouncement to Jane on their first and failed wedding day, while she is still a governess and thus before coming into an inheritance that would allow her to be a woman of independent means. Jane says, "Rochester took me into the dining-room, surveyed me keenly all over, pronounced me 'fair as a lily, and not only the pride of his life, but the desire of his eyes.'"[51] Jane is indeed as a lily among thorns at Thornfield. Earlier in the novel, Rochester proposes to her for the first time, saying, "My bride is here . . . because my equal is here, and my likeness. Jane, will you marry me?"[52] His assertion of equality matches Jane's declaration in the same scene that "it is my spirit that addresses your spirit; just as if both had passed through the grave, and we stood at God's feet, equal,—as we are!"[53] And, of course, Rochester's claim that Jane is his equal and "likeness" foreshadows, and is fulfilled by, Jane's biblically tinged assertion that "I am my husband's life as fully as he is mine. . . . Absolutely bone of his bone, and flesh of his flesh." It is through these echoes of the Bible, including the Song of Songs, that Rochester and Jane articulate and reaffirm mutual love and equality in their relationship.

Brontë's novel of true companionate marriage, which exemplifies the ideal of mutual love, intellectual compatibility, and deep friendship and intimacy, anticipates J. S. Mill's words twenty years later during the House of Commons debate on the Second Reform Bill. On this occasion, Mill tabled a parliamentary motion for a gender-blind franchise, which John Tosh argues was "the

---

49. Peters, "We Stood at God's Feet," 53.
50. Peters, "We Stood at God's Feet," 53.
51. Brontë, *Jane Eyre*, 362.
52. Brontë, *Jane Eyre*, 319.
53. Brontë, *Jane Eyre*, 318.

climax of a lifetime's commitment to the cause of women's emancipation."[54] In Mill's speech, one might be forgiven for discerning echoes of Jane Eyre's words about her marriage to Rochester:

> Women and men are, for the first time in history, really each other's companions. Our traditions respecting the proper relations between them have descended from a time when their lives were apart—when they were separate in their thoughts, because they were separate equally in their serious occupations. In former days a man passed his life among men; all his friends, all his real intimacies, were with men; with men alone did he consult on any serious business; the wife was either a plaything or an upper servant. All this, among the educated classes, is now changed. The man no longer gives his spare hours to violent exercises and boisterous conviviality with male associates; the two sexes now pass their lives together; the women of a man's family are his habitual society; the wife is his chief associate, his most confidential friend, and often his most trusted adviser.[55]

Tosh argues that when Mill gave his speech, "domesticated husbands and supportive wives [had] become central to the self-image of the Victorians. . . . Mill's generation liked to believe that their domestic relations were about love, comfort and morality."[56] Yet rather than reciprocity, the reality was maintained by a legacy of the Evangelical movement, the assumption that wives have a moral duty to provide their husbands with loving support.[57] In contrast, the marriage between Jane and Rochester is sustained by mutual intellectual interests and equality of support. In other words, the moral duty of providing comfort and companionship in *Jane Eyre* is shared equally between husband and wife.

HARDY, PASTORAL LOVE, AND SHEEP

Like Brontë, Hardy certainly understood the value of the Song of Songs. But as we saw in the introduction, with Sue Bridehead's condemnation in *Jude the Obscure* of the allegorical and typological interpretations of the Song of Songs, the influence of higher criticism played an undeniable role in Hardy's use of the biblical text. As such, Hardy emphasized less the theological meaning than

---

54. Tosh, *Man's Place*, 53.
55. Cited in Tosh, *Man's Place*, 53.
56. Tosh, *Man's Place*, 54.
57. Tosh, *Man's Place*, 54.

its earthly one. Whereas Barrett Browning's phrase from *Aurora Leigh*, "Love is God," might for Brontë have meant that "God is Love," for Hardy, its meaning had a more literal—and increasingly painful—sense. Like Jude, who in courting Sue used the Song of Songs to express desires unattached to "ecclesiastical abstractions,"[58] Hardy borrowed expressions of human desire from the Song of Songs in his courtship of Emma Gifford, the woman who would become his first wife. In October 1870, Emma wrote him a letter in which she spoke of their love as "this dream of my life—no, not dream, for what is actually going on around me seems a dream rather."[59] And to a disappointingly undemonstrative moment by Hardy, declared, "I take him (the reserved man) as I do the Bible; find out what I can, compare one text with another, & believe the rest is a lump of simple faith."[60] Upon receiving the letter, Hardy "immediately" marked her initials in his Bible against Song of Songs 4:2–3, which says, "Thy teeth are like a flock of sheep that are even shorn, which came up from the washings; whereof everyone bear twins, and none is barren among them. Thy lips are like a thread of scarlet, and thy speech is comely."[61] Tactile and figurative, specific and displaced, ripe and delicate, the startling passage from the biblical text is "at once voluptuous and reticent,"[62] which is how Ariel Bloch and Chana Bloch describe the language of the Song of Songs. Spoken by a shepherd to describe the precious countenance of his lover, the aforementioned passage signals a blossoming erotic awareness between Hardy and Emma. In the Song of Songs, there is no shame in nakedness (of being shorn, as it were), for the lovers are "conveyed as animals . . . in a celebration of the richness and multiplicity of a shared world between humans and animals, or a world where humans too are animals."[63] By initialing the passage from the Song of Songs, Hardy tactfully draws attention to the earthy, carnal, or animal side of desire—one that mirrors what theologian Roland Boer might describe as "a fecund, sensual, and pulsating world, eager to get on with the job of sprouting, pollinating, mating, and reproducing."[64] It is a desire that colors Hardy's description of landowner Bathsheba Everdene's "exact arch of . . . upper unbroken . . . teeth, and . . . the keenly pointed corners of her red mouth," in a scene where she is the singular "feminine figure" among a group

---

58. Hardy, *Jude the Obscure,* 157.
59. Cited in Millgate, *Thomas Hardy,* 121.
60. Cited in Millgate, *Thomas Hardy,* 121.
61. Millgate, *Thomas Hardy,* 121.
62. Bloch and Bloch, introduction to *The Song of Songs,* 14.
63. Strømmen, "Animal Poetics," 414.
64. Boer, *Earthy Nature of the Bible,* 42.

34 · CHAPTER 1

of "heavy yeoman."[65] It is noteworthy that *Far from the Madding Crowd* was published in the year that Hardy and Emma were married and was therefore written during their courtship.

The combining of the human with the animal in the Song of Songs is in concert with Hardy's representations of the natural or nonhuman world as one that is "fully embedded into and inextricable from the human and social world."[66] The term shepherd incorporates the animal into the human, or merges the animal with the human.[67] Sheep are emblematic of Hardy's own interest in the natural world and of his reputation among his reviewers (for better or for worse) as an author of the pastoral. Henry James's somewhat critical review of *Far from the Madding Crowd* declares facetiously but tellingly, "Everything human in the book strikes us as factitious and insubstantial; the only things we believe in are the sheep and the dogs."[68] Hardy was well aware of—and frustrated by—his status as a specialist of pastoral literature. Thus, according to his biography, "he had not the slightest intention of writing forever about sheepfarming."[69] In following the success of *Far from the Madding Crowd* with *The Hand of Ethelberta* (1876), a decisive step away from the pastoral mode, he wryly explains that there was "general disappointment at the lack of sheep and shepherds."[70]

Nonetheless, as Hardy would have known (by initialing Emma's name in his Bible against Song of Songs 4:2–3), the pastoral tradition is one in which sheep, love, bodies of lovers, and the Song of Songs are coterminous. Indeed, "pastor," from which we derive the word "pastoral," originates from the Latin for "shepherd." The genre of the invitation poem was influenced by the Song of Songs and flourished in medieval and early modern literature. It includes Christopher Marlowe's well-known "The Passionate Shepherd to His Love," an early modern poem that Erik Gray argues "combine[s] the pastoral tradition of the gift-giving shepherd with the sublimated eroticism of the Song."[71] As with the Song of Songs, Marlowe's speaker repeatedly calls on his beloved to "Come" and take as much pleasure in the landscape as with each other. And like the Song of Songs, Hardy associates the female lover with the pastoral landscape and with sheep, as illustrated in the following scene from *Far from the Madding Crowd*. Gabriel Oak, a sheep farmer, though later reduced to

---

65. Hardy, *Far from the Madding Crowd*, 91, 90.
66. Kreilkamp, "Pitying the Sheep," 474.
67. Kreilkamp, "Pitying the Sheep," 477.
68. Cited in Beach, *Method of Henry James*, 117.
69. Hardy, *Life of Thomas Hardy*, vol. 1, 135.
70. Hardy, *Life of Thomas Hardy*, vol. 1, 136.
71. Gray, "Come Be My Love," 378.

the status of a shepherd when tragedy strikes, shears a ewe in the admiring presence of its owner, Bathsheba, Gabriel's employer and the woman he loves: "The clean, sleek creature arose from its fleece—how perfectly like Aphrodite rising from the foam should have been seen to be realized—looking startled and shy at the loss of its garment, which lay on the floor in one soft cloud."[72] Robert M. Polhemus draws an intriguing link between this amusing image of shorn sheep and the disrobing of the Greek goddesses Hera, Athena, and Aphrodite in the presence of the shepherd, Paris, who is to decide which among them is the fairest.[73] "The shepherd is not only a key man in the economy on which culture was built," Polhemus says, "he is also a key figure in the custom of religious ritual. Different deities try to gain the allegiance of the pastor. This tie between Aphrodite and Paris the keeper of flocks joins the erotic to the pastoral."[74] One could also compare Hardy's analogy of Aphrodite "rising from the foam" to Botticelli's famous *Birth of Venus,* "very likely the best-known image of erotic love in the world," which became famous from the 1860s and 1870s when the likes of Walter Pater, John Ruskin, the Brownings, and the Pre-Raphaelites rediscovered the masterpiece.[75] Polhemus argues that the main reason for the revival of interest in the masterpiece "is precisely that it *does* express religious feeling: reverence for love."[76] Ruskin said of Botticelli that "he understood the thoughts of Heathens and Christians equally, and could in a measure paint both Aphrodite and the Madonna."[77] Thus, Love is God and Love is also a goddess. The shorn ewe is Hardy's humble ode to the goddess of love and, in all probability, a homage to his then-beloved Emma whose teeth "are like a flock of sheep that are even shorn."

CAMARADERIE VERSUS COVERTURE

Hardy appeals to Song of Songs 8:6–7 in order to illustrate the ideal romantic union within a pastoral context: a combination of companionate marriage and shared labors. Following Bathsheba and Gabriel's confession of love, chapter 56 ends thus:

---

72. Hardy, *Far from the Madding Crowd,* 145–46.

73. Polhemus, *Erotic Faith,* 225–26.

74. Polhemus, *Erotic Faith,* 226. In *Far from the Madding Crowd,* shepherds can be ideal lovers, just as they are in the Song of Songs. The novel compares Gabriel to Eros, the god of love and the son of Aphrodite. Hardy, *Far from the Madding Crowd,* 131.

75. Polhemus, *Erotic Faith,* 7.

76. Polhemus, *Erotic Faith,* 7.

77. Letter 22, 19 September 1872, in Ruskin, *Fors Clavigera,* 428.

36 • CHAPTER 1

Theirs was that substantial affection which arises (if any arises at all) when the two who are thrown together begin first by knowing the rougher sides of each other's character, and not the best till further on, the romance growing up in the interstices of a mass of hard prosaic reality. This good-fellowship—*camaraderie*—usually occurring through similarity of pursuits, is unfortunately seldom superadded to love between the sexes, because men and women associate not in their labours but in their pleasures merely. Where however happy circumstance permits its development the compounded feeling proves itself to be the only love which is strong as death—that love which many waters cannot quench, nor the floods drown, beside which the passion usually called by the name is evanescent as steam.[78]

Significant here is the narrator's description of Bathsheba and Gabriel's relationship as a "good-fellowship—*camaraderie*—usually occurring through similarity of pursuits." These words strongly propose a partnership between equals, a love match based on compatibility and friendship, on similar and mutual "labours" rather than "pleasures merely." It is a relationship requiring time to develop and mature, as each person comes to learn not simply the other's most desirable qualities but also "the rougher sides of each other's character." Moreover, it is unlike the unrequited and obsessive love that Broadwood holds for Bathsheba. Though he calls his love "a thing strong as death,"[79] it is Gabriel and Bathsheba's love which we are told is "the only love which is strong as death."

Despite the increasing emphasis on mutual affection in marriage throughout the century, the ideal kind of relationship I have been talking about is not based on fleeting passions alone (which is "evanescent as steam") but on an intermixing of emotion and additional factors that together form a complete experience or "compounded feeling" of love. This critique of fleeting passions and, by association, reckless sexual abandon is a convention we have witnessed elsewhere, famously in Jane Austen's *Pride and Prejudice* (1813), concerning the elopement of Lydia with Captain Wickham; in the ill-advised marriage of Bathsheba with Sergeant Troy; and in Jude's sexual attraction to Arabella. In comparison, the "labours" by which "men and women associate" reflect, I would argue, both the typical work of keeping the relationship alive and the "labours" on the land, such that the shared work fosters a partnership between equal players. Like the Shulamite and her beloved who labor on the land, Gabriel and Bathsheba likewise work the land toward a common goal; Troy, however, has no interest in farming, preferring to gamble instead, just

---

78. Hardy, *Far from the Madding Crowd*, 383–84; emphasis added.
79. Hardy, *Far from the Madding Crowd*, 199.

as Bathsheba had unwisely gambled away her heart to him. In stark contrast is the relationship between Bathsheba and Gabriel, which is like a sturdy and enduring oak tree—reminiscent of Gabriel's surname—and has its roots deep in the land that brought them together and sustains them. In using the Song of Songs in the quoted passage, Hardy strips the biblical text of its religious associations and returns it to its pastoral roots. In so doing, he elevates the human aspect to the final and, perhaps, only meaning of the Song of Songs. Given that God is not mentioned in the Song of Songs, the love that is "strong as death" could well be the only God we can claim to know.

While *Far from the Madding Crowd* concludes with an ideal marriage, *Jude the Obscure,* published just over twenty years later, shows, to devastating effect, that not all couples live out their final days in happy marriages. Sexologist Havelock Ellis declared in a review from 1896, "In *Jude the Obscure* we find for the first time in our literature the reality of marriage clearly recognized as something wholly apart from the mere ceremony with which our novelists have usually identified it."[80] Likewise, the reality is that when Hardy was writing his novel, his marriage to Emma was undergoing one of its worst periods.[81] He stated in the year of the novel's publication, "I feel that a bad marriage is one of the direst things on earth, & one of the cruellest things."[82] The first marriage in the novel, that of Jude and Arabella, fails because it lacks the camaraderie that would render it "the only love which is strong as death." In the words of the narrator,

> Their lives were ruined, he thought; ruined by the fundamental error of the matrimonial union: that of having based a permanent contract on a temporary feeling which had no necessary connection with affinities that alone render a life-long comradeship tolerable.[83]

The sexual attraction that brought them together does indeed prove to be "evanescent as steam."

The novel's frank depiction of unhappy marriages reflects the shift around the concept of coverture. Coverture made two people legally one upon marriage ("bone of my bones, and flesh of my flesh"), as the wife's legal identity was subsumed into that of her husband. This merging of man and woman was a legal minefield for married women over much of the century in relation to access to their money and property, which by law was absorbed by the husband upon marriage. In other words, "the family was a locus of male

---

80. Ellis, "Concerning *Jude the Obscure,*" 48.
81. Daleski, *Paradoxes of Love,* 188.
82. Hardy, *Collected Letters of Thomas Hardy,* vol. 2, 98.
83. Hardy, *Jude the Obscure,* 69.

power sustained by the judicial authority of the state."[84] Victorian feminists agitated for legal reforms, which led to some property protections for separated and divorced women through the Matrimonial Causes Act of 1857. Yet this act was one of "compromise, not revolution."[85] Emma and Hardy met in 1870, the year that saw the passing of the Married Woman's Property Act, which decreed that income a wife earned through her own work would be regarded as her separate property but that any property she acquired before and after marriage belonged to her husband. It was only with the 1882 Married Women's Property Act that married women were able to retain full legal control of everything they owned or earned before and after marriage. Given these reforms, it is unsurprising that the rise in the ideal of companionate marriage over the course of the century was accompanied in the latter half by a rise in the divorce rates, which brought to increasing public attention the existence of unhappy marriages and the increasing financial independence of women. The spectacle of divorce raised questions about whether marriage was indeed a union "as strong as death," though no doubt many more divorces would have been filed had social and religious norms made it possible and had legislation allowed for full legal equality between husband and wife. For instance, though the legal reforms granted married women more control over their personal property, the reforms did not grant a married woman feme sole status, recognition of her own legal identity. Moreover, the diminution of coverture over the second half of the century did not necessarily have a material impact on the lives of unhappy wives. Jane Thomas reminds us that throughout Emma and Hardy's long marriage, "Hardy held the purse strings, and held them rather tightly by all accounts" and that the income Emma received through bonds seems to have been administered by Hardy.[86] Despite their unhappiness, the pair did not divorce. Emma died in 1912, and Hardy married Florence Dugdale after an appropriate period of time, in 1914.

In her review, "The Anti-Marriage League," Margaret Oliphant deemed *Jude the Obscure* "an assault on the stronghold of marriage, which is now beleaguered on every side."[87] Hardy's novel expresses such a profoundly tragic outlook toward legal marriage that the freedom a divorce might adumbrate seems redundant. Life seems irrevocably tainted once the wedding vows have been exchanged, such that divorce makes little difference to one's future happiness. Happiness seems possible only if the matrimonial bond is avoided altogether. In short, it is not divorce that requires reform but marriage itself; marriage is the cause of tragedy. Yet in the novel, Hardy is uninterested in

---

84. Shanley, *Feminism, Marriage, and the Law*, 4.
85. Chase and Levenson, *Spectacle of Intimacy*, 191.
86. Jane, "In Defence of Emma Hardy," 48.
87. Oliphant, "Anti-Marriage League," 141.

reformist thinking in marriage law.[88] He is much more interested in proposing alternatives to marriage, as I will explore. Given the novel's dim view of marriage, it is without surprise that the most completely realized relationship in the novel is between Jude and Sue—before they finally decide to legalize their relationship. As the narrator says of them at an outing, "That complete mutual understanding, in which every glance and movement was as effectual as speech for conveying intelligence between them, made them almost the two parts of a single whole."[89] Sue calls Jude "my comrade."[90] The two demonstrate ample camaraderie without the marriage bond, possibly because they are already united by blood. Moreover, in arguing against what she calls the "vulgar" and coercive institution of legal marriage, Sue says to Jude, "I really am yours and you really are mine."[91] This phrase echoes those from the Song of Songs, which we explored earlier in the chapter: "My beloved is mine and I am his" and "I am my beloved's, and my beloved is mine" (2:16; 6:13). It is when Sue and Jude finally decide to legalize their marriage, after a few years of delay, that their lives shift toward tragedy. The first sign is Sue's "dull, cowed and listless manner for days,"[92] suggesting her loss of vitality as her legal identity becomes subsumed into that of her husband. When their neighbors learn of their marriage, Jude loses his job and the family is cast out from its lodgings; the family descends into poverty; Sue and Jude's eldest son kills himself and his two siblings; their last child is stillborn; Sue and Jude leave their pastoral home and remarry their first spouses; Jude dies. "Weddings be funerals," portends a widow.[93]

For much of the novel, it is Sue who proposes alternatives to marriage and its attendant sufferings. Critics associate her with the New Woman, a term first used in 1893.[94] Indeed, Hardy had proposed the title "The New Woman" for a dramatization of the novel.[95] As "a sign of the changing aspirations of women,"[96] the New Woman seems both unfeminine and engaged in apparently male pursuits. Sue herself does not "talk quite like a girl," as Jude tells her when he recognizes the extent of both her intellect and her reading.[97] She also possesses "strange ways and a curious unconsciousness of gender."[98] And in

---

88. Claybaugh, "Irrelevance of Marriage Law," 50.
89. Hardy, *Jude the Obscure*, 306.
90. Hardy, *Jude the Obscure*, 357.
91. Hardy, *Jude the Obscure*, 285.
92. Hardy, *Jude the Obscure*, 313.
93. Hardy, *Jude the Obscure*, 420.
94. Claybaugh, "Irrelevance of Marriage Law," 55, 54.
95. Wright, *Hardy and the Erotic*, 120.
96. Burdett, "New Woman," 363.
97. Hardy, *Jude the Obscure*, 152.
98. Hardy, *Jude the Obscure*, 154.

their early days, she asserts, "I at least don't regard marriage as a Sacrament."[99] Amanda Claybaugh argues that the novel proposes three alternatives to marriage.[100] In my view, these alternatives are chiefly specific to Sue. The first is Sue's preference, which is sexless companionship; the second is the free love union into which she and Jude eventually enter once they decide not to marry; and the third is collective child rearing extending beyond the couple and immediate family.[101] Sue's following words to Jude exemplify her modernity: "Everybody is getting to feel as we do. We are a little beforehand, that's all."[102]

The scholarly focus on Sue's modernity has obscured the undeniable biblical influence on her identity. Yet as we have seen in the introduction, Jude utters a description from Song of Songs 1:8 to describe what Sue means to him: "You know *you* are fairest among women to me, come to that!"[103] Sue's first name means "lily," while her surname recalls maidenhead, potentially implying a conflict between virginity and marriage.[104] The two names recall the description of the Shulamite in the Song of Songs as "the lily of the valleys" and "as the lily among thorns" (2:1–2), and as a "garden inclosed" and "fountain sealed" (4:12), respectively. With Sue's first name, Hardy slips into a symbolism that has its origins in allegorical readings of the lily in the Song of Songs and hence finds himself still chained to biblical interpretations that his characters decry (as discussed in the introduction). But for Sue, the lily implies more than physical virginity; it suggests freedom from both intellectual restraint and marriage, in much the same way that celibacy afforded women advantages such as career advancement through freedom from maternity.[105] At once a New Woman and the "fairest among women," Sue is "a refined creature, intended by Nature to be left intact."[106]

Sue embodies the tension between ideals. She represents, on the one hand, freedom of intellectual and bodily autonomy and, on the other hand, subjugation to marital convention. Where once she had held "scorn" for "convention," she has now, in returning to Phillotson after living happily with Jude, become "creed-drunk."[107] Jude mourns this "sad, soft, most melancholy wreck of a promising human intellect that it has ever been my lot to behold."[108] Jude compares her now-dimmed intellectual faculties to light: "She was once a

---

99. Hardy, *Jude the Obscure,* 173.
100. Claybaugh, "Irrelevance of Marriage Law," 56.
101. Claybaugh, "Irrelevance of Marriage Law," 56.
102. Hardy, *Jude the Obscure,* 301.
103. Hardy, *Jude the Obscure,* 158.
104. Page, *Thomas Hardy,* 43.
105. Heilmann, "Marriage," 357.
106. Hardy, *Jude the Obscure,* 362.
107. Hardy, *Jude the Obscure,* 411.
108. Hardy, *Jude the Obscure,* 410.

woman whose intellect was to mine like a star to a benzoline lamp; who saw all my superstitions as cobwebs that she could brush away with a word."[109] But like Lucifer the light bearer, Sue has become a fallen star: "bitter affliction came to us, and her intellect broke, and she veered round to darkness."[110] In preparing to do her "penance" and "duty"[111] by finally consummating her marriage to Phillotson, Sue informs Jude, "I've wrestled and struggled, and fasted, and prayed. I have nearly brought my body into complete subjection."[112] To this, Jude responds, "O you darling little fool; where is your reason? You seem to have suffered the loss of your faculties!"[113] Sue's loss of intellectual reasoning and her subjection to Phillotson represents her "enslavement to forms," her enchainment to a blinkered understanding of the Bible and of marriage.[114] As Jude puts it, by quoting the Bible in the process, "We are acting by the letter; and 'the letter killeth.'"[115] Hardy draws a parallel here between the perils of marriage and biblical exegesis if they both produce constraints on individual freedoms. At the conclusion of *Jude the Obscure,* God is nowhere to be found, and Sue readies herself to finally consummate her loveless marriage to Phillotson. In other words, in the city of Christminster, there is no God and there is no love.

In *Jane Eyre,* Brontë emphasizes a particular aspect of Christian discourse, notably the centrality of love in all relationships, whether human or divine. The foundation of all meaningful forms of love is God. *Jane Eyre* is a means of articulating its author's ideals of companionate marriage and the union of like minds. To this end, Brontë deploys the authority of the Song of Songs to reinforce the role of middle-class women as equals in their romantic partnerships. *Far from the Madding Crowd* and *Jude the Obscure* demonstrate that the Song of Songs remained relevant in the nineteenth century, whether in depicting companionate marriage or the perils of entering an incompatible one. While the earlier novel ends with an ideal marriage, Hardy's final novel shows us that not all couples are happy. The unspoken question in *Jude the Obscure* is, if Love is God, and if God is dead, then what does that mean for the Bible's canonical book on love?

---

109. Hardy, *Jude the Obscure,* 422.
110. Hardy, *Jude the Obscure,* 422.
111. Hardy, *Jude the Obscure,* 416.
112. Hardy, *Jude the Obscure,* 410.
113. Hardy, *Jude the Obscure,* 410.
114. Hardy, *Jude the Obscure,* 422.
115. Hardy, *Jude the Obscure,* 410.

CHAPTER 2

Violence, Eroticism, and Art

Edward Burne-Jones and Phoebe Anna Traquair

We saw in the previous chapter that Victorian marriages elicited the gamut of human emotions, from happiness to unhappiness. In this chapter, I turn to visual culture to further explore relationships between men and women in the context of social and intellectual concerns. In the first half, I elucidate a darker or hidden side of marriage. In particular, I am interested in the obstacles on the road to marriage as well as the "destructive power of love,"[1] that is, violent unions. I begin with the Pre-Raphaelite Edward Burne-Jones, who visualizes the Song of Songs as a love story in which Solomon is one of the protagonists. Burne-Jones's reputation as a "dreamer" and what that term might mean forms the connecting thread between the works. Beneath the veneer of beautiful dreamlike images lie distortions of tales of love and happy marriages. In his extant unpublished drawings of the Song of Songs, the lovers are often physically separated or show little physical affection. I then shift my attention to a stained-glass church window at St. Helen's, Darley Dale, and Burne-Jones's partial depiction of a "dream" sequence from the Song of Songs: a nightmarish scene of violence against the Shulamite. This image reminds us of other often-forgotten examples of violence against women in the Bible. Furthermore, we can read the window within the context of the increasing social and legal attention paid to marital violence in the Victorian era, including

---

1. Faxon, "Pre-Raphaelites and the Mythic Image," 77.

attempts to define and legislate against it. The general invisibility of marital violence in middle-class discourse did not erase its presence in reality. After all, the middle-class Victorian home contained many secrets and sometimes unspoken horrors.

In the second half of the chapter, I explore the theme of separation and reunion in a work by Phoebe Anna Traquair, a leading exponent of the Arts and Crafts movement in Edinburgh. Here, the relationship between lovers and the hidden side of love are not as dark as they were for Burne-Jones. Instead, Traquair depicts joyful reunion and erotic desire after the pain of separation. I have chosen to focus on a commissioned work, a painted grand piano that combines biblical and classical myths. In a series of panels around the piano, Traquair successfully marries the arts of music, painting, and literature. Yet unlike the disjointed nature of Burne-Jones's drawings and stained-glass panels, Traquair's narrative about a love triangle tells the story of obstacles in the way of union and the triumph of love. In this narrative, Solomon separates the woman from her lover in his attempt to seduce her, leading the two lovers to spend most of their time apart, yearning to be together and uncertain as to whether they will return to each other. Traquair's desire-driven narrative of lovers separated and reunited might be interpreted allegorically as the soul's separation and reunion with Christ. Yet she also draws attention to the hidden and sexual nature of marriage by transposing the eroticism of the Song of Songs onto the function of the piano, an instrument of sympathetic vibration, flirtation, and courtship. She also transfers the erotic onto the figure of the earthy god Pan, a nature deity whose music plays a role in uniting not simply nature with the divine but also Traquair's spiritual, ecological, and scientific belief systems.

DREAMER

Edward Burne-Jones was born in Birmingham in 1833, just before Victoria ascended the throne. His mother died six days after giving birth to her only son. Burne-Jones's father, a carver and gilder, could not bear to hold his son for the first few years of his life. The son's guilt over his mother's death persisted until his death. Burne-Jones acknowledged that his melancholic or depressive tendencies "began with my beginning" and became "a deep sunk fountain in me."[2] Studious and an avid reader, he was frequently bullied at school. During school prayers, a fellow student surreptitiously stabbed him in the groin, but

---

2. Cited in MacCarthy, *Last Pre-Raphaelite*, 4.

the incident was never officially reported. In the latter years of his schooling, Burne-Jones did extremely well in Greek, Latin, history, and religion. He won prizes for drawing and mathematics and in 1851 was promoted to the top of his school. At school he admired the bas-reliefs in the Nimroud or Assyrian room of the British Museum. "He loved the close written inscriptions and the scenes of violent action on the bas-reliefs," argues a biographer: "scenes of hunting, scenes of battle, tremendous sieges."[3] By the time Burne-Jones went up to Oxford in 1853, he had formed an ambition to enter the church as a follower of the Oxford Movement and an ardent admirer of Robert Wilberforce and John Henry Newman (despite Newman's secession to Rome). Shortly after Burne-Jones arrived, he met William Morris, who would become his lifelong friend and fellow artist. The two men were born romantics with a passion for the medieval and a desire for ordination.

In 1854 Burne-Jones and Morris underwent spiritual crises after reading Thomas Carlyle's concept of the hero or man of vision who interprets for ordinary mortals the transcendental will. Additionally, the two men were persuaded by Ruskin's claim that the artist was uniquely qualified to fulfil the prophetic role by use of the imagination, which could offer profound insights into the nature of God. The friends' aspirations turned away from the church, as they resolved to enact change in the world through their art.[4] Ruskin's writing led them to the Pre-Raphaelites and their leader, Dante Gabriel Rossetti, whose medievalist and romantic watercolor *The First Anniversary of the Death of Beatrice* (1853) had them in raptures. Rossetti was to become Burne-Jones's mentor and would encourage him to leave university, move to London, and take up art under his supervision. Burne-Jones's wife, Georgiana, writes that after his pilgrimage to "the shrine of Rossetti in Blackfriars . . . there was no more talk of Edward's going back to Oxford for his degree: Rossetti's encouragement and advice had decided him to give his whole life to Art."[5] Throughout his career, Burne-Jones was prolific and remarkably versatile. Besides large-scale paintings and sequences of pictures,

> he made thousands of designs for stained glass, embroidery and tapestry, hand-painted furniture, clothes, shoes and jewellery. Loving music, Burne-Jones even started a campaign for the reform of piano design. In collaboration with William Morris he made numerous illustrations for books.[6]

---

3. MacCarthy, *Last Pre-Raphaelite*, 19.
4. Rager, "'Smite this sleeping world awake,'" 445.
5. Burne-Jones, *Memorials of Edward Burne-Jones*, vol. 1, 136.
6. MacCarthy, *Last Pre-Raphaelite*, xx.

Burne-Jones was made a baronet in 1894, much to the displeasure of Morris and Georgiana, both socialists. He died in 1898, and a memorial service was held at Westminster Abbey—an unprecedented honor for an artist.

Victorian art critic Cosmo Monkhouse praised Burne-Jones in 1894, saying, "He has created a new world with the breath of his own genius, a world wondrously beautiful and beautifully wondrous."[7] Declaring the painter's "grand series of pictures on the legend of 'The Briar Rose,' or 'Sleeping Beauty,' the masterpiece of his lighter fancy," Monkhouse states, "from beginning to end it is not only a dream, but a dream of dreams."[8] He concludes by calling Burne-Jones "the arch-dreamer of the nineteenth century."[9] Burne-Jones himself associated love with dreams. In 1892 he wrote about the effect of his unfulfilled infatuation with long-time friend Frances Horner, née Graham: "And I am living in a dream—is it a month ago? how unpremeditated it all was—I glided into this heavenly land as perhaps we glide into a new life."[10] The characterization of Burne-Jones as a dreamer, removed from the world, has persisted over the years, "but its connotation has shifted from praise to dismissive denigration," notes Andrea Wolk Rager.[11] By privileging the decorative and fantastical, Burne-Jones has been marginalized in scholarship as an escapist withdrawing from modernity into a world of sleep, dreams, and legends.[12] Rager challenges the assessment of escapism in Burne-Jones's work. She argues that with paintings of stillness, such as *The Briar Rose,* Burne-Jones created "a liminal space from which to reflect back on the ills of the modern world rather than retreat from them."[13] The knight at the far end of the first canvas stands in for Burne-Jones's "struggle for personal, social, artistic, and even environmental awakening."[14] For these reasons, *The Briar Rose* is a "radical" painting.[15] In similar fashion, I would argue that Burne-Jones's depictions of the Song of Songs pull back the curtains to reveal relationships that are contrary to the Victorian middle-class idealization of marriage.

Marriage evoked complex and contradictory feelings for Burne-Jones. For him, it seemed unlikely to afford lasting pleasure or happiness. His celebrated *King Cophetua and the Beggar Maid* (ca. 1883) appears to celebrate the love-match between a king and a beggar maid, but the narrow room is suggestive of

---

7. Monkhouse, "Edward Burne-Jones," 152.
8. Monkhouse, "Edward Burne-Jones," 146–47.
9. Monkhouse, "Edward Burne-Jones," 147.
10. Dakers, "Yours affectionately, Angelo," 20.
11. Rager, "'Smite this sleeping world awake,'" 438.
12. Rager, "'Smite this sleeping world awake,'" 438.
13. Rager, "'Smite this sleeping world awake,'" 441.
14. Rager, "'Smite this sleeping world awake,'" 441.
15. Rager, "'Smite this sleeping world awake,'" 441.

a tomb, while the anemones are linked to the tears of Venus.[16] Above the pedals of an upright piano gifted to him and Georgiana on the occasion of their wedding in 1860, Burne-Jones painted a design of seated women, with some playing instruments and others bent over and possibly asleep—all unaware of the crowned female figure of Death at the gate.[17] The macabre image on a musical instrument implies discord as opposed to harmony, a reminder of "the impossibility of perfect love"[18] and that dreams of marital happiness cannot last. Indeed, Burne-Jones once joked to his wife about marriage being a lottery and whether it should be outlawed.[19] The piano was a deliberate choice for this painting because of its centrality in the domestic sphere and its association with women. Burne-Jones claimed in a letter from 1880, "I have been wanting for years to reform pianos, since they are as it were the very altar of homes, and second hearth to people, and so hideous to behold."[20] Beyond household aesthetics, however, Burne-Jones's images of the women playing instruments confirm that it is "almost impossible to separate nineteenth-century images of music from issues of gender and sexuality."[21] Music was associated with women at a number of levels and included the idea of music as a domestic accomplishment.[22] By painting the wedding present, was Burne-Jones drawing a link between marriage, the role of women, and the need for marital reform?

VIOLENT MARRIAGES

Many Victorian wives suffered physical and sexual abuse, despite the middle-class idealization of marriage and family.[23] The equivalent nineteenth-century terms for marital or domestic violence included "marital cruelty," as a legal term, or "wife beating," as a colloquial one.[24] Lisa Surridge notes that marital violence, which may have been physical or sexual, "formed part of a web of Victorian issues surrounding marital power—coverture, married women's property law, divorce law, conjugal rights."[25] I mentioned in the previous chapter that the Victorian era saw improvements to the rights of women in regard

---

16. Arscott, "Edward Burne-Jones (1833–1898)," 233.
17. Crawford, "Victorian Artist-Dreamer," 6.
18. Black and Exum, "Semiotics in Stained Glass," 320.
19. Burne-Jones, *Memorials of Edward Burne-Jones*, vol. 2, 193.
20. Burne-Jones, *Memorials of Edward Burne-Jones*, vol. 2, 111.
21. Cooper, "Liquefaction of Desire," 189.
22. Cooper, "Liquefaction of Desire," 189.
23. Bourke, "Sexual Violence, Marital Guidance," 419.
24. Lawson and Shakinovsky, *Marked Body,* 2.
25. Surridge, *Bleak Houses,* 4.

to property laws and divorce. These improvements belonged to broader historical shifts toward greater protection for women and children. For instance, the 1853 Criminal Procedure Act, also called the Act for the Better Prevention of Aggravated Assault upon Women and Children, set a clear limit for what was tolerable in relation to family chastisement and bodily harm inflicted on children under the age of 14.[26] In 1856 J. W. Kaye wrote an article, "Outrages on Women," partly as a response to a parliamentary bill that proposed flogging penalties for marital violence.[27] Kaye describes the prevalence of marital violence among the working classes and claims that, "in the criminal annals of England, outrages upon women have of late years held a distressingly prominent position."[28] The screams of the working-class wife echo in "the close alley or teeming courtyard," piercing the "thin, dilapidated partition-walls" of multihousehold quarters.[29] Joanne Begiato believes that Kaye "contrasted the visibility of working-class wife-beating with the invisibility of middle-class abuse."[30] In the words of Kaye, the middle-class home "is screened and guarded by closed doors and obscuring curtains; and from the penetralia of such houses no voice can come without the consent of aides and abettors. . . . Everything is secret as death."[31] Yet when the 1857 Divorce Act took effect, shortly before Burne-Jones was to design the stained-glass windows at St. Helen's, Darley Dale, middle-class assaults received the same level of publicity and reporting in the daily press as did the working class.[32]

We see, then, that despite the ideology of the angel in the house, marriage did not automatically protect women from harm; in fact, it could be a cause of harm. Marital law "allowed for significant levels of injury," observes Joanna Bourke.[33] Until the case of Kelly v. Kelly in 1870, "legal accusations of violence within marriage were assumed to involve extreme physical (as opposed to psychological or emotional) brutality."[34] Women could only turn to the law of assault and battery because marital rape was legal.[35] As Bourke explains,

The "marital rape exemption," commonly ascribed to Sir Matthew Hale in 1736, meant that a wife was presumed to have granted lifelong consent to

---

26. Moon, "Domestic Violence," 8.
27. Kaye, "Outrages on Women," 344; Surridge, *Bleak Houses,* 4.
28. Kaye, "Outrages on Women," 233.
29. Kaye, "Outrages on Women," 236.
30. Begiato, "Beyond the Rule of Thumb," 54.
31. Kaye, "Outrages on Women," 236.
32. Surridge, *Bleak Houses,* 8.
33. Bourke, "Sexual Violence, Marital Guidance," 421.
34. Bourke, "Sexual Violence, Marital Guidance," 421.
35. Bourke, "Sexual Violence, Marital Guidance," 421.

48 • CHAPTER 2

sexual intercourse with her husband. Under the marriage vows, husband and wife became "one person under the law." It was a contract that "she cannot retract." Thereafter, as James Schouler explains in *A Treatise on the Law of Domestic Relations* (1870), "wilfully declining matrimonial intimacy and companionship" was nothing short of a "breach of duty, tending to subvert the true ends of marriage." Emotional coldness, irritability, and "sallies of passion" were supposed to be met with calm resignation by good wives.[36]

Individual instances of sexual violence are part what could be considered "the larger system that makes rape and other forms of sexual violence possible."[37] Such a culture would lead feminist thinkers like John Stuart Mill and Harriet Taylor to write in protest against the legal status of women that had inevitably led to wrongs such as wife beating. In parliament and in the ecclesiastical, divorce, criminal, and magistrates' courts, as well as in domestic manuals and the printed press, Victorians debated how to prevent and punish marital violence.[38] This public scrutiny of private conduct shone a spotlight on dangers lurking within an often-idealized domestic space.

THE SONG OF SONGS AND VIOLENCE IN A STAINED-GLASS WINDOW

It has been argued that the Song of Songs was "a natural choice of biblical subjects for Burne-Jones, having little overt religious content but much in the way of lyrical word-painting and allegorical allusion."[39] Despite the insinuation of secularism here, Burne-Jones did not shy away from religious subjects. In fact, although he abandoned the church as a career in 1855, "he did not abandon its visual language" and once declared, "I love Christmas Carol Christianity, I couldn't do without Medieval Christianity."[40] Two surviving sketchbooks in the British Museum and the Morgan Library and Museum include drafts of scenes from the Song of Songs.[41] In viewing either these or other drawings of the Song of Songs, Ruskin declared them "entirely masterful" and "as tranquil

---

36. Bourke, "Sexual Violence, Marital Guidance," 421–22. I have deleted in-text references from the original quotation.

37. Graybill, *Texts after Terror*, 2.

38. Surridge, *Bleak Houses*, 6.

39. Wildman and Christian, "Seven 'Blissfullest Years," 189.

40. Cited in Crawford, "Victorian Artist-Dreamer," 8.

41. Burne-Jones, *Secret Book of Designs*; and Burne-Jones, *Sketchbook*.

and swift as a hawk's flight."[42] As literal "lyrical word-painting," these illustrations combine the source material with visual imagery of figures in medieval attire. The accompanying text is either from the Vulgate or an English translation from the Catholic Douay Bible, in keeping with the Pre-Raphaelite Brotherhood's medievalism and Burne-Jones's youthful Tractarian leanings. Some sketches were eventually transformed into displayed works. Thus *Awake O North Wind* (ca. 1876), at the Birmingham Museum and Art Gallery, was converted into a large watercolor under the Latin title *Sponsa di Libano* (*The Bride of Lebanon*) (1890).[43]

Burne-Jones was drawn to the Song of Songs for reasons that are not entirely celebratory or aesthetic. This approach to the text is in contrast to that of his mentor, Dante Gabriel Rossetti, whose sumptuous and well-known painting *The Beloved* (1856–66) features the Shulamite as a paragon of desirability gazing at the viewer. Indeed, Burne-Jones's extant images are unlikely to depict the source text's most soaring passages of beauty and desire, though one would believe that a man who described beauty in the following manner would seek out its most poetic scenes: "I mean by a picture a beautiful romantic dream of something that never was, never will be—in a light better than any light that ever shone—in a land no one can define or remember, only desire—and the forms divinely beautiful."[44] Burne-Jones largely spurned beautiful images of union when he turned to the Song of Songs. In a sketchbook containing a page of quotes from the biblical text, he curiously combines two different passages so that together they read, "Flee away O my beloved, for love is strong as death" (8:14; 8:6).[45] The insinuation is that love is that from which one should flee. Held at the Morgan Library and Museum, the sketchbook features lilies, along with the sealed fountain and walled garden from 4:12.[46] These images appear to stress the impenetrability of the lover. Similarly, the sketchbook at the British Museum entitled "The Secret Book of Designs" (1885) depicts the following passage from 4:8: "Come from Libanus, my spouse, come from Libanus, come: thou shalt be crowned from the top of Amana, from the top of Sanir and Hermon, from the dens of the lions, from the mountains of the leopards" (Douay translation).[47] The composition, specifically the general placement of the figures and the steep verticality,

---

42. Anonymous, "Professor Ruskin on Burne-Jones," 224. I would like to thank Elizabeth Cumming for drawing my attention to this piece.

43. Wildman and Christian, "Seven 'Blissfullest Years,'" 190.

44. Cited in MacCarthy, *Last Pre-Raphaelite*, xx.

45. Burne-Jones, *Sketchbook*, n.p.

46. Burne-Jones, *Sketchbook*, n.p.

47. Burne-Jones, *Secret Book of Designs*, n.p.

presages that of *King Cophetua*. Additionally, Solomon stands between a dead tree and a lily plant. He holds up a branch, perhaps from an olive tree, and gestures toward the bride, who is standing on vertical rocks, her hands clasped together. Situated between the lovers is a pond, a lion, and a leopard with cubs. Again, one senses the obstacles in the way of love, including a literal lion's den. Likewise, an illustration for the line "my beloved to me and I to him who feedeth among the lilies" (2:16) features the lovers facing each other, arms raised, but their bodies separated by lilies.[48]

Typological interpretation provides little joy for Burne-Jones. A translation from the Douay Bible, "The new and the old my beloved, I have kept for thee" (7:13), inspires an image of lovers standing on either side of a tree, reminiscent of the angel Gabriel and the Virgin Mary in Burne-Jones's *The Annunciation* (1858–61).[49] In *The Annunciation*, the action takes place in a walled garden, which alludes to the Song of Songs and Eden. The typological link between the Old and New Testaments suggests a redemptive theology, whereby "the process of Redemption is an inverse parallel of the Fall."[50] A typological reading also holds to Mary's virginity, as opposed to Eve's implied sexuality. In the nineteenth century, Newman revived the ancient concept of Mary as the Second Eve.[51] Burne-Jones's sketchbook drawing seems to depict a character picking fruit from a tree, thereby enacting both Song of Songs 4:16 and the story of Adam and Eve, in which the serpent tempts Eve to eat the fruit from the forbidden tree (Genesis 3). She in turn encourages Adam to eat, and thereafter the two are expelled from the garden. Thus, the Song of Songs evokes for Burne-Jones a great deal of ambivalence.

Biblical violence lurks in the background of Burne-Jones's images surrounding the feminine and the Song of Songs. In a later version of *The Annunciation* (1872), a cartoon for stained glass at Castle Howard Chapel in Yorkshire, Burne-Jones draws the female-headed serpent writhing down a tree. The convention of depicting the serpent with a female head connects the feminine with seduction and evil.[52] Seduction, or the possibility of it, is punishable by violence. In iconography, the serpent's head is crushed beneath Mary's foot to signal Mary's "immaculacy and triumph over original sin."[53] The beauty of a female biblical figure is often the cause of sexual violence against her. Such is the case of Susannah in Daniel 13. One wonders if there is

---

48. Burne-Jones, *Sketchbook*, n.p.
49. Burne-Jones, *Sketchbook*, n.p.
50. Bullough, "Serpent, Angels and Virgins," 474.
51. Bullough, "Serpent, Angels and Virgins," 466.
52. Bullough, "Serpent, Angels and Virgins," 474.
53. Bullough, "Serpent, Angels and Virgins," 474.

a link between the serpent, Susannah, and the Shulamite. The Song of Songs includes a scene of violence that has puzzled and confused many readers. In 5:2–6, the lover is awakened by the voice of her beloved knocking on the door. She opens to him, but he has disappeared. In 5:7, the lover leaves the house and becomes a victim of violence: "The watchmen that went about the city found me, they smote me, they wounded me; the keepers of the walls took away my veil from me." These watchmen seem to be the same men from 3:3 who at first seem harmless yet later prove violent. The scene from 5:7 appears to be part of a dream sequence and hints at possible rape, particularly with the reference to the lost veil.

Burne-Jones depicts the violent scene in a stained-glass window at St. Helen's. Fiona C. Black and J. Cheryl Exum have discussed the scene at length, so these scholars provide a starting point for my discussion. The panel is one of twelve located on three adjacent columns, with each column containing four panels. Each panel combines the written text and its visual representation from the Song of Songs. Inspired by the Oxford Movement and shaped by the Gothic Revival, the Victorian era saw a revival in the medieval art of stained-glass windows.[54] The artistic medium aligned with Burne-Jones's medievalism. As Black and Exum note, however, stained-glass windows are generally devoted to biblical narratives, and therefore the depiction of scenes from the Song of Songs is unusual.[55] The memorial window was commissioned by Colonel William James Gillum, either in 1861 or 1862 through Morris, Marshall, Faulkner and Co., for whom Burne-Jones started designing in 1861.[56] It is likely that Burne-Jones was responsible for the subject matter, as he usually selected the subjects for his work.[57] The windows are laid out in table 1.

On the whole, Burne-Jones elected not to depict the most poetic, amorous, and joyous passages from the source text. Black and Exum speculate that the reasons include the facts that, given much of the subject matter of his paintings, "a story of two lovers, separated by difficult circumstances, would have appealed to him" and that he "shared with his Pre-Raphaelite counterparts an interest in the medieval period and its age-old theme of unrequited love."[58] Burne-Jones's windows largely ignore the fulfilment of love, leaving the lovers' reunion until the final pane.[59] For the majority of his window panels, including the entire middle column, the "arch-dreamer" chose the two

---

54. Crawford, "Victorian Artist-Dreamer," 8.
55. Black and Exum, "Semiotics in Stained Glass," 315.
56. Black and Exum, "Semiotics in Stained Glass," 319.
57. Black and Exum, "Semiotics in Stained Glass," 319.
58. Black and Exum, "Semiotics in Stained Glass," 319.
59. Black and Exum, "Semiotics in Stained Glass," 320.

52 • CHAPTER 2

TABLE 1. Sequence of the Song of Songs panels at St. Helen's, Darley Dale*

COLUMN 1	COLUMN 2	COLUMN 3
1. As the apple tree among the trees of the wood so is my beloved among the sons [Song 2:3]	5. I charge you O daughters of Jerusalem if ye find my beloved that ye tell him that I am sick of love [Song 5:8]	9. As the lily among thorns so is my love among the daughters [Song 2:2]
2. My mother's children were angry with me they made me keeper of the vineyards [Song 1:6]	6. I sleep but my heart waketh It is the voice of my beloved that knocketh [Song 5:2]	10. Whither is thy beloved gone O thou fairest among women [Song 6:1]
3. Behold he standeth behind our wall he looketh forth at the windows shewing himself through the lattice [Song 2:9]	7. I opened to my beloved but my beloved had withdrawn himself and was gone [Song 5:6]	11. Who is that cometh up from the wilderness leaning upon her beloved [Song 8:5]
4. By night on my bed I sought him whom my soul loveth I sought him but I found him not [Song 3:1]	8. The watchmen that went about the city found me they smote me they wounded me [Song 5:7]	12. Go forth O ye daughters of Zion and behold King Solomon [Song 3:11]

* Adapted from Black and Exum, "Semiotics in Stained Glass," 326.

related dream/nightmare sequences from Song of Songs 3:1–5 and 5:2–6:3. These dreams depict "encounters sought but missed."[60] Moreover, one of the moments of physical contact with a man—this time unsought—is with the watchman. While the woman is not in a relationship with the watchman and, furthermore, the violence takes place outside the domestic space, the specter of male violence in a text commonly associated with love and marriage would have been recognizable to those familiar with the topic of gendered and marital violence. After all, marital violence lies on a spectrum of interpersonal violence most often inflicted against women. In addition, a viewer's eyes would have first beheld the image of a man dominating a fallen woman before settling on the words informing the viewer that he is a watchman. The decision to show only one watchman instead of two or more watchmen allows for the mind to automatically see the woman and man as a couple. The watchman provides an acceptable class-based depiction of marital violence, as it would have been inappropriate to suggest that someone as esteemed as Solomon would be a violent spouse. Indeed, the watchman's physiognomy prefigures sexological theories of a wife beater from the laboring classes: coarse facial features, voluminous lower jaw, abundant and red hair.[61]

Why would Burne-Jones choose to depict a disturbing scene of violence from the Song of Songs in a highly visible and religious location? The scene

---

60. Black and Exum, "Semiotics in Stained Glass," 332.
61. Bourke, "Sexual Violence, Marital Guidance," 424.

would have been difficult to ignore by virtue of its location at the bottom of the middle column and because "its dynamic quality and violent nature contrast sharply with the panels around it."[62] The image of violence can be seen as a literal window into the world of gendered and sexual violence, not just in the era but also in the Bible. This depiction in a church setting invites the viewer to draw a parallel with Biblical examples of violence against women. In the words of contemporary biblical scholar Rhiannon Graybill, the Hebrew Bible is "dense with misogyny, sexual violence, and rape culture."[63] This "rape culture" includes sexual violence more broadly understood:

> sexual exploitation other than rape, stories where rape is hinted at but not explicitly described, stories of forced sex, unwelcome sex, and unwanted sex, *was it or wasn't it?* stories, stories about forced marriage, stories about sexual trafficking and exchange, stories that assume the same gendered logic as rape without, however, describing rape explicitly.[64]

As I have said, the Song of Songs contains a scene where sexual violence "is hinted at but not explicitly described." In panel ten, the lover is humbled and kneeling, as if she were begging the women of Jerusalem for her beloved's whereabouts. Black and Exum observe that she is wearing her nightdress without her robe, which the watchmen had taken from her in Song of Songs 5:7. Her disheveled, indecorous, and immodest appearance has been inflicted against her will by men. Black and Exum hold that, while Burne-Jones thought it important to include the beating in panel eight, he was either not entirely comfortable with it or he felt that he could not represent it explicitly.[65] Thus, despite the citation "they smote me, they wounded me," the watchman is not delivering any blows. Instead, he grabs one of the woman's wrists and with his other hand points a lantern to her face. I would argue that the Victorian preference for obliqueness in the depiction of indelicate matters renders this window sufficient in representing gendered violence. Due to the invisibility of the handle, the male hand that raises the lantern is clenched as if it were a large fist. While the lantern might remove the action from a direct punch, it also allows for a startling illumination into the woman's plight. Together with both the hold on the woman's wrist and her crouched state, possibly from being pushed, the scene becomes shockingly violent, especially taking into account the context of its location—a countryside church—and its source material: a text commonly interpreted as a homage to love and marriage.

---

62. Black and Exum, "Semiotics in Stained Glass," 336–37.
63. Graybill, *Texts after Terror*, 10.
64. Graybill, *Texts after Terror*, 2.
65. Black and Exum, "Semiotics in Stained Glass," 337–38.

54 · CHAPTER 2

The window draws attention to the relationship between violence and unequal power relations. We witness a fallen and cowering woman, her right foot exposed, her physical state in dishevelment. The towering man bends and moves toward her in a menacing pose. His clasping of her wrist renders the woman helpless. Indeed, the wrist is held in such a way that the woman's raised hand might also be read as a feeble attempt to ward off the attacker. There is an element of the woman having transgressed—notably as a woman wandering the streets at night, which in the eye of street surveillance potentially locates her in the same category as a prostitute: a woman socially out of place. In contrast, men could walk the streets and enter public locations with impunity. Indeed, masculinity as a social status required the full ability to move freely in society.[66] This masculine freedom of movement also allows men to defend patriarchal privilege, which is "positioned within a broader culture of physically aggressive masculinity involving drink, male sociability, and predatory heterosexuality."[67] While the watchman might be said to be doing his job, his is a role upholding patriarchal privilege over women who walk the streets at night, who have stepped out of line, and who as a result are physically assaulted and punished. Like marital rape, this is legally sanctioned violence. Burne-Jones was certainly radical in his depiction of this scene of violence in a church window.

TRAQUAIR'S AMBITION

The Shulamite's lowly social position meant she was especially vulnerable to patriarchal privilege. Middle-class Victorian women had privileges and social connections that their working-class sisters did not. As an ambitious artist involved with the Edinburgh Arts and Crafts scene, Phoebe Anna Traquair thrived as a middle-class woman in a world of men. She "occupies a unique position" as "Scotland's first significant professional woman artist of the modern age."[68] Like Burne-Jones, Traquair was accomplished in a range of media: painting, book illustration and binding, embroidery, manuscript illumination, enameling, and mural decoration. She painted the interiors of at least six public buildings, including the giant mural of biblical scenes (1893–1901) in the former Catholic Apostolic Church, now known as the Mansfield Traquair Centre in Edinburgh. Admired by Ruskin and W. B. Yeats, among others, she networked, negotiated commissions, and exhibited in Britain, Europe, and

---

66. Brady, *Masculinity and Male Homosexuality*, 213.

67. D'Cruze, *Crimes of Outrage*, 21.

68. Cumming, *Phoebe Anna Traquair*, 9. The biographical information originates from this volume by Cumming.

North America. Elizabeth Cumming argues that Traquair's Ruskin-influenced ideas of "the minutiae of the natural world . . . as [being] part of one vast grand plan" were underpinned by Christian faith and intended to "reflect the immensity of spiritual life and culture."[69] Traquair and her husband's intellectual circles included luminaries such as T. H. Huxley, Charles Darwin, and the Edinburgh sociobiologist Patrick Geddes.[70] Demonstrating her ability to reconcile evolutionary science with Christianity, Traquair included an image of a dinosaur in her mural schemes in two places of worship.[71]

Phoebe Anna Moss was born in Dublin in 1852 to a surgeon, William Moss, and Teresa Richardson. The family visited local collections at the Trinity College library. Showing a talent for art and encouraged by her parents, she received art training at the Department of Science and Art of the Royal Dublin Society in the late 1860s. She won a student prize, leading to an assignment illustrating the research papers of Scottish paleontologist Dr. Ramsay Heatley Traquair, who was a professor of zoology at the Royal College of Science. The attraction was immediate, and Phoebe announced to her family her intention of marrying the academic. The couple married in 1873 and moved to Edinburgh a year later, where Ramsay was appointed the first keeper of natural history at the Museum of Science and Art. Traquair provided meticulous pencil drawings of the fossil fish at the center of her husband's research papers until his retirement in 1906. Traquair was also engaged in Edinburgh's literary scene and became a close friend of John Miller Gray, the first curator of the future Scottish National Portrait Gallery. Gray was friends with the likes of Walter Pater and Michael Field, and he had a hand in influencing Traquair's poetic tastes. Her literary influences included Dante, Wordsworth, Blake, Tennyson, Carlyle, Pater, Dante Gabriel Rossetti, Burne-Jones, and Morris. She initiated a correspondence with Ruskin in 1887, ostensibly to seek his advice on medieval illumination. Through his public lectures in the 1850s, Ruskin promoted the revival of manuscript illumination within the context of Victorian visual medievalism.[72] Ruskin loaned Traquair manuscripts from the thirteenth century, while Traquair sent him originals and copies of her work. She was to illuminate major works, including the Song of Songs in 1897 (the copy is now lost)[73] and *The Psalms of David* (1884), along with Elizabeth Barrett Browning's *Sonnets from the Portuguese* (1897–98), Dante Gabriel Rossetti's *The House of Life* (1898), and Dante's *La Vita Nuova* (1902). In 1920 Traquair became the

---

69. Cumming, *Phoebe Anna Traquair*, 10.

70. Huxtable, "Drama of the Soul," 25.

71. Huxtable, "Drama of the Soul," 26.

72. Coluzzi, "Illuminating the *Vita Nuova*," 191–92.

73. For a photograph of the book cover, see Morris, "Versatile Art Worker," 342. I wish to thank Elizabeth Cumming for drawing my attention to this essay.

56 · CHAPTER 2

first honorary woman member of the Scottish Royal Academy, reflecting her status as a leading professional designer in a field dominated by men. She died in Edinburgh in 1936.

Throughout her career, Traquair maintained "the ideal of the artist who alone can realize her concepts and thus positioned herself at the 'art' end of the Arts and Crafts movement," notes Cumming.[74] The movement had its roots in the late nineteenth century. Its leading proponents, such as William Morris, trained as architects and worked toward unity in the arts, believing that all creative endeavor was of equal value.[75] With the spirit of reform, they sought to rekindle a sense of harmony between architect, designer, and craftsman in the production of everyday objects.[76] Ruskin was a proponent of the movement. Decrying the commercial- and machine-oriented society of the Victorian era, he believed that the builders and craftsmen of the later middle ages enjoyed complete freedom of expression.[77] The formal beginnings of the Edinburgh Arts and Crafts movement took place in October 1889, with the second congress of the National Association for the Advancement of Art and its Application to Industry, which met in the new Scottish National Portrait Gallery.[78] The delegates numbered several hundred and included a new generation of artists, architects, and sculptors, among them James McNeill Whistler, Walter Sickert, William Lethaby, C. F. A. Voysey, George Frampton, and Albert Gilbert.[79]

THE PIANO AND THE SONG OF SONGS

Piano decoration was a feature of Victorian decorative art, as we saw with Burne-Jones's painting of his wedding gift. It was also a standout feature of the Arts and Crafts movement. Pianos and their predecessor, the harpsichord, have a history of craftsmanship, as accomplished artists often sought to beautify the cases of their instruments with painting and mottoes.[80] It is notable that Sébastien Érard, who made his first piano in 1772 and was the first piano maker in France to prioritize the grand piano model, ascribed his success to his early training in architecture and design.[81] Traquair is known to have decorated only three pieces of furniture, and one of these was a Steinway grand

---

74. Cumming, "Patterns of Life," 16.
75. Cumming and Kaplan, *Arts and Crafts Movement*, 6.
76. Cumming and Kaplan, *Arts and Crafts Movement*, 6.
77. Cumming and Kaplan, *Arts and Crafts Movement*, 12.
78. Bowe and Cumming, *Arts and Crafts Movements*, 17.
79. Bowe and Cumming, *Arts and Crafts Movements*, 18–19.
80. Purcell, "Design of Grand Pianos," 63.
81. Purcell, "Design of Grand Pianos," 63.

piano.[82] The piano was commissioned by Frank Tennant in 1908 for restorations of Lymphe Castle in Kent. Traquair would describe her work in progress as the "best *painting* I have done, wood is so delightful to work on."[83]

The piano case became a canvas of sorts for several independent series of paintings. The first includes nine panels of the Song of Songs wrapped around three sides of the piano. The second comprises three scenes along the keyboard panel, set in the ghostly location of the "Willowwood" sonnets from Dante Gabriel Rossetti's *The House of Life* (1876). The third has a tree of life on the outside of the lid. In the words of Kathleen Purcell, the Arabesque tree of life rises "from a world full of flowers, with Cupid sleeping in the centre. Among the branches of the tree are fauns, angels, centaurs, dragons and birds, while behind the world is a sea full of fishes."[84] This delightful painting is indicative of Traquair's penchant for combining mythologies with detailed natural imagery. Her painting of Pan playing the pipes to Psyche and Eros on the inside of the lid was partially repainted with vine and putti decoration, as Psyche's nude torso offended Mrs. Tennant.[85] Photographs indicate that the repainting completely erased the presence of a fully clothed Eros floating in the corner above Psyche's head. His comparatively small size and position in the painting renders him a secondary and distant figure, in contrast to Psyche and Pan, who are both nude. Furthermore, it is Pan the musician who holds Psyche in his thrall. With the piano, Traquair successfully marries the arts of music, painting, and literature. The illustrations were positively received, with critics comparing the piano to other pieces such as Burne-Jones's piano decoration for William Graham, one of Burne-Jones's most devoted patrons.[86] Constructed in the 1880s, the instrument was a present for Graham's daughter Frances, with whom, as we saw, Burne-Jones was long infatuated. On the piano case, Burne-Jones painted the tragic story of Orpheus and Eurydice. Like Pan, Orpheus is a musician and thus a fitting subject for a musical instrument.

As with Burne-Jones and his stained-glass windows at St. Helen's, Traquair combined text from the Song of Songs beneath the panel of its visual rendering. Unlike Burne-Jones, however, she chose a linear narrative faintly suggested by the source text. Her narrative depicts a love triangle, in which Solomon separates the Shulamite from her shepherd lover. Nonetheless, the Shulamite's love for her beloved is undimmed, and the two are ultimately reconciled. August Renan understood the Song of Songs to be a story of a love triangle but discounted the allegorical and mystical interpretation of the

---

82. Cumming, *Phoebe Anna Traquair*, 85.
83. Cited in Cumming, *Phoebe Anna Traquair*, 85.
84. Purcell, "Design of Grand Pianos," 65.
85. Cumming, *Phoebe Anna Traquair*, 86.
86. Purcell, "Design of Grand Pianos," 65.

text.[87] A viewer unfamiliar with the allegorical interpretation of the Song of Songs is unlikely to recognize any religious significance in Traquair's rendering, especially since the panels are to be read from left to right, like a novel. Allegorical readings of the Song of Songs are typically propelled by discrete images and moments of passionate outburst rather than a strong narrative structure. Indeed, Traquair took liberties by inserting narrative tension that moves the plot toward its resolution, such as with the passage, "Return, return, O Shulamite; return, return, that we may look upon thee" (Song of Songs 6:13). Here, we see a crowned Solomon, arms crossed, looking on from the edge of his palace as maids force the Shulamite toward him. At the same time, her shepherd lover moves in their direction with arms outstretched, beseeching, his sheep behind him and his shepherd's crook flung on the ground. Allegorically, it is possible to interpret Solomon as the material world, the shepherd as Christ, and the Shulamite as the soul literally struggling between the two forces. In other words, Traquair is devoted to telling a desire-driven narrative of lovers separated and reunited, a narrative that could be interpreted allegorically as the soul's reunion with Christ. The Shulamite bears some resemblance to Psyche, who loses her lover Cupid (or Eros), undergoes trials to win him back, and in the end reunites with him.[88] In like manner, the book cover of Traquair's lost illuminated manuscript of the Song of Songs shows the beloved ascending stairs to reunite with his lover. The Shulamite holds to her heart her beloved's hands as they gaze into each other's eyes. The accompanying text around the couple is, "My beloved is mine and I am his" (Song of Songs 2:16), signifying the union of two into one.

I believe it useful to describe Traquair's sequence of illustrations so that the reader can appreciate their uniqueness and thematics. Her Song of Songs is a romantic quest narrative set in a landscape influenced by her Scottish surroundings. The progression of events is marked by a shift from dawn to midday, through night, and to the brightness of a new day."[89] In the first scene of the narrative, beginning at the treble end of the piano, the two maids bring the Shulamite before Solomon, who sits on the porch of his palace. A procession of musicians follows them, and the king looks distinctly bored, his head leaning on his hand. The accompanying text is, "We will be glad and rejoice in thee . . . While the king sitteth" (Song of Songs 1:14, 1:12). In the second panel, Shulamite is with the king in his banqueting hall, while three maids stand to the side. A verdant and mountainous landscape is visible through the windows. The caption below is an extension of the previous quote: "at his table, my spikenard sendeth forth the smell thereof" (Song of Songs 1:12).

---

87. Renan, *Song of Songs Translated*, xi.

88. Apuleius, *Golden Ass*, books 4–6.

89. Purcell, "Design of Grand Pianos," 66.

Next is a panel of the Shulamite locked in a room with two women, one of whom is playing a lute while the other is overseeing the seated Shulamite who leans against the window, inching toward her beloved. The shepherd stretches his hands through the bars of the windows to touch his lover's face. The text below reads, "The voice of my beloved! behold, he cometh" (Song of Songs 2:8). In the adjoining panel, we glimpse the dream sequence. The Shulamite is asleep in bed, while her dream of meeting her beloved in the town at night-time is painted in the encircled corner picture. The mountains and moon are visible behind the bars of her window. The caption is, "By night on my bed I sought him whom my soul loveth" (Song of Songs 3:1). Purcell classifies the next extended panel at the end of the piano as two panels. It comprises two scenes separated by the image of a staircase. The first sees Solomon returning from war, accompanied by his army. In the foreground, the Shulamite bends over her knees, distressed, as musicians play nearby. This scene represents the passage "Who is this that cometh out of the wilderness like pillars of smoke" (Song of Songs 3:6). In the next scene, Solomon holds onto the Shulamite, pressing his suit, while she looks away, again distressed. The text below reads, "Behold, thou art fair, my love, behold, thou art fair" (Song of Songs 4:1)

The remaining three panels show the return of the shepherd (the afore-mentioned scene from 6:13), the release of the Shulamite and the reunion of the lovers, and, finally, the wedding feast. In the penultimate panel, the lovers are reunited in passionate embrace: heads close, his right hand touching her face, his left arm around her shoulder, her right arm around his hip, and her left hand holding his left hand on her shoulder. Behind them are fellow countrysiders carrying fruit and wheat. Ahead of them are children playing instruments. The accompanying text is, "I am my beloved's, and his desire is toward me: let us go forth into the field" (Song of Songs 7:10, 7:11). The final panel befits the marriage plot. The joyous marriage feast depicts the couple in the center of both the panel and a u-shaped table. They are surrounded by friends and family. A musician sits to the side and plays a lyre. The concluding text is, fittingly, "Many waters cannot quench love, neither can the floods drown it" (Song of Songs 8:7). Behind the wedding party we catch sight of the fields and mountains. The triumphant reunion with the beloved is replete with images of jubilation, community, and fecundity.

HARMONIZATION

By providing a recognizable narrative arc, Traquair's Song of Songs sequence appears to sacrifice many poetic and erotic elements of the text. Nonetheless, one might argue that these elements have been remediated or transposed onto other features of the piano. Indeed, the piano itself acts as another canvas to convey both literal and musical art. The very name, the Song of Songs, allows us to consider the text as a piece for the ear, either as music or poetry or both, and it is one of the reasons why musicians feature extensively in Traquair's panels. Similarly, the sensuousness of song is manifested through the sense of touch, namely, piano playing. Piano playing is another artistic creation, like arts and crafts. The hand as metonym of the creative laborer[90] is the same hand that plays the piano, sews, embroiders, binds, illustrates, and paints. As a "digital" technology (from the Latin *digit,* or finger), the nineteenth-century piano keyboard provided a conceptual and practical model for new media technologies such as the telegraph and typewriter.[91] Ivan Raykoff argues that these writing instruments "can be seen as comparable technologies of the fingers: by physically touching their keys, one produced expressive messages that could also 'touch' a reader or listener through something like the 'language' of music."[92]

The users of these digital technologies were usually women. In the nineteenth century, the piano had a range of feminine associations, such as the process of acculturation or education into middle-class girlhood and the passage into marriage and womanhood.[93] Regarding the latter, the piano had potential "as a site for flirtation, courtship and protosexual dalliance,"[94] which is the likely reason as to why Burne-Jones painted women and women musicians on the piano gifted to him and Georgiana. Thus, the piano could be used as an effective device for a range of purposes, including seduction, that is, drawing the eyes, ears, and perhaps even the male body toward the female pianist. Yet for girls enjoying the visibility of being on display, one Victorian commentator found it necessary to warn them to "wait till [the music] carries you away with *its* loveliness, but don't try to carry it away before the right moment with *your* loveliness."[95]

Music lent itself to the metaphorical language of touch in phrases such as "to strike a chord" and "to pull on the heart-strings."[96] In the nineteenth century, however, this language was more than metaphorical; it was a matter of scientific inquiry and theological appropriation. As I have explored elsewhere, sound literally resonates within our bodies in a manner that objects of

---

90. Colligan and Linley, "Introduction," 5–6.
91. Raykoff, "Piano, Telegraph, Typewriter," 160.
92. Raykoff, "Piano, Telegraph, Typewriter," 159.
93. Burgan, "Heroines at the Piano," 51–52.
94. Solie, *Music in Other Words,* 98.
95. Goddard, "How to Play the Piano," 166.
96. Raykoff, "Piano, Telegraph, Typewriter," 161.

vision cannot.[97] The natural philosopher Hermann von Helmholtz compared the ear to the piano, saying, "The end of every fibre of the auditory system is connected with small elastic parts, which we cannot but assume to be set in sympathetic vibration by the waves of sound."[98] The concept of sympathetic vibration is brought together with magnetic attraction and romantic passion in George Eliot's *The Mill on the Floss*, wherein Stephen's singing—"the inexorable power of sound"—causes Maggie's body to be "played on" like a musical instrument: "You might have seen the slightest quivering through her whole frame as she leaned a little forward, . . . her eyes dilated and brightened," says the narrator.[99] Eliot's use of music in her novels reflects her engagement with science.[100] Electromagnetism was a reasonably fresh concept in the nineteenth century,[101] though it effects had been observed for centuries. Thus, according to Aristotle, Thales "seems . . . to have supposed that the soul is something productive of movement, if he really said that the magnet has a soul because it produces movement in iron."[102] Nineteenth-century religious commentators used the Song of Songs to appeal to the concept of magnetic attraction. In his explication of the line "Draw me after thee" (Song of Songs 1:4), Anglo-Irish clergyman Richard Frederick Littledale argues:

> For Thou hast said in Hosea the Prophet, "I drew thee with cords of a man, with bands of love;" and in Jeremiah, "I have loved thee with an everlasting love, therefore with loving-kindness have I drawn thee." And in this drawing, which consists in leading the human will into union with the Divine will, as the magnet draws the iron to itself, the Three Persons of the Holy Trinity co-operate. . . . [A] threefold cord which is not quickly broken.[103]

In Traquair's Song of Songs sequence—and in the constant presence of musical instruments—the lovers are continually drawn to each other, ultimately reuniting as with a magnet to a lodestone. Like Maggie in relation to Stephen, the Shulamite is drawn to a voice: the caption for one of the painted panels is, "The voice of my beloved! behold, he cometh" (Song of Songs 2:8). As we have seen, she leans against the window toward the shepherd, who stretches his hands through the bars of the windows in order to touch his lover's face.

---

97. Dau, *Touching God*, 89. The following examples of sympathetic vibration are drawn from pages 90–91.

98. Cited in Picker, *Victorian Soundscapes*, 87.

99. Eliot, *Mill on the Floss*, 416.

100. Da Sousa Correa, "Music Vibrating in Her Still," 542.

101. Rudy, *Electric Meters*, 137–38.

102. Aristotle, *De Anima*, 405a.

103. Littledale, *Commentary on the Song of Songs*, 15–16.

62 • CHAPTER 2

Another erotic transposition of the Song of Songs is through the compelling figure of the musician, herdsman, and goat-god, Pan. Dennis Denisoff argues that Pan "not only leaves his mark throughout the modern history of decadence, but . . . [he also] rose during the Victorian and Edwardian periods to become the most popular pagan deity of the age."[104] Fiona Richards notes that "the sheer diversity of representations of this god in English literature is astonishing, from Aleister Crowley's incantatory 'Hymn to Pan' to Francis Thompson's 'Pastoral' and Lawrence's rustic god lurking 'with a goat's white lightning in his eyes' [from 'Pan in America']."[105] Women poets also wrote of the deity: Elizabeth Barrett Browning features "the great god Pan" (a refrain) in her poem "A Musical Instrument" (1860), while Michael Field includes him in a series of poems in the volume *Wild Honey from Various Thyme* (1908), published in the year Traquair was commissioned to paint the piano. Traquair's depiction of Pan is a romanticized vision in the tradition of Walter Crane's cover illustration for composer Theo Marzials's *Pan Pipes* (1883),[106] which combines illustrations with lyrics or poetry set to music, as well as Burne-Jones's *Pan and Psyche* (1872–74) and *The Garden of Pan* (1886–87).[107] Despite his romanticized, youthful, and beardless appearance in the Traquair representation, Pan embodies the erotic, fecund, and pastoral elements of the Song of Songs. This interpretation is reinforced by the deity's long-held association with sexuality and fertility, as depicted on the other side of the piano lid: the tree of life, abundant with the fruits of creation, populated with centaurs and fauns.

As the goat-god who lends his name to the pan pipes, Pan is also the god of shepherds. It is no coincidence that Psyche is drawn to his music in the same way that the Shulamite is drawn to the voice of her beloved shepherd. Pan's music is a song of songs that harmonizes nature, hastening it toward union with the divine. Certainly, it is possible to see Pan as a syncretization of other gods; in the Orphic Rhapsodies he is called Eros, along with the names of other gods.[108] Traquair is at pains to emphasize the musical element of the scene, including music's ability to enchant the listener. I leave it to Purcell to describe Traquair's painting:

Pan, who symbolises the music of Nature[,] . . . is seated on the round green world, surrounded by water, on which Psyche stands, looking at him with

104. Denisoff, *Decadent Ecology,* 102.
105. Richards, "Goat-God in England," 90.
106. Marzials and Walter Crane, *Pan Pipes.*
107. Richards, "Goat-God in England," 91.
108. West, *Orphic Poems,* 205.

a gaze instinct with wonder. Pan, however, is absorbed in the music of his pipes and does not observe her; but Eros with his bow surveys them both.[109]

Traquair follows visual precedent by depicting Pan on a small island, surrounded by reeds and water. Her love of nature, and most likely her long history of drawing fossilized fish for her husband, ensured that her eye for detail did not neglect the fish in the water. Like Psyche, the fish are facing Pan, as if they, too, are drawn to his music. Pan is a nature deity, so his music plays a role in uniting—through sympathetic vibration—not simply nature but also Traquair's spiritual, ecological, and scientific belief systems. These are her myths of truth turning art into praise. In Neoplatonic thought, music and harmony are a means of returning to unity from multiplicity and division.[110] With the help of musician gods, music can guide the human soul back to the origin of reality.[111] Yet, it is not simply the human soul that harmonizes through music. For Traquair, Pan, whose name means "all," is the ideal god to reunite all of nature with God. Traquair herself wrote in 1893, "Perfect harmony, is that not what we all strive after? Seek deeply and is it not perfect, union with the Divine."[112]

Burne-Jones and Traquair demonstrate how the visual representation of the Song of Songs in the Victorian era could take on many forms, whether in relation to artistic materials or interpretative response. Both artists focused on relationships between men and women, yet the differences in approach were at times stark. I have focused on Burne-Jones's ambivalence toward the common interpretation of Song of Songs as a text about joyous romantic love. His Song of Songs emphasizes obstacles in the way of love, along with the dark and discordant nature of relationships, including the often-hidden instances of violence. Traquair understood the challenges within relationships but chose to prioritize the moments of joy that couples take in each other's company. Her interweaving of myths, especially the trope of music from classical and biblical source materials, amplifies the message of harmonious union between husband and wife, nature and humans, the soul and the divine. Her Song of Songs is ultimately one of harmony and pleasure.

---

109. Purcell, "Design of Grand Pianos," 65.
110. Moro Tornese, "Philosophy of Music," 52.
111. Moro Tornese, "Philosophy of Music," 230–31.
112. Cited in Huxtable, "Drama of the Soul," 33.

CHAPTER 3

Celibacy, Sisterhoods, and Women's Poetry

Augusta Theodosia Drane and Christina Rossetti

Sisterhood offers a space of religious nurturance and common devotion to Christ. In this chapter, I explore the poetry of Augusta Theodosia Drane and Christina Rossetti, two women who found divine love and the possibility of agency within chastity and sisterhood. Scholars have paid little attention to Drane, despite her being a model of an accomplished Victorian whose many published works include poetry, histories, essays, and biographies. That she is religious author whose poetic output numbered only one volume of poetry might help explain the lack of critical attention. In contrast to Drane, Rossetti's preeminent status in Victorian poetry remains undisputed. Nonetheless, the many readings of Rossetti's "Goblin Market" usually pay scant attention to the religious dimensions of the poem. As Emma Mason notes, however, the Tractarian doctrine of reserve dictates that poetry "represents God's truths indirectly like a parable, allowing only those armed with faith and knowledge to recognise what Keble . . . called 'parabolical lessons of conduct' within its 'symbolical language in which God speaks to us of a world out of sight.'"[1] "Goblin Market" exemplifies such a work. The writing of these two women bears a resemblance to what readers today might call the erotic, simply as a result of the creative freedoms afforded by their celibacy. With this in mind, I turn to the role of the Song of Songs in the verse of the two authors, whose

---

1. Mason, "Christina Rossetti," 200.

lives were devoted to both God and female communities: Drane, as a convert and prioress at St. Dominic's Convent, Stone, and later, as Mother Provincial, and Rossetti, mostly within her domestic setting but also as volunteer Sister Christina at St. Mary Magdalene, a refuge for so-called fallen women. The two women were born within years of each other and died in the same year.

I begin the chapter by exploring the emergence of Tractarianism and the growth of Roman Catholicism in the nineteenth century. The rise of the two provided the conditions for the rapid growth of religious houses in each denomination. Religious celibacy encouraged Drane's special devotion to Mary, whose existence is interpreted in Song of Songs 2:1. I also argue that the religious life led Drane to be at odds with mainstream English society, by allowing her freedom from the bondage of traditional marriage. Most religious communities were active rather than contemplative, which meant that working nuns obtained relative financial security from the world of men. The independent nature of being a working and celibate nun comes to the fore in the comparison between nuns and heroic warriors, which finds credence in militaristic imagery from Song of Songs 4:4, 6:4, and 6:10. In the final section on Drane, I turn to her poetry, particularly poems inspired by John of the Cross. Drane's emphasis on love, her espousal to Christ, and the necessity of the dark night of the soul are compelling reasons as to why she would gravitate toward the work of the Spanish mystic. In a sense, the dark night—a period of purgation and tribulation—reflects her own preoccupation with the necessary travails of the heroic life of a nun.

In the second half of the chapter, I return to the exploration of sisterhood in Rossetti's most famous poem, "Goblin Market," published in *Goblin Market and Other Poems* (1862). This bond is deeply, even startlingly, intimate, and is not a substitute for, or even a precursor to, marriage. For Rossetti, religious devotion is intertwined with sisterhood. In her case, it exists largely within a domestic setting comprising her mother Frances, sisters, and Frances's unmarried sisters. "Goblin Market" is a poem that empowers women to reserve the right to remain unmarried and to prioritize relationships with either direct family members or a community of women. I focus on two elements from the Song of Songs in the poem: sweetness and the aspect of invitation. The Song of Songs refers often to two activities of the mouth—eating and kissing—and on the interconnection of the two with the taste of sweetness. I explore these elements, particularly the history of sugar and fruit consumption, asserting that the poem argues for salvation in Christ obtained through a religious community of sisters. The poem's suspicion of material sweetness explains its wariness of cultures of consumption, as exemplified by pornography, which promotes the sweetness of physical delights. I compare and contrast images of sweetness

66 • CHAPTER 3

in pornography with those in Rosetti's poetry. For Rossetti, bitterness exists for its own sake, just as hardship has a defined purpose in Drane's writing: they both work to draw one closer to Christ.

CELIBACY AND SISTERHOOD

A chapter on Rossetti and Drane's faith and association with sisterhoods should be understood within the context of the Catholic revival of the Church of England and the growth of Roman Catholicism in England. Both women had an affiliation, either short- or long-term, with Tractarianism, that is, the Oxford Movement, which started in the early 1830s at Oriel College, Oxford, and was led by academic churchmen John Henry Newman (before his defection to Rome), Edward Bouverie Pusey, and John Keble. The Oxford Movement led to the revival of the Church of England's Catholic identity and eventually developed into Anglo-Catholicism. Denouncing the increasing secularization of the Church of England, Tractarians sought to return the church to its heritage of apostolic order, the teachings of the early church fathers, and the sacraments and the liturgy, along with more frequent public references to the Virgin Mary. Originally designed to save the Church of England, Tractarianism often became a stepping stone to Rome, thereby generating a degree of apprehension and suspicion among Protestants.

Drane's conversion and subsequent entry into conventual life was made possible by changes to the status of the Catholic Church in mid-nineteenth-century England. These changes wrought a good deal of anxiety among many Anglicans who feared their national church, and by extension their country, was in retreat before its old religious foe.[2] The gradual process of removing the many restrictions imposed on Catholics culminated in the Roman Catholic Relief Act 1829 (also known as the Catholic Emancipation Act 1829), which gave Catholics full civil rights, including the right to sit in Parliament, though they were still barred from studying at Cambridge and Oxford. The growth of the Catholic Church was largely the result of migration, mainly from postfamine Ireland in the 1840s, complemented by a comparatively small but steady stream of converts from the Church of England. The reestablishment of the Catholic hierarchy in 1850 gave rise to fears of papal aggression and subsequently lent more fuel to anti-Catholic sentiment. It was also the year that Drane entered the church. The First Vatican Council (1869–70) proclaimed the doctrine of Papal Infallibility, creating further alarm among Anglicans. It

---

2. See chapter 1 of Wheeler, *Old Enemies*.

was the doctrine of the Immaculate Conception (Mary's preservation from the guilt of Original Sin), declared in 1854, that had a lasting impression on Drane, who not long after would take on the religious name of Francis Raphael of the Immaculate Conception, so as to signal her devotion to the mother of Christ. The new name was a decisive demonstration of allegiance to her new church, given that Mary was a figure of dispute between Catholics and Protestants. Mary's image contributed to the division between the two groups in the Reformation, which had only hardened by the mid-nineteenth century.[3] Drane joined an order with a special devotion to Mary and that was overseen by a woman with the title of Mother, a powerful mantle that she herself would eventually inherit as Mother Superior and Mother Provincial. Additionally, Mary might have reminded Drane of her own beloved mother, who died in 1848 and of whom she wrote, "My mother was the most beautiful being I ever beheld, the kind of face that an artist might select as a model for a Madonna."[4]

Drane's decision to choose Mary, the celibate life, and sisterhood signaled her commitment to her new faith. The Song of Songs enabled her to embrace the role of celibacy. Carol Engelhardt argues that Mary "repudiated Victorian family values. Her virginity opposed the family system, within which women were expected to marry and bear children."[5] Catherine of Siena, a fellow Dominican who consecrated her own virginity to Christ, provided Drane with a blueprint for considering Mary and sacred virginity. In the first volume of her history of the saint, Drane quotes a passage in which Catherine adapts the phrase "Ego flos campi" to execute a fecund Marian reading of Song of Songs 2:1:

> Hear her describing our Lady as "the sweet field in which was sown the seed of the Divine word. In that sweet and blessed field of Mary, the Word made flesh was like the grain which is ripened by the warm rays of the sun, and puts forth its flowers and fruit, letting its husk fall to the earth. It was so He did when, warmed by the fire of Divine Charity, He cast the seed of the Word into the field of Mary. O Blessed Mary! It was you who gave us the flower of our sweetest Jesus! That flower yielded its fruit on the Holy Cross, because there it was that we received the gift of perfect life."[6]

---

3. Engelhardt, "Paradigmatic Angel in the House," 159; and Engelhardt Herringer, *Victorians and the Virgin Mary*, 2.

4. Drane, *Memoir*, part 1, 6.

5. Engelhardt, "Paradigmatic Angel in the House," 162.

6. Drane, *History of St. Catherine of Siena*, vol. 1, 188.

68 • CHAPTER 3

Similarly, the nun is able to bear spiritual fruit for the sake of Christ. In a letter to a convent dated 18 May 1888, Drane alludes to garden images from Revelation 22:2 and Psalm 1:3 and concludes with Song of Songs 4:12–13 and 16:

> May the Holy Spirit of God Himself produce in us an abundance of these delicious fruits, and so make of our religious homes "a garden enclosed, a fountain sealed up, a paradise of pomegranates, with all the fruits of the orchard," that our Beloved may Himself "come into His garden, and eat the fruits thereof"![7]

Reiterating that the fruits are the results of labors reserved for Christ, she paraphrases from Song of Songs 7:13 in a set of retreat notes of the same period: "'All the fruit, new + old, I have kept for thee, my Beloved.' The old fruit is the work of [the] last six years: the new those of the three to come."[8] If the Song of Songs could be used for conventional marriage, it could also be used for celibate marriage.

Both Tractarians and Catholics held to the virtues of celibacy, especially in their attempts to reestablish monastic orders in England. Sisterhoods in particular came under great suspicion. "Most disturbing of all to Protestant England was the development of sisterhoods by the Tractarians, the enemy within," Michael Wheeler has argued.[9] Anglicans were wary of sisterhoods in their church because they challenged the primacy of the family system, for the following reasons: they too closely resembled Roman Catholicism (thereby acting as a stepping stone to Rome) and they were relatively independent of ecclesiastical authority.[10] Sisterhoods were part of the "women's movement in the Church," which Brian Heeney believes "was against belief in women's subordination to a male ruling class, against automatic submission to husband, father, or brother."[11] Yet for women who joined Anglican sisterhoods, "vocations were as likely to be motivated by practical concerns, including a desire to remain single and to have useful work, as for religious reasons."[12] Whether she stayed for a few months or a lifetime, becoming a sister allowed an Anglican woman to circumvent social norms and restrictions experienced by her married counterparts. In particular, as Susan Mumm writes, membership afforded her the possibility of leaving the family home

---

7. Drane, *Memoir*, part 2, 278–79.
8. Drane, G/FRD/ii/1b "Examen" notebook, n.p.
9. Wheeler, *Old Enemies*, 218.
10. Heeney, *Women's Movement*, 66–67.
11. Heeney, *Women's Movement*, 6.
12. Engelhardt, "Revival of the Religious Life," 393.

without marriage, of participating in the government of an institution, and of undertaking meaningful though often demanding work in social welfare.[13] With around ten thousand women passing through more than ninety communities between 1845 and 1900, Anglican sisters became the largest group of full-time organized women church workers within the Church of England.[14] A number of sisterhoods continued to flourish long after the deaths of the original founders of the Oxford Movement, and they were central to perpetuating the spirit of Tractarianism.[15]

Catholic sisterhoods were threatening because they were Roman Catholic, "led by women and [apparently] open to unspeakable abuses."[16] The second half of the nineteenth century saw a remarkable increase in the number of Roman Catholic women entering convent life in England.[17] Engelhardt believes that this interest in convent life reflects, first, an interest in a return to pre-Reformation culture and values and, second, a larger resurgence in vowed religious life among women in Europe.[18] Moreover, these communities were chiefly active rather than contemplative groups. By focusing on areas of community need, such as education (in particular), nursing, orphans, fallen women, the elderly, prisons, sewing, foreign missions, or a combination of any of the above, the working nuns obtained relative financial security. The women, then, helped finance their convents through church work rather than a dowry.[19] Nonetheless, Catholic clergy were sometimes reluctant to be involved with convents, believing that nuns should live an enclosed rather than active life.[20] But, these women came to develop a system "outside that defined by church or culture—the convent system."[21] Once established in an area, the congregations tended to set up satellite houses in other districts, which, while requiring the approval of the clergy, were directly responsible to their female superior at the Motherhouse.[22] Based on a continental model, this style of management gave considerable power to the women in charge of the organization of their sisterhoods.[23]

---

13. Mumm, *Anglican Sisterhoods*, xii.
14. Mumm, *Anglican Sisterhoods*, 3.
15. Mumm, *Anglican Sisterhoods*, 5.
16. Wheeler, *Old Enemies*, 214.
17. McAdam, "Willing Women," 412.
18. Engelhardt, "Revival of the Religious Life," 388.
19. McAdam, "Willing Women," 413–16.
20. McAdam, "Willing Women," 421.
21. McAdam, "Willing Women," 431.
22. McAdam, "Willing Women," 417.
23. McAdam, "Willing Women," 417.

70 • CHAPTER 3

DRANE: LOVER AND WARRIOR NUN

Drane was born to a prosperous family three years after the birth of Victoria. She was a precocious child and was what she calls in her memoir a "nature-worshipper," with a strong interest in natural history.[24] A prolific reader, Drane's childhood readings reflected her later interests and works in literature, history, and religion. In her words, "Up to the age of nineteen, I had few friends, but I had read many books."[25] Drane's family was Anglican. She became interested in Tractarianism in her late teens and then underwent a few years of spiritual torment and internal "self-inspection," describing herself as "[a] barren fig-tree, with leaves upon leaves, but no fruit."[26] She would later repeat the image of the barren fig tree by way of contrast to the abundant fruit trees in Song of Songs 4:13.[27] Drane finally converted to Roman Catholicism in 1850, at the age of twenty-six, and a year later was received into the Third Order of St. Dominic, as a secular tertiary living in the world. In 1852 she joined the Dominican Congregation of St. Catherine of Siena, which had received papal approval only a year earlier. Her superiors recognized and encouraged her writing talents. She wrote several books before becoming Prioress of Stone in 1872. Nineteen years later, she became Prioress Provincial, in charge of all the houses of the congregation. Drane died in 1894.

Love is a key theme from the very first page of Drane's memoir. Editor Bertrand Wilberforce begins the book thus:

> Only three days before her death, which happened on April 29 1894, Mother Francis Raphael wrote the following words in a confidential letter to a friend:—
>
> "Write, read, and study—do what you will, there is only one real thing to do in this world, and that is, to love; all else must be centred in this, and flow from it, or it will be like a tinkling cymbal. Six months of pain have taught me that, in a way I hardly realised before. It will be our life in heaven, and we must begin it here on earth, without excluding the active life, which loves by working for Him we love."[28]

The image of the "tinkling cymbal" originates from 1 Corinthians 13:1, in which Paul famously upholds love's preeminence by declaring, "Though I speak with the tongues of men and of angels, and have not charity, I am

---

24. Drane, *Memoir*, part 1, 42.
25. Drane, *Memoir*, part 1, 21.
26. Drane, *Memoir*, part 1, 38.
27. Drane, *Memoir*, part 2, 279.
28. Drane, *Memoir*, part 1, 3.

CELIBACY, SISTERHOODS, AND WOMEN'S POETRY · 71

become as sounding brass, or a tinkling cymbal." Wilberforce draws the following conclusion from Drane's letter:

> The lesson taught by her life is thus expressed in golden words just before her death. Love is the centre from which all must flow, love for God only and for all others for His sake, was the only thing valuable in her eyes at the end. "Vanity of vanities, and all is vanity, except to love God. He is truly great who has great love."[29]

The profound love between the individual and God is a realization that came to Drane early in her religious career. As a novice, she heard the Bishop of Birmingham, William Bernard Ullathorne, give a speech on the personal love of Christ for each soul. His words had a profound impact on her spiritual devotion, and she would eventually become the editor of his autobiography and letters. In her words, "When in my cell alone, I lay prostrate on the floor in a sort of ecstasy. I could not sleep for three nights, but lay broad awake, thinking, 'He loves me! He loves *me myself* with a personal love!' I could hardly touch food. There was a complete revolution in my spiritual life, and the solid grace lasted when the sensible devotion was withdrawn."[30]

Drane's words both at the end of her life and at the start of her religious vocation inform us that the life of a Victorian nun was intimately bound up with love. Yet it was by no means an easy kind of love, given that the life of a working nun required fortitude. Such a love must be actively maintained, not unlike one's virginity and work ethic: Drane exclaims in her poem "Sensible Sweetness," "We dare not shrink from work in His dear Love begun" (line 41).[31] Likewise, she writes in an unpublished booklet, "The advancement of the soul consists not in thinking much on God, but in loving Him greatly. And this love is got by readiness to Do and to Suffer, for God's sake."[32] In the poem "Josue," the biblical Joshua finally sets his eyes on the promised land, which Drane depicts as a virgin landscape. She says,

> He gazes on the stream
> Through which 'twas his to lead the Hosts of God

---

29. Drane, *Memoir,* part 1, 3. In addition to alluding to Ephesians 1:2, the final quotation is the English translation of the memoir's first epigraph, which is the Latin from book 1 of Thomas à Kempis's *The Imitation of Christ.*

30. Drane, *Memoir,* part 1, 68.

31. Drane, *Songs in the Night and Other Poems.* Future references to Drane's poems are from this volume.

32. Drane, Flores Sanctorum, n.p.

72 • CHAPTER 3

To lead where foot of man hath never trod.
And scale those haughty walls that yonder gleam. (lines 13–16)

The "haughty walls" are reminiscent of the walls in Song of Songs 2:9, 4:12, and 8:9, which represent the bride's virginity or chastity. Indeed, in a letter addressed to convents, Drane alludes to the walled garden of 4:12 when she describes the convents or "homes of [Christ's] chosen spouses" as "retreats, sheltered from the cold, cutting winds of worldly temptation, in which these lovely flowers might blossom and flourish as in a garden enclosed."[33] A certain hardness of exteriority is necessary to protect the soft heart of the lover. As Drane declares, the religious life "tread'st a harder way" ("Dartmoor," line 38). This life is far removed from the traditional realm of women and children and thus from the domestic sphere. For Drane herself, "The human home, the earthly rest, / Is not for thee!" ("Loss and Gain," lines 120–21). She had understood from an early age that she was not destined for London seasons and their superficialities, nor for courtship and marriage. Such things she "held in abhorrence."[34]

The quality of hardness translates to the notion of the lover nun as a warrior nun and, at times, masculinized. Playing the active part of a lover-as-warrior was an important aspect of a life dedicated to religious celibacy. The concept derives part of its language from the Song of Songs, which describes the bride's neck as "like the tower of David," armed with the shields of warriors (Song of Songs 4:4). Guarding the citadel, the shields display both impenetrability and strength. A similar image is of the bride being as majestic as an army with banners (Song of Songs 6:4; 6:10). In some of Drane's poems, the speaker is clearly male. The inference is that manliness, like Drane's acquired male name, Francis Raphael, is a characteristic or quality achieved rather than being innate. Indeed, one definition of the word "manly" in the *OED* captures the qualities of the ideal Victorian nun: "Of a person: having those qualities or characteristics traditionally associated with men as distinguished from women or children; courageous, strong, independent in spirit, frank, upright, etc. Occas. in early use: having those qualities or characteristics associated with fighting men (*obs.*)."

The garb of masculinity enabled Drane to describe herself and her vocation in the language of a warrior, that is, as a socially recognized embodiment of strength. Drane was not the only one of her time to understand her vocation in military terms. Written evidence demonstrates that "stamina in the

---

33. Drane, *Memoir*, part 2, 276.
34. Drane, *Memoir*, part 1, 36.

face of difficulty was prized in convent circles and that nuns saw themselves not entirely as the woman of Victorian womanhood."[35] After all, these nuns often risked health and safety in the slums of England or the remote corners of empire.[36] As McAdam puts it,

> Frequently, a superior's directive to her Sisters was to be as men; for example Cornelia Connelly wanted her Sisters "to have a masculine force of character and will," whilst Janet Erskine Stuart called for her novices to be as "warrior maidens"; and much of the literature produced by nuns reiterates just such an image.[37]

Drane had another source for the "warrior maiden" analogy. Her wide-ranging interests included religious warfare and military orders, as demonstrated in the publication of her book about the Knights Hospitaller. Published anonymously in 1858, the book was admired by military men who were shocked to discover its author was a nun.[38] The preface praises members of the order for their "determined courage and heroic devotion."[39] Drane's book on the life of St. Dominic notes that in its early days, and before the admittance of women, the Third Order of St. Dominic "was essentially military."[40] Known by the title of the Militia of Jesus Christ, it was established to fight against the heresy of Catharism.[41] Drane holds the life of a nun to be as valorous and active as that of the heroes in the military orders: "Wring out the sweetness from thy life, / And gird thy loins for nobler strife," she says ("Dartmoor," lines 29–30). In "Dartmoor," the poem's speaker chooses to turn away from the "murmuring streams" of pastoral scenes that "[lull] each manlier sense to sleep" (lines 3, 4). Drane was familiar with the sublime beauty of Dartmoor, a place she visited several times in her childhood.[42] The speaker seeks a higher cause and resolves to live a heroic life by turning her back on the "soft, voluptuous green" (line 19). She favors instead "scenes more desolate and stern. / Some lone and mountain solitude" (lines 8–9), represented by the rocky tors. In short, Drane shifts from the allure of a "soft" setting to an absolute commitment to one's religious vocation or calling:

---

35. McAdam, "Willing Women," 430.
36. McAdam, "Willing Women," 430.
37. McAdam, "Willing Women," 430–31.
38. Drane, *Memoir,* part 1, 75.
39. Drane, *Knights of St. John,* iii.
40. Drane, *History of St. Dominic,* 245.
41. Drane, *History of St. Dominic,* 243–44.
42. Drane, *Memoir,* part 1, 29.

The hero's life, the hero's death;

He gives, in answer to thy call. (lines 58–59)

The celibate life for the sake of Christ is heroic. In the words of the Tractarian Frederick William Faber, it is a feat of "religious manliness," for it seeks not the tender comforts of domesticity.[43]

The heroic solitude of religious life restricted the number of close friendships in one's personal life. Such friendships could be especially passionate, mirroring the broader social acceptance of friendships as relationships of greater equals than were often found in many marriages. Espousal to Christ required both a turning inward and a concomitant detachment from the world, while also allowing for friendships in Christ. Drane argues that, for a religious, the relationship with Christ takes priority over all others: "a Religious must of necessity lock up a good many inner chambers, and keep them for the One Friend."[44] At the same time, the realization that the religious life is a lonely one enhanced the need for human companionship within the context of one's love for Christ. Thus, Drane's dearest friend and mentor, Mother Imelda Poole, addressed her in a letter as "my very dear sister, and true yoke-fellow," expressing gratitude to God for granting, "even in this world, such a great blessing as a perfect union of two hearts in Him!"[45] On the unexpected death of Newman's beloved Ambrose St. John, Newman responded to Drane's letter of sympathy, declaring, "I do not expect ever to recover from it; and that I do believe to be the intention of it on the part of our loving Lord: it is the infliction in love of a wound that will never close."[46]

At first glance, these intimate friendships might seem queer to the modern reader, but in their historical context, they appear to have been far from queer or "strange" in the Victorian sense. (Either that or the Victorians were queerer than we are today.) That the depth of the friendship between Drane and Poole, as between Newman and St. John, could be discussed so openly in letters and in a published memoir for a Catholic and potentially general readership suggests that these or similar relationships were publicly known about, accepted, and almost certainly admired. The direct link between such friendships and the celibate's relationship with Christ, "the One Friend," renders the former orthodox and, even, analogous to the love for Christ. Indeed, given their inseparability, one kind of friendship could serve to strengthen the

---

43. Letter to the Rev. J. B. Morris, 26 January 1841, in Faber, *Life and Letters*, 81. See also Dau, "Perfect Chastity," 80–81.

44. Drane, *Memoir*, part 1, 209.

45. Drane, *Memoir*, part 1, 97.

46. Drane, *Memoir*, part 1, 106.

other. "People who thought of God as a friend easily linked friends to God," observes Sharon Marcus in her paradigm-shifting study, *Between Women: Friendship, Desire, and Marriage in Victorian England.*[47] Marcus argues that a range of relationships between women, including those about which they simultaneously "wrote of love for God and love for female friends with equal erotic fervor,"[48] formed an essential rather than outlawed element of Victorian society. Likewise, Newman could speak freely and without shame with Drane, and others,[49] of his love for St. John because he knew that Drane would understand the combined nature of romantic friendships and the loneliness of the religious life. He recognized that she could comprehend the blessings of love and its associated loss as the "intention" of God.

THE SONG OF SONGS AND JOHN OF THE CROSS

The Song of Songs appears in surprising places in Drane's writings to reinforce ideas of her espousal to Christ. In an unpublished piece, Drane incorporates Song of Songs 6:3 with a reflection on the Eucharist:

> He worked, I know not how many miracles, to humble Himself into that little form [i.e., the Eucharist],—not for the world, or the Church, but for <u>me</u>. I to my Beloved, & my Beloved to me. O what a thought! What speciality in His love! How it singles me out from the Mass & speaks to me—as a man speaketh with his friend.[50]

The merging of different kinds of love in Christ, between the erotic and the platonic, is found elsewhere in Drane's writings, such as her meditations on the prodigal son parable. For Drane, the return of the son to the father recalls the beloved's wish for the Shulamite to return: "Return, return, O Sulamitess, return, return!" she quotes (Song of Songs 6:13).[51] "Return" reminds one of the etymology of conversion (to turn around): "Return to grace, return to life, return to your father's home; return to God."[52] The juxtaposition of the parable and the Song of Songs eroticizes the nature of the relationship between the believer and God and reinforces the idea of nuns as espoused to Christ.

---

47. Marcus, *Between Women,* 63.
48. Marcus, *Between Women,* 63.
49. Ekeh, "Newman's Account," 5.
50. Drane, G/FRD/ii/1a Album, n.p.
51. Drane, *Memoir,* part 2, 25–26.
52. Drane, *Memoir,* part 2, 26.

76 • CHAPTER 3

Like the Song of Songs, the story of the prodigal son is essentially a love story: "How his father had loved him!" says Drane of the son.[53]

For *Songs in the Night and Other Poems,* Drane drew on John of the Cross's use of spousal imagery from the Song of Songs. Her source text was the two-volume *The Complete Works of Saint John of the Cross,* published in 1864 and translated by David Lewis.[54] Lewis was a friend of Newman and a former Tractarian who defected to Rome. A clipping from volume two of the complete works is found in one of Drane's notebooks, and it offers a clue as to why she possessed a strong feeling for the Spanish mystic.[55] Containing the final paragraph of "Prayer of the Enamoured Soul," we find a characteristic assertion by John of the Cross, which is of being united as a bride to Christ. With veiled images of seduction and sexual euphemism from female-centered texts, Ruth 3:7 and Song of Songs 2:6 and 8:3, he says,

> O my God, how sweet to me Thy presence, who art the Supreme Good. I will draw near to Thee in silence, and will uncover Thy feet, that it may please Thee to unite me to Thyself, making my soul Thy bride: I will rejoice in nothing till I am in thine arms.[56]

Beneath the cutting is a passage from Charles Borromeo concerning three things one must do to "make progress in the service of God."[57] The status of the two men as Counter-Reformation figures might explain, at least in part, their significance in Drane's eyes. The counter-Reformation was a period of renewal and reform in the Catholic Church. Drane might have believed that a similar, love-based revival was being staged during her own lifetime, of which she herself was a part.

Songs in the Night and Other Poems was first published in 1876, followed by a second and expanded edition in 1887. The volume had an impact on readers. As Drane remarks, "It is the only book of mine that I know for certain has done good to others, because they have told me so."[58] I will focus largely on the first section of the volume, as these poems are in dialogue with the poetry of John of the Cross. Apart from the first poem, which both adapts and embellishes his "The Canticle of the Soul Rejoicing to Know God by Faith" (Drane's title), the provenance of almost all of the other fourteen poems in the sec-

---

53. Drane, *Memoir,* part 2, 26.
54. John of the Cross, *Saint John of the Cross,* vol. 1.
55. Drane, G/FRD/ii/1a Album, n.p.
56. John of the Cross, *Saint John of the Cross,* vol. 2, 390.
57. Drane, G/FRD/ii/1a Album, n.p.
58. Drane, *Memoir,* part 1, 82.

tion are, as Drane claims, "suggested" by individual passages from John of the Cross's "The Spiritual Canticle,"[59] a poem that displays the pervasive influence of the Song of Songs in content and structure. Drane argues her poems are likewise written in the first person, "as best fitted to convey the experience of each individual soul."[60] Her poems are therefore as much attempts to engage in dialogue with the Spanish saint as they are with God. Each poem begins with an epigraph of two or three lines from John of the Cross, followed by Drane's poetic response to the spiritual significance of his words.

Following the style of "The Spiritual Canticle," Drane's poems describe the natural world in order to detail both the beauty of the beloved[61] and the dark night of the soul. It is on the latter that I wish to focus. Drane's landscapes are emblematic of emotional and spiritual states, including abandonment, despair, and spiritual aridity. She appears to have experienced depression in her past—an "intense inward trial and darkness"[62]—which influenced her writing. For instance, "Light on the Hill-Tops" draws on a capricious northern landscape, "whose sky / No changeless azure wears, / But varies like a wayward child" (lines 9–11). In keeping with the title of her volume, Drane introduces darker material from the second poem onward to reflect John of the Cross's concept of the dark night of the soul, a state in which the soul resides before it is reunited with Christ. Drane declares in reflections on Psalm 106 that the dark night is an experience of purgation and tribulation:

> If He loves our soul, He will perfect it; and if He means to perfect it, He must chasten and purge it. Not by the sweetness of consolation, but by the hard ways of darkness, aridity, temptation, and weariness of spiritual things, it may be that He will purify and perfect His chosen ones. "Our souls abhor all manner of meat;" and, so far from feeling nearer to God, we feel as it were at death's door. The sensitive part of our soul, that wherein self-love makes its very nest and hiding-place, is torn to atoms. We cannot pray, or at least we think we cannot. And yet prayer is the only refuge, the only remedy. So, in the dark night of our purgation, whilst God seems so far away, we yet do cry to Him in our tribulation, and once more He delivers us out of our distress.[63]

---

59. Drane, *Songs in the Night and Other Poems*, v.

60. Drane, *Songs in the Night and Other Poems*, v.

61. Speaking of the pastoral landscape in "The Fairest Fair," F. Elizabeth Gray argues that by giving her female speaker "the power to praise and woo her own beloved, Drane turns both Song of Solomon and secular pastoral lyric traditions to new account, through their combination." Gray, *Christian and Lyric Tradition*, 149.

62. Drane, *Memoir*, part 1, 77.

63. Drane, *Memoir*, part 2, 99.

The dark night is an extension of the heroic life of a hardened warrior. It is a progression toward "perfect[ion]" by means of a sacrifice, specifically, an emptying of the old self and the cares of the world for the love of God.

Drane says elsewhere, "There must be darkness before there can be light. This darkness is the forgetting of all things—of oneself, one's good and one's bad—past sins, past everything. And simply fastening the point of one's heart + mind and ask on God, in desire."[64] One must lose what is valuable in this world to obtain the ultimate prize in the next. This sacrifice is necessary to receive Christ:

> All this, as I see it, is only part of the price we have to pay for an inestimable treasure. Our Lord, when He takes possession of us, infuses into all earthly things a something which prevents our ever belonging to them again. He makes a great void in them, and in our own hearts, just because He means to fill that void with Himself. I have expressed it somewhere in the "Songs in the Night;" indeed it is the keynote of most of [the poems]. . . . They acknowledge the sense of loss—of separation from what was prized before— of loneliness in the world, and death to the world.[65]

Drane's understanding of the dark night adheres to her esteem for other forms of emptying and sacrifice—an example set by Catherine of Siena, who sought a life of remarkable austerity.[66] And of course, it follows the first of the three conditions of the spiritual life described by John of the Cross in his exposition of "The Spiritual Canticle": the purgative, illuminative, and unitive ways. The first way pertains to beginners (the purgative); the second to the advanced (the spiritual espousal); the final to the perfect (the spiritual marriage).[67] The hard landscape of "Light in the Hill-Tops" provides a suitable backdrop for the dark night and its promise of the illuminative way:

> I see the dull, dark cloud,
> And I feel the heavy air;
> But I lift my eyes to the mountain-top.
> And I know there is sunshine there. (lines 33–36)

The God of the dark night is a hidden God. His absence is like the end of summer in "Abandonment": "I wander through the meadows, / But their beauty all is gone" (lines 1–2). The soul's response is loneliness and longing,

---

64. Drane, G/FRD/ii/1c The Imitation of Christ: Text and notes, n.p.

65. Drane, *Memoir*, part 1, 209–10.

66. Drane, *History of St. Catherine of Siena*, vol. 1, 31.

67. John of the Cross, *Saint John of the Cross*, vol. 1, 12.

CELIBACY, SISTERHOODS, AND WOMEN'S POETRY · 79

as shown in Drane's "Forgotten among the Lilies," a response to John of the Cross's "The Obscure Night of the Soul."[68] With the exception of a few missing commas, the epigraph of Drane's poem comprises Lewis's translation of the final three lines of the Spanish poem: "I fainted away abandoned; / And amid the lilies forgotten / Threw all my cares away." What makes Drane's poem a fascinating reworking of themes from the source material is the fact that Lewis appears to have mistranslated a couple of crucial moments in these three lines, consequently leading Drane to emphasize God's desertion. Modern translations suggest that the final stanza describes a moment of blissful union, in which one is finally at rest and all cares are abandoned:

I remained, lost in oblivion;
My face I reclined on the Beloved.
All ceased and I abandoned myself,
Leaving my cares forgotten among the lilies.[69]

In contrast, the Lewis translation suggests the speaker has been abandoned and forgotten among the lilies:

I continued in oblivion lost,
My head was resting on my Love;
I fainted away, abandoned,
And, amid the lilies forgotten,
Threw all my cares away. (lines 36–40)

As a result of this mistranslation, Drane understandably turns her poetic dialogue with this stanza into an extension of the dark night rather than an entry into the illuminative or unitive way. "Forgotten and abandoned," her speaker declares, "It is a weary thing to be forgot— / A tearful, weary melancholy thing / To lie here like a bird with a wounded wing" (lines 51, 36–38). Left with no choice, the speaker makes peace with her abandonment: "Yet there is something, though I know not what, / That makes me lie at rest, and love my lot. / *Forgotten 'mid the lilies*" (lines 39–41). And later,

A sad, sweet lot—I needs must call it sweet;
My cares, like withered buds, I cast aside,
And reck but little what may next betide;

---

68. John of the Cross, *Saint John of the Cross*, vol. 1, 323–24.
69. See translation by E. Allison Peers in John of the Cross, *Dark Night of the Soul,* 34.

The days and years fly past on pinions fleet,
Amid these lilies crushed beneath His feet. (lines 46–50)

Passively, she must wait among the lilies for him to return, like Apollo on his chariot: "I am content to stay / Until once more the Bridegroom passes by, / And hither turns His gracious, pitying eye" (58–60).

Despite her heartbreak, the speaker holds on to the hope that the object of her desire will one day return. Given the poignancy of Drane's poem, which reminds one of Hopkins's sonnets of desolation, it is probable that Lewis's mistranslation and withholding of a happy ending enabled Drane's poem to be a more powerful work than it might otherwise have been. Relatedly, the poem assists in setting the tone for the volume's repeated reference to the beloved's flight and the lover's search for him, as expressed in Song of Songs 2:14 and much of "The Spiritual Canticle." As Drane would write in "Abandonment," "Where art Thou fled, Beloved One? / Where dost Thou hide thy face?" (lines 25–26). Likewise, she concludes "The Search for the Beloved" with the following:

So I live as one not living
    In a world all dead and cold,
Sighing for the longed-for hour
    When His face I may behold:
Sighing for the day of freedom
    When my chain shall be unbound,
And in ever-verdant pastures
    At His Feet I may be found! (lines 49–56)

After the dark night, the face of the hidden God will reveal itself in fulfilment of 1 Corinthians 13:12 and Song of Songs 2:14. Drane says of the wise men that, upon entering the stable in Bethlehem, "they were to have the joy beyond all other joys of seeing Him face to face."[70] Likewise, the dark night of the soul concludes with the sight of Christ's loving gaze.

SWEETNESS AND BITTERNESS IN ROSSETTI'S "GOBLIN MARKET"

Drane challenged the domestic roles expected of women, though she would have argued that she was simply following her vocation. She would have also

---

70. Drane, *Memoir,* part 2, 115.

CELIBACY, SISTERHOODS, AND WOMEN'S POETRY · 81

claimed that her provocative notion of being a manly warrior and bearing spiritual fruit for Christ's pleasure originated, at least in part, from the canonical Song of Songs. In turning to Rossetti, one can see resonances of Drane in Mary Arseneau's assertion that "Rossetti's most assertive, most feminist, most political, and most egalitarian statements are formulated not in resistance to her religion, but rather are firmly grounded in it."[71] C. C. Barfoot believes that a number of Rossetti's religious poems contain a spiritual eroticism linked to the tradition of the Song of Songs and poets such as John of the Cross and John Donne.[72] Nilda Jiménez points out that the Song of Songs was Rossetti's most favored source for direct biblical quotation in her poetry.[73] While Jiménez's concordance of the Bible in Rossetti's poetry does not include references to the Song of Songs in "Goblin Market," I believe that the fairy tale quality of the poem determines that biblical references should be echoes rather than direct quotations.

A rhyme dating from the early nineteenth century tells us that boys are "made of snips & snails and puppy-dogs' tails," whereas girls are "made of sugar & spice & all things nice."[74] This gendering of sweetness is not as innocent and "sweet" as it seems, as we shall see from the consequences that befall the sexualized and gluttonous Laura in Rossetti's cross-audienced "children's fairy tale and adult erotic fantasy."[75] Succumbing to the temptation of the goblin costermongers, we are told that Laura "sucked and sucked and sucked the more / Fruits which that unknown orchard bore; / She sucked until her lips were sore" (lines 134–37).[76] Girls might be "made of sugar," but one cannot forget the added element of "spice," despite its rhyme with "nice." Because of the intimacy of ingestion and the association of sweet foods with excess and pleasure, sweet foods were highly sexualized and moralized among the middle classes over the course of the century.[77] Among the middle classes in the 1860s, sugar changed from being seen as nutritious in moderation to being regarded as dangerous or, even, poisonous food.[78] Sweet food posed a

---

71. Arseneau, *Recovering Christina Rossetti*, 3.

72. Barfoot, "In This Strang Labourinth," 243.

73. Jiménez, *Bible and the Poetry of Christina Rossetti*, x.

74. Cited in Matthews, *Blake, Sexuality and Bourgeois Politeness*, 78.

75. Kooistra, "*Goblin Market* as a Cross-Audienced Poem," 185.

76. Rossetti, *Complete Poems of Christina Rossetti*, vol. 1. Future references are to this volume.

77. Of the feminized Oscar Wilde at the fin de siècle, I am reminded of Julia Skelly's argument that the public's obsession with his mouth and decaying teeth, and with what he spoke and consumed, especially in relation to anxieties around sexual acts, food, and drink, points to the interconnected discourses of consumption, addiction, and excess. Skelly, "Paradox of Excess," 140–43.

78. Tate, "Aesthetics of Sugar," 164.

82 • CHAPTER 3

moral danger to children (and adults) by causing cravings. Hence, we are told the goblin fruits are "like honey to the throat / But poison in the blood" (lines 555–56). Unsurprisingly, Laura's "passionate craving" (line 267) for goblin fruit after the first sugar hit resembles the symptoms of drug addiction.[79] She says, "I ate and ate my fill / Yet my mouth waters still" (lines 165–66).

Combining the act of eating with the taste of sweetness made sugar a potent commodity. Sugar consumption among women and children of the working classes skyrocketed in the second half of the nineteenth century, due largely to its dramatic decrease in price and greater availability.[80] Rosemary Tate argues that "the growing popularity of sugar as a commodity provoked new modes of representation for sweetness both as a taste and as a literary and aesthetic category."[81] As an imported product from tropical climates, sugar crossed the literal boundaries of geography and the cultural borders of decorum and "taste." We recognize this border crossing in a "nursery rhyme" published in *The Pearl* (1879–80), an erotic periodical to which Algernon Charles Swinburne anonymously contributed flagellation pornography:

> There was a young lady of Troy,
> Who invented a new kind of joy:
>   She sugared her thing
>   Both outside and in,
> And then had it sucked by a boy.[82]

This ditty intermixes the twin impulses of eating and sex. To "suck" a sugared "thing" is to taste its sweetness. Taste is traditionally considered one of the lowest of the senses. Etymologically, the word "taste" is connected to "touch," another lowly sense associated with the body and animality. I do not mean to suggest that Rossetti was familiar with the ditty from *The Pearl,* but I use it to illustrate how she was not alone in creating an adult nursery rhyme that employs the sensuous language of sweetness to reference sexual matters.

Critics tend to agree that the central symbol of "Goblin Market" is the goblin fruit.[83] The taste that the goblins and Laura both attribute to the fruit is sweetness.[84] Rossetti uses the word "sweet" seven times to paint a picture of "sweet-tooth Laura," lured by the sweet goblin fruit that she discovers to be

---

79. Tate, "Aesthetics of Sugar," 163.
80. Mintz, *Sweetness and Power,* 6.
81. Tate, "Aesthetics of Sugar," 2.
82. Anonymous, "[There Was a Young Lady of Troy]," 31.
83. D'Amico, *Christina Rossetti,* 69.
84. Tate, "Aesthetics of Sugar," 160.

"Sweeter than honey from the rock" (lines 115, 129). These unnatural parcels of sweetness—which "all ripe together" unseasonably (line 15)—lure her away from the sisterhood. For Rossetti, religious devotion is coterminous with sisterhood; to stray from one is to stray from the other, thereby endangering the purity of the soul. Diane D'Amico notes that the comparison "Sweeter than honey from the rock" echoes Psalm 81:16: "And with honey out of the rock should I have satisfied thee."[85] If the rock denotes Christ,[86] then the implication is that Laura either confuses the sweetness of the world with that of Christ or prioritizes the former before the latter. In the context of the poem, I argue that sweetness is a focus on the pleasures and sensations of the body, at the expense of sisterhood and the nurturance of the soul.

In both the Song of Songs and "Goblin Market," the beckoning to "come" and eat of the fruit is significant, though the reasons and consequences differ enormously. In the first text, love is the paramount reason, while in the second it is malice (until it is replaced by sibling love, as we shall see). In the Song of Songs, the lover uses the language of nature to invite, and wish for, her beloved to eat her "fruit": "Come, my beloved, let us go forth into the field" (7:11) and "Let my beloved come into his garden, and eat his pleasant fruits" (4:16). The romance is lost in "Goblin Market," as the goblin men's repeated calls of "Come buy, come buy" resemble the London costermongers who cried out for buyers on the street. Food vendors were dangerously seductive because their "iterated jingle[s]" (line 253) might ring in susceptible ears. "We must not buy their fruits" (line 43) is Laura's first utterance.[87] Lizzie takes appropriate cautions: "She thrust a dimpled finger / In each ear, shut eyes and ran" (lines, 67–68). The poem participates in the tradition of Aunt Busy-Bee's book, *New London Cries* (1852), and other books urging young readers to be wise consumers, thereby suggesting a multidimensional literacy that is aural, oral, and moral.[88] The skilled reading of a vendor's cry was important at a time of rapid industrialization when exotic foods found their way to English tables and public fears abounded over food adulteration.[89] Within a literary context, one might understand the cry as a variation on the invitation poem through the homonym of "come by." It is therefore useful to compare "Goblin Market" with Rossetti's poem "Echo" (1862), which begins with an imperative, "Come to me" (line 1), and repeats the word "Come." Like the Song of Songs, which

---

85. D'Amico, *Christina Rossetti*, 71.
86. D'Amico, *Christina Rossetti*, 71.
87. Tucker, "Rossetti's Goblin Marketing," 120.
88. Norcia, "Come Buy, Come Buy," 38.
89. Norcia, "Come Buy, Come Buy," 26.

84 • CHAPTER 3

is the first and most influential text of the invitation genre,[90] Rossetti's poems beckon to the reader.

Rossetti both critically reflects upon and knowingly partakes in the wielding of sweet and pleasurable words. The Song of Songs refers often to the taste of sweetness, especially from fruit and occasionally honey. Indeed, the biblical text begins, "Let him kiss me with the kisses of his mouth: for thy love is better than wine" (1:2) and later says, similarly, "His mouth is most sweet: yea, he is altogether lovely" (5:16). With its emphasis on oral sensations, "Goblin Market" is one of the most sensuous poems of the era, rivaling the Song of Songs in its eroticism. But unlike the goblin men, Rossetti uses her mastery of words toward a moral and didactic end. In her poem, she appeals to the senses, even if she is also wary of them. The goblins' advertisement begins as a shopping list of domestically available fruits, like apples, cherries, raspberries, and cranberries (lines 5–14), but then quickly moves to rarer ones not native to Britain:

> Our grapes fresh from the vine,
> Pomegranates full and fine,
> Dates and sharp bullaces,
> Rare pears and greengages,
> Damsons and bilberries,
> Taste them and try:
> Currants and gooseberries,
> Bright-fire-like barberries,
> Figs to fill your mouth,
> Citrons from the South
> Sweet to tongue and sound to eye;
> Come buy, come buy. (lines 20–31)[91]

Rossetti offers us the seductive rhythm of the goblins' "cry" before she presents us with descriptions of any of the characters. Through alliteration and parallelism, respectively, the goblin men beseech their listeners to "Taste . . . and try" the wares, which are "Sweet to tongue and sound to eye"—utterances to fill the mouth, just like fruit. It was a tactic also used by London sellers: cries such as, "All round and sound my Ripe Kentish Cherries."[92]

Rossetti's abovementioned passage displays an almost over-ripeness of the aural, such as in the use of feminine rhymes, hyphenated descriptions, and the seductiveness of "s" sounds. This is complemented by the unusual and

---

90. Gray, "Come Be My Love," 370.
91. Lysack, "Goblin Markets," 152.
92. Norcia, "Come Buy, Come Buy," 30.

irregular rhyme and metrical scheme that offers greater freedom of sounds. The seeming excessiveness of rhyme and of irregular rhythm and meter break away from the Victorians' preference for regularity in rhyme and meter. The deviation draws our attention to the materiality of sound and fruit such as "Citrons from the South." The citron is a fruit that varies in taste, from sour to sweet, and its uses include candied fruit, jam, and liqueur. Its inclusion in the poem reflects the multivalent nature of fruit in the text. "Goblin Market" conforms to the principle of using "fruit forbidden" (line 479) for moral instruction on proper conduct. Laura succumbs to the temptation of goblin fruit that appears to represent the "joys brides hope to have" (line 314), but if consumed out of wedlock, leads to sickness and death. Like other transgressive and diseased women, Jeanie from "Goblin Market" and the lady in Swinburne's "The Leper" (published four years later, in 1866), Laura witnesses her golden hair turning gray and she becomes "cankered and goblin-ridden" (line 480). For her transgression and subsequent "ruin" (line 483), Laura swiftly finds herself at death's door. This interpretation views the poem within the so-called fallen woman narrative, a lens through which the poem is often read,[93] especially given Rossetti's work with Magdalen homes.

What I have been alluding to is that "Goblin Market" possesses elements that many readers today would interpret as pornographic. Indeed, *Playboy* published explicit illustrations of "Goblin Market" by Kinuko Craft in the 1970s.[94] One thing, however, separates Rossetti's poem from Victorian pornography. In pornography, there is little if any bitterness; everything and everyone tastes deliciously sweet. Any pain that exists, whether through flagellation, masochism, or defloration, is simply a prelude to greater pleasure. But in Rossetti's poetry, pain and bitterness exist for their own sakes, just as solitariness and hardship have a defined purpose in Drane's writing. In contrast, there is no comparable bitterness in the following (saccharine) nursery rhyme from *The Pearl*:

There was a young lady of Rheims,
Who was terribly plagued by wet dreams;
    She saved up a dozen,
    And sent them to her cousin,
Who ate them and thought they were creams.[95]

---

93. Scholl, *Hunger, Poetry and the Oxford Movement*, 140.

94. Kooistra, *Christina Rossetti and Illustration*, 241–43.

95. Anonymous, "[There Was a Young Lady of Rheims]," 31.

"Cream" was consumed with tea and cooked fruit; today, we call it sweetened condensed milk.[96]

With its own "iterated jingle / Of sugar-baited words" (lines 233–34), pornography advertises the repetition of sweet delights, always ripe, always sweet for consumption. Just as goblin merchants must continually advertise the sweetness of their products in order to break down the walls of consumer resistance, pornography whitewashes realities by telling us that bodily juices are always sweet. Ironically, the very marginalization of pornography would have enhanced its own allure as forbidden fruit, as something delicious to be consumed. Advertising, that most conspicuous of marketing practices of the technologies of capitalism, entails a "redescription of the commodity in terms that boost its value by deepening its mystique, a property that Victorians ordinarily associated with the exotic in space or time (with empire, that is, or history)."[97] Pornography was immersed in the capitalist impulses of the Victorian era. By the mid- to late nineteenth century, it was a mass-cultural product, cutting across class lines in both print and visual mediums.[98] According to Alison Pease, mass production contributed to pornography's "democratization" by making items of erotica increasingly cheaper and more obtainable than ever before.[99] Like sugar. Pornography acts in the same way as advertising. In other words, if marketing citrons from the south offers the customer the exoticism of the south, pornography offers charms from the body's own south.

Rossetti demystifies the allure of sweetness that exists within systems of commodification and, indeed, pornography. The goblins' marketing strategy is to aurally seduce Laura into buying a product that is entangled with a romance of fulfilled desires, like the love story in the Song of Songs. Professional seducers that they are, the goblins lure their victim with sweet utterances, mellifluous words and "tones as smooth as honey" (line 108). Susceptible and enticed, Laura believes the goblins bear only harmless offerings of love: from her perspective, "They sounded kind and full of loves / In the pleasant weather" (lines 79–78). Unlike her sister, Lizzie does not fall for the goblins' act. As the moral-minded sister, she warns Laura, "Their offers should not charm us, / Their evil gifts would harm us" (65–66). The goblins' jingle, "Come buy, come buy," is a dangerous charm, a spellbinding incantation; as Rossetti's rhyme suggests, "charm" is but one letter—and one bite—away from "harm."

---

96. Mintz, *Sweetness and Power*, 143.
97. Tucker, "Rossetti's Goblin Marketing," 121.
98. Pease, *Aesthetics of Obscenity*, 52.
99. Pease, *Aesthetics of Obscenity*, 52–53.

SISTERHOOD VERSUS BROTHERHOOD:
"MY SISTER, MY SPOUSE"

Rossetti ultimately rejects the temptations of mellifluous language and what it represents in order to uphold the double sanctity of celibacy and sisterhood, whether conventual or familial. "In the literature and life of Christina Rossetti, we find a woman who entered Victorian Anglo-Catholic discourse as a champion of female virginity," argues Frederick Roden.[100] Ultimately, "Goblin Market" reverses the story of Eden, whereby the snake seduced Eve into eating the fruit from the tree of the knowledge of good and evil (Genesis 2:16–17). The relationship between fruit eating and the "knowledge" or experience of sexual relations is one that finds resonance in the Song of Songs and "Goblin Market." While Rossetti's poem could be understood as a cautionary tale against premarital sex, one could also read it as one that upholds sisterhood above marriage—even if Lizzie and Laura eventually marry and have children. After all, the poem is largely one of women and of cozy homosocial domestic spaces. In the words of Herbert Tucker, "An epilogue fast-forwards to later years: both sisters now being married, Laura makes a habit of summoning her daughters and nieces—nephews, sons, and husbands somehow need not apply—to hear her tale of trespass, waste, and redemption and to learn its lesson that 'there is no friend like a sister'" (line 562).[101] Any male figures who are given a voice are external to family and familiarity; these are the "queer brother[s]" (line 94)—the "goblin men" (repeated six times)—who mean harm. Sisterhood triumphs over the goblin brotherhood, and the domestic space trumps the goblin marketplace. Indeed, religious sisterhoods paved the way for the liberated new woman at the turn of the century.[102] On a similar note, Lynda Palazzo argues that Rossetti cared little for hierarchical distinctions and thereby disliked that priests were universally considered the guardians of national morality.[103] Thus, in "Goblin Market," we find that women—sisters—are the moral guardians and teachers of lessons.

The critical enterprise of locating Rossetti primarily within the "androcentric" world of the Pre-Raphaelite Brotherhood has tended to obscure the importance of sisterhood in her life and poetry.[104] In contrast, critics attentive to Rossetti's religion have spoken at length about the importance of both sisterhood and female familial relationships. Faith was foundational in the

---

100. Roden, *Same-Sex Desire,* 35.
101. Tucker, "Rossetti's Goblin Marketing," 119.
102. Roden, "Sisterhood Is Powerful," 63–64.
103. Palazzo, *Christina Rossetti's Feminist Theology,* 2.
104. Arseneau, *Recovering Christina Rossetti,* 18.

88 • CHAPTER 3

self-identities of the Rossetti women—mother Frances, sisters Christina and Maria, and Frances's unmarried sisters—and their domestic setting. This primary community was a microcosm of the other homosocial communities with which Rossetti was associated.[105] As a community of women filled with a common love for Christ, whether it be in the domestic space or outside the home, sisterhood consumed Rossetti's life and writing. The world of the Rossetti women existed on the same plane as the religious-based affiliations that Rossetti maintained in her charity work as a secular outer sister of an Anglican order involved with Magdalen homes for so-called fallen women. Her sister Maria entered the Anglican Sisterhood of All Saints in 1873, making her a sister twice over—as Rossetti's sibling and as a member of a religious community. Rossetti also wrote influential poems about nuns, such as "The Convent Threshold" (1858), which inspired Gerard Manley Hopkins to respond with a poem of the same title. Her poem "Three Nuns" (1850) reworks lines from Genesis, indicating what Elizabeth Ludlow calls her "opposition to the Victorian prioritization of maternity over a life of dedicated service to God."[106] Lines 131–37 of the poem use the language of the fountain sealed and well of living waters from the Song of Songs (4:12; 4:15),[107] images alluding to virginity and spiritual plenitude. D'Amico rightly argues that Rossetti "consider[ed] the consecrated single life spiritually superior to married life" and that "numerous" poems written between 1850 and 1870 suggest that she viewed the institution of marriage "with a cynical eye."[108] By extension, in choosing to maintain her virginity, Rossetti chose not an impoverished, solitary life typically associated with "spinsters" or nuns alike but rather a life of salvific devotion to Christ in the presence of other women.

In the Song of Songs, the Shulamite is called "my sister, my spouse" (4:9; 4:10; 4:12; 5:1). "Goblin Market" depicts the vital importance of the sororal bond as if it were a marriage. This bond is deeply and startlingly erotic and intimate, at least to readers today. Theologically, however, suggestions of incest are not so different from the typological readings that posit Mary as the New Eve and Christ as the New Adam. Alliteratively named Laura and Lizzie are bonded by blood; they work together during the day and at night lie in each other's arms on "their curtained bed; / Like two blossoms on one stem" (lines 187–88). By repeating "Like two" thrice and including images of the sisters sleeping "Cheek to cheek and breast to breast / Locked together in one nest"

---

105. Arseneau, *Recovering Christina Rossetti,* 3–5.
106. Ludlow, *Christina Rossetti and the Bible,* 84.
107. Ludlow, *Christina Rossetti and the Bible,* 85.
108. D'Amico, *Christina Rossetti,* 67.

(lines 197–98), Rossetti makes it abundantly clear that the sisters' affinity is unbreakable. It is stronger than any other relationship and, indeed, as we shall see, strong as death. The relationship between Lizzie and Laura is not a substitute for, or even a precursor to, marriage, which led middle-class brothers and sisters to be socialized into their gendered roles as children. Valerie Sanders argues that brother-sister relationships prepared children for their future roles in marriage and were sometimes fraught with intense romantic feelings combined with a general sense of the girl's social and intellectual inferiority.[109] In contrast, sisters "essentially exist as equals: educated in the same way, and subject to the same constraints imposed on them as women in a male-dominated society."[110]

For Rossetti, sisterhood is complete as a relationship, and indeed sufficient as a reflection of one's relationship with Christ. As she says in her concluding lines of "Goblin Market":

> For there is no friend like a sister
> In calm or stormy weather;
> To cheer one on the tedious way,
> To fetch one if one goes astray,
> To lift one if one totters down,
> To strengthen whilst one stands. (lines 562–67)

Sisterhood literally rewrites the well-known lines of the Song of Songs to be, "Let her kiss me with the kisses of her mouth." The mouth both sins and redeems. Etymologically, to redeem means to buy back, and Lizzie redeems Laura through a kiss. In the poem's climax, Lizzie seeks out the goblin fruit for the sake of her beloved sister. Lizzie resists the goblins' attempts to force her to eat the fruit, and this leads to her physical assault and the smearing of fruit over her face and closed lips. Her bravery shows her to be as heroic as any warrior nun. Lizzie returns home, calling to Laura *up the garden*:

> Did you miss me?
> Come and kiss me.
> Never mind my bruises,
> Hug me, kiss me, suck my juices
> Squeezed from goblin fruits for you,

---

109. Sanders, *Brother-Sister Culture*, 4–5, 11–31.

110. Sanders, *Brother-Sister Culture*, 31.

90 • CHAPTER 3

> Goblin pulp and goblin dew.
> Eat me, drink me, love me;
> Laura, make much of me:
> For your sake I have braved the glen
> And had to do with goblin merchant men. (lines 464–74; emphasis added)

Lizzie's call to Laura "up the garden," a reminder of "the voice of my beloved" (Song of Songs 2:8), begins to undo the charm of the poison. Marylu Hill argues that Lizzie's "invitation to eat/love is almost playful,"[111] though Hill does not mention the invitation poem, a genre that harks back to the Song of Songs. Responding to her sister's "invitation to eat/love," Laura "clung to her sister, / Kissed and kissed and kissed her" and "kissed and kissed her with a hungry mouth" (lines 485–86, 492). The repetition of "kissed" is not incidental, as it draws us to the act and ultimately the goal of the repeated kissing, which is to eat the fruit in its transformed state.

Typologically, the fruit combined with the garden image not only reverses the original seduction by fruit in the garden of Eden; it also alludes to the arousal of the lover under the tree in Song of Songs 8:5. Each of these trees could be understood as a type of cross. What is therefore at stake is not simply Laura's life but also her soul. Critics, such as Hill, Arseneau, D'Amico, and Ludlow, have spoken about the importance of Eucharistic imagery in "Goblin Market." I add that, just as bread and wine are transformed into Christ's body, so the goblin fruit is transmuted into an antidote through contact with Lizzie's sacrificial body (note the trinitarian "Eat me, drink me, love me," indicating unity between the three verbs). The antidote is transmitted in kisses, ensuring the act becomes an unmistakable sign of redemptive love. In other words, the kisses reveal that Lizzie's love for Laura is "strong as death" (Song of Songs 8:6); in fact, her sacrifices made in the name of sororal love grant Laura "Life out of death" (line 524). Lizzie's kisses transmit love's "most vehement *flame*" (Song of Songs 8:6; emphasis added) to her sister's heart, the seat of love, acting as a "*fiery* antidote" (line 559; emphasis added) to save her life and soul. Moreover, the healing juices from Lizzie's kisses are bitter: Laura "gorged on bitterness without a name" (line 510). The sweetness of the fruit hides a bitter core. By exposing the reality of the fruit's bitterness, Rossetti strips it of everything that makes it seductive. In other words, she strips it of its false sweetness. Christ is the only permitted sweetness, and this sweetness is best found through sisterhood.

---

111. Hill, "Eat Me, Drink Me, Love Me," 465.

Drane and Rossetti chose to live within sisterhoods dedicated to Christ. They wrote of heroic women who lived without compromise and displayed nothing short of absolute commitment to their religious vocation, celibacy, and sisterhood. The Song of Songs provides a number of examples from which to consider the women's relationship to Christ and the world, most notably in relation to spiritual fecundity, heroic virginity, independence from men, and sisterly devotion. Indeed, "there is no friend like a sister," because sororal love is truly strong as death.

CHAPTER 4

Queer Hands, Bodies, and Masculinities

Simeon Solomon and John Gray

The poet John Gray wrote to French art critic Félix Fénéon in 1890, saying, "We shall see everything there is to see in London; we shall seek out drawings by a fellow named Simeon Solomon, a pre-Raphaelite [*sic*], but also something else—something like Verlaine if what they say is true. . . . People no longer speak of him, except in whispers, but he was one of the great artists of the School (sometimes)."[1] The letter strongly implies that Gray was familiar with Solomon's reputation, spawned by the reception of his homoerotic art and confirmed sensationally with his 1873 arrest in a public urinal on a sodomy charge. The arrest led to Solomon's social downfall, and the man born in 1840 into a well-to-do London Jewish family would in his later years be blighted by alcoholism until his death in a workhouse in 1905. Along with the trials of Oscar Wilde—who owned a copy of Solomon's prose poem, *A Vision of Love Revealed in Sleep* (1871)—Solomon's social ostracism might have contributed to Gray's decision to seek the priesthood and a life without infamy.[2]

In this chapter, I look at the relationship between the Song of Songs and the queer body in the art of Simeon Solomon and the ekphrastic poetry of John Grey. I begin by exploring the nature of hands as communicators of human feeling and cultural meaning in Solomon's homoerotic art. I regard the hand as a potential instrument of queer touch, specifically, handholding

---

1. Cited in McCormack, *John Gray,* 28.
2. Wilde's copy of the Solomon work is held in the British Library.

in visual depictions of Sappho and the Song of Songs, which sometimes overlap through intertextual references and Solomon's penchant for combining the Hebraic and Hellenistic. In his art, Solomon demonstrates the queer and erotic potential of hands and handholding. He subverts the interpretation of the Song of Songs as a heterosexual love triangle, such that the beloved daringly expresses bisexual or same-sex attraction through the placement of his hands. With their limp wrists, the male lovers exude a certain kind of effeminacy that, in other works, repelled some critics, but from which one could draw a link between concepts of Jewishness, the *effeminatus,* and Hellenism. The classical and Hebraic elements in Solomon's works, whether combined or mirrored, had religious and sexual significance for him. Not only did classical and Biblical subjects fall under the prestigious field of history painting, but ancient Greece and the Bible furnished Solomon with precedents and legitimizing models of same-sex desires. Combining the Song of the Songs with classical settings or figures forms a kind of handholding between forms usually kept apart, like that of two men. Indeed, Solomon's triads did little to obscure same-sex desire, serving, rather, to highlight the element of same-sex attraction in his works.

Like Solomon, Gray was same-sex attracted and possessed a highly attuned aesthetic sensibility. Indeed, I argue that Gray's decadent Catholicism was an aestheticized faith, reconstructed by art. The visual focus of the chapter places a spotlight on Gray's ekphrastic poetry, mostly concerning the body of Christ. Gray wrote several poems about the quintessential Catholic object of devotional gaze and desire: the crucifix. These poems are reminiscent of waṣf poetry, an ancient Arabic style of poetry found in the Song of Songs to describe and celebrate a lover's body from head to toe. Gray, however, uses the waṣf style to highlight the moment of Christ's greatest ugliness, humiliation, and suffering. In so doing, he maintains a queer devotional gaze reconceptualized through a French decadent reception of the medieval depiction of Christ's vulnerable body. Christ's feminized body falls into closer alignment with that of a dandy priest than a muscular Christian ideal. I conclude the chapter with an exploration of the influence of John of the Cross's poems, which depict the vulva-like wounds of Christ's eternally crucified body as the entrance to the seat of love, which is the Sacred Heart.

SOLOMON'S QUEER HANDS

Why focus on the hand? It is a body part that both acts and signals a great deal. In Song of Songs 5:4, the beloved places his hand "by the hole of the door," an act that excites his lover. She rises to meet him, her hands dripping with myrrh as she touches the door handle (5:5). Earlier in the text, it is the hand that she mentions in the act of embracing: "His left hand is under my head, and his right hand doth embrace me" (2:6). Thus, the hand expresses and elicits human feelings. It is a versatile instrument of the body, conveying tenderness and cruelty, delivering strokes and strikes. With handshakes we offer a welcome, and with a helping hand we offer assistance. In everyday language, the hand follows a constellation of complex images and attendant meanings: to give with an open hand is to be generous; to be tightfisted is to be miserly; to sit on one's hands is to do nothing; to join hands is to cooperate; to seek more hands is to ask for help. The final example also suggests that the hand in everyday language can be a synecdoche for a person. Hands can also demonstrate our literal humanity: "hand privileging" still remains within Western anatomical and philosophical conceptions of human identity.[3] It is no surprise then that if a single person's hand can hold so many meanings, then the meeting of hands in a handhold can convey, evoke, and mean a great deal more.

The hand is the body part most commonly associated with touch. The Victorians were acutely aware of the power of touch to cross cultural boundaries. By outlining "the proper decorum for almost every type of interaction," Victorian etiquette and conduct manuals "provide an explicit taxonomy of touch," argues Ann Gagné.[4] Why did touch need to be monitored and policed? Touch, in particular the touching of hands, embodies a plethora of emotional meanings, particularly of togetherness. In the images I will look at, handholding—the embrace of hands—stands in for the body's embrace of another. In the body's embrace, we mutually adjust and shape our bodies to fit each other. In turn, contact is able to influence our emotions, enhancing them. Hands and emotions might become each other's mirror. This orientation of hands demonstrates "towardness" rather than "awayness," to use terms by Sara Ahmed. "Emotions are relational: they involve (re)actions or relations of 'towardness' or 'awayness' in relation to such objects," she says.[5] Emotions, including desire, affect the movement and spatial orientation of bodies in relation to each other—whether toward or away.

By directing my attention to queer hands, I follow Christopher Craft's reading of the homoerotic touch in Alfred Tennyson's *In Memoriam* (1850), with his provocatively titled chapter, "'Descend, and touch, and enter': Tennyson's Strange Manner of Address."[6] In relation to queer touch, I think of

---

3. Capuano, *Changing Hands,* 130.
4. Gagné, *Embodying the Tactile,* 9.
5. Ahmed, *Cultural Politics of Emotion,* 8.
6. Craft, *Another Kind of Love,* 44–70.

the erotic potential of deviant hands—hands that undress, and touch, and enter. Kimberly Cox deploys the term "queer touch" to consider tactility "in nonnormative ways" that make the different forms of queer touch—homosocial, homoerotic, and homosexual—"multiple and irreducible to singular conceptions of tactility—familial *and* sexual, homosocial *and* homoerotic."[7] Cox insists that pleasure is central to queer touch.[8] As instruments of pleasure and desire, hands might be considered the primary symbol of female homoeroticism in the nineteenth century. Writing specifically about lesbian codes in Victorian poetry, Virginia Blain has warned us "not to overlook the importance of hands as signifiers of erotic power."[9] This is especially important in the discussion of Sappho; however, Sappho's influence over male poets and artists, including Solomon, means that her reach extends beyond representations of women and female audiences.

Solomon was attentive to hands over the course of his career. A group of undated works in ink from around 1854 to 1855, when the artist was between the ages of thirteen and fifteen, demonstrates from early on Solomon's attention to handholding and attendant body language such as embracing. Depicting figures from the Hebrew Bible, he includes Joseph embracing Jacob, the son whom he thought dead (*The Meeting of Joseph and Jacob*); Delilah reaching for Samson's hand in their embrace (*Samson and Delilah*); Tobias meeting and embracing his father's kinsman Raguel (*Tobit and the Angel with Relations*); Abraham tenderly touching his son and kissing his hand (*Abraham and Isaac set out for Mount Moriah*); and two images of David and Jonathan embracing (*David and Jonathan*). The David and Jonathan images are especially important. They furnish us with early examples of Solomon's queer interpretation of sacred scripture and of the famous friendship "passing the love of women" (1 Samuel 1:26). Of this friendship, we are told, "the soul of Jonathan was knit with the soul of David, and Jonathan loved him as his own soul" (1 Samuel 18:1). Solomon presents this knitting of souls through the touching of hands in one image and a tender embrace in the other. In both images, David has long hair, wears a dress (though he is stripped to his waist in the second illustration), and could be mistaken for a woman, while Jonathan is dressed in armor and looks down protectively at his friend. Gayle M. Seymour believes fifteen-year-old Solomon would have identified with David, with David being an eighth son and Solomon the youngest of eight children.[10] In the first image, David's body is turned timidly away from Jonathan, but his face and right

---

7. Cox, *Touch, Sexuality, and Hands*, 148.

8. Cox, *Touch, Sexuality, and Hands*, 148–49.

9. Cited in Thain, "'Damnable Aestheticism,'" 319.

10. Seymour, "Simeon Solomon," 100.

96 • CHAPTER 4

hand are turned to him while Jonathan holds David's hand to his armored chest. With the dynamic between David and Jonathan, Solomon was already pushing the boundaries of the related norms of desire and masculinity. He was engaging in what Richard Dellamora might have called "the production of revisionary masculine discourses . . . that attempt to enlarge masculine capacities for relationships."[11]

These early queer pictures of David and Jonathan make way for same-sex handholding in Solomon's later works on the Song of Songs. Thais E. Morgan argues that Solomon reads the Song of Songs as a "paean to same-sex love instead of heterosexual love."[12] As I have discussed elsewhere in relation to his queer prose poem, *A Vision of Love Revealed in Sleep*, Solomon assigns a queer interpretation to the Song of Songs.[13] Same-sex handholding in Solomon's drawings *The Bride, the Bridegroom and Sad Love* (1865) and *The Bride, the Bridegroom and the Friend of the Bridegroom* (also known as *The Song of Solomon*) (1868) offer daring expressions of same-sex attachment and, perhaps even more daringly, of bisexuality. The handholding between the groom and the male figure in these drawings echoes other images featuring same-sex hand clasping in Solomon's oeuvre, including *Sappho and Erinna in a Garden at Mytilene* (1864) and *A Youth Relating Tales to Ladies* (1870), along with several works with religious and (mixed-gender) romantic allusions, such as *Dante's First Meeting with Beatrice* (1859–63) and *Faust and Marguerite* (ca. 1865). Through these visual echoes of handholding, Solomon demonstrates that physical intimacy moves beyond the confines of heteronormativity and religious dogmatism to encompass heterogeneity and homoeroticism.

SAPPHO AND THE SONG OF SONGS

Solomon was interested in creating visual echoes in his works, sometimes visiting the same theme and images more than once. Likewise, the placement of hands—specifically the act of handholding—allows us to find a point of connection across works and time. For instance, Solomon's watercolor painting *Sappho and Erinna in a Garden at Mytilene* might at first seem unrelated to the topic of the Song of Songs, but a closer inspection suggests otherwise. It is probable that Solomon came across Sappho through his friendships in the 1860s with intellectual elites and classicists familiar with same-sex desire in ancient Greek literature: Walter Pater at Oxford, Oscar Browning at Eton,

11. Dellamora, *Masculine Desire*, 5.
12. Morgan, "Perverse Male Bodies," 68.
13. Dau, "Song of Songs for Difficult Queers," 34–39.

and Algernon Charles Swinburne.[14] Solomon was likely aware of the surge of interest in Sappho in French literary circles from the mid-1840s onward.[15] Yopie Prins argues that the Victorian period "is an important moment in Sappho's reception," largely because "the recovery of 'new fragments' of Sappho in the course of the nineteenth century coincided with the Romantic aesthetic of fragmentation and the rise of Classical philology, culminating in the idealization of Sappho herself as the perfect fragment."[16]

Sappho is a part-portrait of imagination and projection. As such, she is a complex and compelling figure for Solomon. Morgan argues that Sappho provided Solomon with "a novel opportunity for representing same-sex desires in a publicly acceptable form."[17] Given that classical subjects were recommended by the Royal Academy, depictions of Sapphism were acceptable under this pretext.[18] As a result, Solomon's *Sappho and Erinna in a Garden at Mytilene* is a "relatively rare explicit early treatment of lesbianism."[19] Indeed, it is "among the few unequivocally homoerotic depictions of Sappho at any time, the only visual representation . . . of the poet actively initiating an embrace with another woman."[20] Sappho's influence also extended beyond the Royal Academy. Solomon's drawing of Sappho and the youth Antinous, the probable lover of Hadrian, decorated the Oxford rooms of initiates in the 1860s, suggesting, perhaps under the influence of John Addington Symonds, Sappho's role as the patron saint of modern homosexuality.[21] On the right-hand side of *Sappho and Erinna in a Garden at Mytilene* is almost certainly a statue of Aphrodite, the goddess of love, whom Sappho and her followers worshipped. Drawing a link between the painting and Swinburne's sadomasochistic "Anactoria," from *Poems and Ballads* (1866), Morgan emphasizes Sappho's "aggressive embrace" and Erinna's reluctance to reciprocate.[22] Even so, the possible aggressiveness of the moment is undercut by its stillness: a rose petal on Erinna's foot remains undisturbed. Moreover, Elizabeth Prettejohn proposes that, while Erinna does indeed seem to shrink from Sappho's embrace, "her drapery falls from her shoulder, and she inclines slightly toward Sappho, as though she may be about to yield."[23] Perhaps Erinna's hesitation, her display of simultaneous toward-

---

14. Cruise et al., *Love Revealed,* 42.
15. DeJean, *Fictions of Sappho,* 265–76.
16. Prins, *Victorian Sappho,* 3.
17. Morgan, "Perverse Male Bodies," 66.
18. Morgan, "Perverse Male Bodies," 66.
19. Dijkstra, *Idols of Perversity,* 153.
20. DeJean, *Fictions of Sappho,* 225.
21. DeJean, *Fictions of Sappho,* 225.
22. Morgan, "Perverse Male Bodies," 67.
23. Prettejohn, "Solomon, Swinburne, Sappho," 119.

ness and awayness, "hints at the difficulty of same-sex desire."[24] Moreover, the pairing appears to be between two great women poets (with Sappho being the greater of the two), despite the fact that Erinna is now thought to have lived at least two centuries after Sappho.[25] Sapphism in this representation is therefore not a displaced equivalent for Greek male *paederastia*, in which a man is dominant to a submissive youth, but offers the possibility of equivalence between partners.[26]

Solomon and Swinburne drew a link between Sappho and the Song of Songs. Prettejohn argues that, with "Anactoria," Swinburne "may have been acknowledging his collaboration with Simeon Solomon, and both men would seem to have been suggesting some deep affinity between Sappho's verse and those of this most sensual book of the Old Testament."[27] Written in the voice of Sappho, the controversial work is Swinburne's "lesbian version" of the Song of Songs, featuring "a brilliant if 'perverse' parody of this biblical text."[28] The two texts portray heightened emotions and sensuous images of love and desire. In his pencil portrait *Study of Sappho* (1862), which served as a model for the poet in *Sappho and Erinna in a Garden at Mytilene*, Solomon makes his dark-skinned poet beautiful, thereby breaking with the ancient literary tradition that describes her as plain. Prettejohn suggests the possibility that Solomon is referencing the well-known line from the Song of Songs, "I am black, but comely" (1:5).[29] Moreover, the prominent appearance of a fawn and the location of Sappho and Erinna within a walled garden filled with abundant plants hint strongly of the Song of Songs.[30] The hybrid nature of the painting is commensurate with Solomon's significant endeavor in the 1860s to balance Hebraic with Hellenic elements in his art.[31] Likewise, this painting of two classical figures echoes a Hebraic image, whereby the embrace between Sappho and Erinna finds a counterpart in a work such as Solomon's *Righteousness and Peace Have Kissed Each Other* (ca. 1863), which the Dalziel Brothers adapted for *Art Pictures from the Old Testament and Our Lord's Parables* (1894). These classical and Hebraic elements, whether combined or mirrored, had religious and sexual significance for Solomon. Not only did classical and Biblical

---

24. Prettejohn, "Solomon, Swinburne, Sappho," 119.

25. Prettejohn, "Solomon, Swinburne, Sappho," 118.

26. Prettejohn, "Solomon, Swinburne, Sappho," 118.

27. Prettejohn, "Solomon, Swinburne, Sappho," 116.

28. Morgan, "Perverse Male Bodies," 68, 67.

29. Prettejohn, "Solomon, Swinburne, Sappho," 109.

30. Prettejohn, "Solomon, Swinburne, Sappho," 118.

31. Prettejohn, "Solomon, Swinburne, Sappho," 109. See also Cruise et al., *Love Revealed,* 39–45.

subjects fall under the prestigious field of history painting, but ancient Greece and the Bible provided him with precedents to legitimize same-sex desires.

In *Sappho and Erinna in a Garden at Mytilene,* Sappho and Erinna sit on a bench. Sappho is leaning in and embracing the younger woman, who faces the viewer. Erinna's right hand gently holds onto Sappho's left hand on the younger woman's shoulder. This handholding suggests a positive response to Sappho's passionate embrace, though the passive placement of Erinna's left arm on her own leg might suggest otherwise. The touching of hands could be compared to the hand clasping between a young man and a boy in *Spartan Boys about to be Scourged at the Altar of Diana* (1865). The young man embraces the naked boy and places a reassuring left hand on the boy's shoulder, which the boy clasps with his left hand, while reaching up to touch the man's face with his other hand. Likewise, in a drawing of Sappho and Erinna from a year later, entitled *Erinna Taken from Sappho* (1865), the placement of Erinna's right hand on that of her embracer strengthens the interpretation of Erinna's emotional towardness with the person embracing her. In the drawing, however, it is a man who draws Erinna into his embrace, while a forlorn Sappho looks on. The scenario has its provenance in Sappho's influential Fragment 31, in which the depth of the speaker's jealous response to her beloved in the presence of a suitor exemplifies the bittersweet nature of love. In Solomon's drawing, Erinna lightly touches her suitor's hand, partially covering it. Her drapery falls to reveal her breast, which would have also been exposed in *Sappho and Erinna in a Garden at Mytilene,* had not Sappho's arm obscured the viewer's line of sight. The existence of both works is at once radical, by suggesting Erinna's bisexual attractions, and conventional, by implying her desertion of her female lover for a man. Again, to the right is a statue of Aphrodite. The love triangle in the drawing is foreshadowed in *Sappho and Erinna in a Garden at Mytilene* by the inclusion, above the women's heads, of two birds touching their beaks, with a dark bird looking on from the side.

QUEER MALE BODIES

Solomon draws on the love triangle to establish a relationship between the Song of Songs and his queer works. As we have seen in chapter 2, one interpretation of the biblical text is that it features a love triangle between the Shulamite, her beloved, and Solomon, whose affections for the Shulamite are not returned. Solomon's relatively heteronormative images of the Song of Songs in *Eight Drawings for the Song of Songs* (1878) feature the bride, bridegroom, and what appears to be the winged male figure of Love, who resides

100 • CHAPTER 4

over the lovers. The artist's most compelling depictions of the Song of Songs, however, show two young men in love with each other, despite or in addition to the presence of the woman. *The Bride, the Bridegroom and Sad Love* and *The Bride, the Bridegroom and the Friend of the Bridegroom* feature an overtly queer love triangle, thereby allowing for daring images of same-sex desire between men. Thus, Solomon's preferred love triangle both resembles and differs from the love triangle of the Song of Songs.

In *The Bride, the Bridegroom and Sad Love,* handholding between the men signals both the towardness of their affections and the awayness of their future—and perhaps imminent—separation. An inscription, once visible in early photographs of the drawing, includes a passage from John 3:29: "He that hath the bride is the bridegroom: but the friend of the bridegroom, which standeth and heareth him rejoiceth greatly because of the bridegroom's voice."[32] There is, however, "an overlay of meaning" from the Song of Song, and its design goes back to Solomon's sketch drawing, *The Favourite Apostle* (ca. 1857).[33] The drawing depicts not only the socially marginalized nature of same-sex relationships but also the bittersweetness of queer love which isn't sanctioned in a heteronormative society that values procreation. Amanda Paxton similarly argues that the bridegroom's turning to the woman "signals the means by which male sexuality and subjectivity is regulated by social strictures elaborated in religious discourse: homoeroticism is proscribed in favor of heterosexual marriage."[34] Each bloom of same-sex love that ends with the marriage of one or both men to women contains the seeds of its ending. This might help account for Solomon's fascination with the entanglement of love with night, sleep, and death. The bittersweetness of love in *The Bride, the Bridegroom and Sad Love* is not unlike the moment of parting in *Mors et Amor* (1865), which shows the separation of lovers. Death, winged and female, holds open a door for a young woman. The woman reaches toward her husband, who kisses her. In the meantime, a youthful and winged Love, bearing a branch as he does in *The Bride, the Bridegroom and Sad Love,* holds the husband's hand, at which Love looks down. The viewer's eyes are drawn to their clenched hands, as the gaze moves down the length of the husband's muscled and mostly bare arm. By embracing his soon-to-be-departed wife and holding the land of Love, the husband appears suspended between death and life, female and male lovers. He would rather hold onto his wife in her death than turn to the winged creature. Even so, there is a thrilling and erotic charge at

---

32. Prettejohn, "Solomon, Swinburne, Sappho," 113.

33. Cruise et al., *Love Revealed,* 155.

34. Paxton, *Willful Submission,* 51.

the moment of love's loss, for loss serves to heighten the awareness of having and not having, regardless of the lover's gender.

Solomon often depicts queer male bodies in various stages of androgyny. In *The Bride, the Bridegroom and Sad Love,* the three figures are naked, apart from diaphanous drapery covering the genitals of the bridegroom and bride. With his body turned toward the bride, left arm around her waist, head touching hers, and eyes closed like Sappho's, the man appears to be in love. And, indeed, he may well be, for why should the presence of same-sex attraction rule out other desires? If this is indeed the case, the drawing provides another example of bisexual attractions. With his right index finger, the bridegroom touches the curled hand of Love, while his little finger almost touches Love's genitals. I do not recall seeing another Victorian image depicting a man's hand so close to the genitals of another male. Love resembles his androgynous counterpart in *Love in Autumn* (1866), which depicts the piteous character of Love from Solomon's *A Vision of Love Revealed in Sleep.* Additionally, Dominic Janes argues that Sad Love is reminiscent of the beautiful nude youth / guardian angel who appears alongside a comparatively shorter and unattractive Socrates in Solomon's *Socrates and his Agathodaemon* (1865), a work of the same year.[35] Socrates was attracted to youths but encouraged the love of the mind. The link between this drawing of Socrates and his companion spirit with that of the love triangle in Solomon's illustration lends an additional spiritual charge and a classical precedent to the latter's homoeroticism. Despite these layered connections with Socrates, however, the melancholy face of Love in *The Bride, the Bridegroom and Sad Love* suggests the bittersweetness of his love for the groom; Love is marginalized, forced to a position behind the bridegroom, who turns away from him toward his new and primary relationship.

An alternative version featuring clothed figures is *The Bride, the Bridegroom and the Friend of the Bridegroom,* often incorrectly titled *The Song of Solomon.*[36] In this drawing, the third figure is not winged Love but a man dressed in something resembling priestly vestments. Christian priests are a subject of Solomon's works, quite possibly because Catholic and Tractarian clergy were demonized by opponents on the grounds that they were, among other things, "of a want of manliness."[37] Compared with his counterpart in *The Bride, the Bridegroom and Sad Love,* the groom in *The Bride, the Bridegroom and the Friend of the Bridegroom* is clearly more inclined toward the man than his bride. The bride is much more passive than her counterpart in the previous

---

35. Janes, "Seeing and Tasting the Divine," 46.

36. Cruise et al., *Love Revealed,* 155.

37. Janes, "Seeing and Tasting the Divine," 44.

drawing; her left arm is locked around her husband's free arm, but her hands are clasped together rather than around her husband's head. Staring somewhat vacantly into the distance, with her mouth slightly open, she stands behind the groom and receives none of his attention. In contrast, the men's arms are interlinked, and their hands are joined. The groom looks down at his friend, whose gaze meets his as he kisses the back of the groom's hand. While the groom is regal and has the literal upper hand, there is tenderness and intimacy in the kiss and a gentleness in the mutual touch and limp wrists. These wrists are part of the men's androgynous beauty and tender masculinity, and they are also a sign of both Jewishness and homosexuality. Daniel Boyarin argues that,

> In direct contrast to the firm handshake approved (for men and business-women) in our culture, a *Yeshiva-Bokhur* [traditional scholar of the Talmud], until this day, extends the right hand with limp wrist for a mere touch of the other's hand. If the handshake is, as frequently said, originally a knightly custom, the counterhandshake of the ideal Jewish male elegantly bears out my thesis of the *Yeshiva-Bokhur* (and his secular grandson, the *mensch*) as antithesis to the knight of romance. Indeed, one of the things that most repelled the Victorian journalist Frank Harris upon meeting Oscar Wilde was that "he shook hands in a limp way that I disliked"—presumably owing to its "effeminacy." The very handshake of the ideal male Jew encoded him as feminized in the eyes of European heterosexual culture, but that handshake constituted as well a mode of resistance to the models of manliness of the dominant fiction.[38]

Limp wrists accompany other controversial and nonnormative features of masculinity in Solomon's male nudes. These nudes are most obviously associated with the intertwined concepts of the *effeminatus* and Hellenism.[39] In a scathing review of Solomon's *Sacramentum Amoris* (1868), one critic writes of a "want [of] firmness of articulation . . . at the knee joints."[40] Regarding the painting, *One Dreaming by the Sea* (1871), another laments the "emasculated personage" and implores the reader to "notice the poor little feet and the 'dandy's legs.'"[41]

Despite displaying a limp wrist, the groom's friend expresses vitality and fecundity. His gown is decorated with delicate flower designs in square panels, and, like sad Love, he holds an upright and blooming branch. Unlike

---

38. Boyarin, *Unheroic Conduct,* 151.
39. See Dowling, *Hellenism and Homosexuality,* 8–12.
40. Cruise et al., *Love Revealed,* 156–57.
41. Cruise et al., *Love Revealed,* 154.

his friend, however, the groom holds a broken and dying branch across his wife's genitals, as if to suggest the sterility or barrenness of their union. The placement of his hand in front of her sex organs is significant, for the fingers holding the branch turn away from her, whereas in the other drawing, the groom's fingers are turned toward the genitals of sad Love. Most of the flowers from the broken branch lie scattered on the ground in front of the bride. The relationship between man and woman is thus depicted—at least by societal standards—in nonideal terms, whereas the same-sex relationship appears to flourish, either sexually or spiritually or both.

GRAY: A LIFE OF CONTRADICTIONS

Solomon was from a prominent Jewish family. In contrast, John Gray was born in 1866 in a working-class area of London. Hailing from the artisan class, the family was upwardly mobile. At the age of twelve, Gray won a scholarship to a grammar school, but after a year his father insisted he leave school to augment the family income. Before leaving school, Gray passed an exam to ensure his admittance to Woolwich Arsenal, where his father worked as an inspector. An autodidact, Gray later passed the exam for the civil service as a boy clerk at the General Post Office. In 1887 he passed London University's matriculation exam and a year later was transferred to the Foreign Office. By this time, he had developed ambitions to develop his gifts as a writer and become part of the dandified and cosmopolitan avant-garde.

His was an intensely homosocial world. Gray's most passionate and romantic friendships were with mentors or father figures, though it is unknown if these relationships were sexual. His closest lifelong friendship was with the wealthy Jewish Parisian and fellow convert Marc-André Raffalovich. Gray admitted to a life of sin that lasted until the middle of the 1890s. Yet as Ian Fletcher notes, converts "are notorious for their delicate sense of having offended against God."[42] A visit to Brittany at the invitation of a friend, a member of an old recusant family, would have a far-reaching effect on Gray's life. In the Brittany countryside, he came across a small chapel, which he entered, finding a priest intoning the mass. A year later, in 1890, Gray was received into Rome, though it did not have a profound effect on his personal conduct. He appears to have become acquaintances with Oscar Wilde and Arthur Symons at around this time. Other acquaintances include artists Charles Ricketts and

---

42. Gray, *Poems of John Gray,* 3. All poems cited are from this volume unless otherwise indicated.

his partner, Charles Shannon. From 1890 Gray began to frequent literary gatherings, thereby extending his acquaintance with fin de siècle writers and artists. He published a few pieces of poetry and prose in literary magazines such as *The Dial* and the *Athenaeum*.

Wilde and Gray were close from 1891 to 1893, with Wilde being a mentor of sorts who offered to underwrite the cost of Gray's first volume of poetry, *Silverpoints* (1893), a book that "was regarded as an epitome of frenchified decadence."[43] Several poems in the volume imply same-sex intimacy, such as "Did we not, Darling, you and I?" which is reminiscent of the love triangle in Solomon's *The Bride, the Bridegroom and Sad Love*. The poem hints at social derision aimed at the speaker and his male friend: "Did we not walk the earth and wonder why / They spat upon us so" (lines 3–4). Rumors insinuated that Gray was the inspiration for the titular character of Wilde's *Dorian Gray*. In 1892 Gray began to distance himself from his mentor, finally breaking with him in 1893. The estrangement resulted in a period of dramatic illness for Gray and thoughts of suicide.

Breaking away from Wilde signaled Gray's intention to remove himself from his decadent past. From the mid-nineties onward, Gray bought up copies of *Silverpoints* to "immobilize" or destroy them.[44] He started to write the sort of Catholic poetry that would appear in *Spiritual Poems* (1896) and *Blue Calendars*, published between 1895 and 1898. Central to his strengthened faith was his friendship with the dying artist Aubrey Beardsley, who was received into the church before his death. In 1898 Gray entered Scots College, Rome, and emerged as Father Gray. He was posted to St. Patrick's Church in the slums of Edinburgh, which was home to much of the city's Irish immigrant community. Raffalovich funded the erection of St. Peters Church in the more affluent suburb of Morningside, over which Gray presided for the remainder of his life. Raffalovich was found dead on Valentine's Day 1934, which was also Ash Wednesday and the forty-fourth anniversary of Gray's conversion to Catholicism. Gray never recovered from the death, and on 14 June that year he died following surgery for an abscess in his left lung. He was remembered as a respected priest, his past largely forgotten.

DECADENT CATHOLICISM AND HOMOSEXUALITY

Although effeminacy is aligned with Solomon's queering of the Song of Songs, most people would regard celibacy and homosexual attraction to be

---

43. McCormack, *John Gray*, 1.
44. McCormack, *John Gray*, 1.

incompatible with the masculinity we see in the biblical text. While I will discuss celibacy and masculinity in relation to the Song of Songs later in the chapter, I believe it would be useful in this section to provide some context to the topic of homosexuality in Gray's milieu, particularly in relation to Raffalovich and the priesthood.

The title of Kristin Mahoney's *Queer Kinship after Wilde* offers a useful starting point for considering Gray's queerness. The book considers how queer twentieth-century decadents "played with the concept of kin, the structure of the family, and the institution of marriage."[45] After falling out with Wilde, Gray's affections shifted strongly to Raffalovich, who called himself Gray's "father & mother."[46] The two men had a close, albeit reserved and likely chaste, friendship. Jerusha Hull McCormack argues that the history between the two men, "for the most part suppressed, is one that evolves into a chaste intimacy, in its duration and commitment comparable to that of brothers."[47] The word "brothers" could potentially diminish a relationship that appears to have been more intimate than that of siblings, unless the familial language is considered within a queer context. As Frederick Roden notes, in an early batch of letters to Gray (written between 1898 and 1901), Raffalovich calls him "notre frère petit" and signs off as "Your most loving brother, Sebastian."[48] Sebastian is not simply Raffalovich's saint name but also the saint who is "significant in homosexual hagiography."[49] For decadents drawn to martyrdom, hagiography, and mysticism, Christ's tortured and homoerotic human equivalent was Sebastian, often depicted in art as an attractive youth tied to a tree or pole, his effeminate and passive body pierced with arrows. Gray owned several paintings of Saint Sebastian.[50] Unsurprisingly, his ekphrastic poem "St. Sebastian" reflects on a painting of the saint. Through a connection with Sebastian, among other things, Gray and Raffalovich "became a model of Catholic homosexual friendship" and "a fulfilment of the monastic friendship envisioned by the Oxford Movement sixty years earlier."[51] Their friendship resembled the intense and culturally sanctioned friendships in Christ, like that between priests or nuns, about which I spoke in the previous chapter (Raffalovich was a third-order, or lay, Dominican). In this way, Gray and Raffalovich became lifelong companions in Christ, like another couple who turned to celibacy following their

---

45. Mahoney, *Queer Kinship after Wilde,* 13.
46. Cited in Hanson, *Decadence and Catholicism,* 318.
47. McCormack, *John Gray,* 7.
48. Cited in Roden, "Michael Field," 63.
49. Roden, "Michael Field," 60.
50. Cevasco, *John Gray,* 86.
51. Roden, *Same-Sex Desire,* 157.

conversion: Gray's close friends Katharine Bradley and Edith Cooper (known as Michael Field), whom I discuss at length in the final chapter.

Like Solomon, Hellenism influenced Gray's understanding of homosexuality. Unlike Solomon, however, he combined his Hellenism with Christianity rather than Hebraism. Gray most likely accepted Raffalovich's dichotomous theory of homosexuality in his book *Uranisme et Unisexualité* (1896). Written in the wake of the Wilde trials of 1895, it maintains that there are two distinct types of inverts or uranists: the "inferior" type, who simply craves venereal pleasure, and the "superior" type, who sublimates his cravings in order to enhance the intellectual and spiritual side of humanity.[52] As an apologist for chaste homosexual friendship, Raffalovich drew upon classical and Christian sources to define a type of noble invert who sublimates sexual desires into art, religion, friendship, and other respectable pursuits; this superior invert "is defined not by sexual acts, but by his flight from them."[53] Raffalovich and Gray appear to have adhered to the latter type of relationship in their "respectable pursuits," for in a letter to Raffalovich about psychologist Charles Féré, Gray writes, "I am curious to know if Féré agrees with me about the overwhelming, superabounding-and-all-that-is-superlative importance of the first sexual act. All the passions of making the discovery that man is naturally chaste comes back to me."[54] The redirection of sexual desires into art, religion, and friendship helps to explain what Ellis Hanson regards as the "ambiguous sexuality that the dandy has always shared with the priest."[55] Hanson argues further,

> what I find extraordinary about Gray is the way in which he integrated his homosexuality, his decadent style, even his dandyism, into a virtually seamless performance as priest. Bradley, the Michael half of Michael Field, must surely have recognized the continuity between the young Gray and the older Canon Gray when she referred to him as "Father Silverpoints."[56]

A celibate Catholic priest like Gray was queer in two senses: first, he was same-sex attracted and, second, like the Catholic nun, the priest exemplified what Roden calls the "cultural queerness of Catholicism."[57] Roman Catholicism was a faith set apart from the religious norm, the Church of England.

---

52. Cevasco, *John Gray*, 8.

53. Hanson, *Decadence and Catholicism*, 320–21.

54. Hanson, *Decadence and Catholicism*, 322.

55. Hanson, *Decadence and Catholicism*, 312.

56. Hanson, *Decadence and Catholicism*, 311.

57. Roden, *Same-Sex Desire*, 6.

QUEER HANDS, BODIES, AND MASCULINITIES · 107

Similarly, in late nineteenth-century England, the Catholic priest was "a man apart," through his lifelong celibacy dedicated exclusively to his spouse, Christ.[58] Raffalovich recognized the attraction of the superior invert to the priesthood and urged the church to welcome such an individual:

> The Catholic Church has, indeed, recognised that inversion was often less scandalous than heterosexual sexuality; she has also always known the extent and ramifications of it; she ought to be the storehouse of rules for the education of inverts, and still today she ought for preference to choose for priests superior inverts, chaste and devoted men; and then heterosexuals who have broken with the world or who have the strength of character necessary; and the coarse invert ought naturally to be one of the worst dangers in any religious institution.[59]

In both their celibacy and the priesthood, decadents like Gray found the "spiritualization of desire."[60] Gray was not simply a Catholic priest, he became so during a unique period in time. The decadent movement probably saw more converts than any other school in English literary history.[61] The foreign status and marginalization of Catholicism fascinated English artists and writers at the end of the century, as they saw themselves likewise at the margins of society.[62] Yet, as Claire Masurel-Murray avers, decadent Catholicism did not reflect much of the reality of English Catholicism, which was by and large a working-class phenomenon, whereas decadent Catholicism was "essentially a fantasised, aestheticised faith, reconstructed by art, which [was] not so much part of the modern world as a literary tradition."[63]

Queer and decadent Catholicism was partial to the aesthetics and erotics of the faith, an example of what Romana Byrne defines as "aesthetic sexuality":

> Aesthetic value indicates a form of sexuality constructed as having aesthetic value, a quality that marks this experience as a form of art. Aesthetic value is apparent in the way in which sexuality is enacted, its composition, characteristics, style, or technique, and the pleasure this produces.[64]

---

58. Healy, "Man Apart," 103.
59. Cited in and translated by Healy, "Man Apart," 114.
60. Hanson, *Decadence and Catholicism*, 7.
61. Masurel-Murray, "Conversions to Catholicism," 105.
62. Masurel-Murray, "Conversions to Catholicism," 117.
63. Masurel-Murray, "Conversions to Catholicism," 124.
64. Byrne, *Aesthetic Sexuality*, 4.

108 • CHAPTER 4

Aesthetic sexuality is "flaunted by the Baudelairean dandy."[65] The aesthetic style of biblical books such as the Song of Songs and Revelation could be called decadent, "with their erotic spectacles, their strange profusion of symbols, . . . and their mesmerizing repetitions."[66] Decadents often found in Catholicism a cult of the imagination in their embrace of the church and its traditions; perhaps as a result, decadent Catholicism "was by turns mystical and witty."[67] St. Peter's Church was built to Gray's specifications and blended asceticism with aestheticism: despite its whitewashed walls, the church held a carved baroque confessional and paintings after the style of the Pre-Raphaelites, along with gray-green marble floors. It is not surprising that Gray's interest in art would seep into his ekphrastic style of poetry, as we shall see in the next section.

THE CRUCIFIED HEART AND THE SUBVERSION OF MASCULINITY

Gray wrote a number of ekphrastic poems about that object of fervent desire: the crucifix. These poems are reminiscent of waṣf poetry, an ancient Arabic style of poetry used in the Song of Songs to describe and celebrate the lovers' bodies from head to toe. The beloved is depicted in beautiful and vital terms:

> My beloved is white and ruddy, the chiefest among ten thousand. His head is as the most fine gold, his locks are bushy, and black as a raven. His eyes are the eyes of doves by the rivers of waters, washed with milk, and fitly set. His cheeks are as a bed of spices, as sweet flowers: his lips like lilies, dropping sweet smelling myrrh. His hands are as gold rings set with the beryl: his belly is as bright ivory overlaid with sapphires. His legs are as pillars of marble, set upon sockets of fine gold: his countenance is as Lebanon, excellent as the cedars. (Song of Songs 5:10–15)

In short, "he is altogether lovely" (5:16). Gray, however, uses the waṣf style to spotlight Christ's moment of greatest ugliness, humiliation, and suffering. This depiction of Christ adheres to a queer devotional gaze reconceptualized through a French decadent rendering of Christ's broken body in medieval art. In Christ's disfigurement and debasement lie his glory and triumph: the miraculous endurance of his love over death. Gray's use of the style is

---

65. Byrne, *Aesthetic Sexuality*, 4.
66. Hanson, *Decadence and Catholicism*, 7.
67. Hanson, *Decadence and Catholicism*, 366.

QUEER HANDS, BODIES, AND MASCULINITIES · 109

deliberate, as seen in the unpublished poem, "Rosary of the Cross." Almost each stanza is devoted in the following order to a body part of the crucified Christ: the swollen feet, the "cramped and palsied" knees (line 9), a "painful waist" (line 13), the "wrung and anxious" breast (line 17), the "outstretched and helpless" arms (line 21), a "marred and ugly" face that is "Furrowed, streaked and spotted, / Bleared with spittle, blood and sweat" (lines 25, 27–28), "the eyes of thy compassion" (29), and the head bearing a garland "with fruit of many a thorn" (line 34). This utterly abject body is gazed upon from the feet to the head, a movement that mimics the upward-moving stare of the "Sinner at thy feet, / Ignorant, besotted" (lines 42–43).

In Catholic iconography, the crucified body of Christ is to be looked at and meditated upon, creating opportunities for believers to reflect on the power of love over death. Just as the heart is metaphorically the central organ of the body, so the Sacred Heart in "A Crucifix," from *Silverpoints,* is brought up almost in the middle of the 28-line poem, on line 13. Based on Paul Verlaine's "Un crucifix" (1888), the poem's setting is a gothic church, which itself imitates the shape of the cross and by extension the crucified body. "At one end of an aisle" (line 1) is a life-size crucifix holding "Christ's unutterable charm" (line 4). Part of this "charm" lies in Christ's humanity, his physicality, which renders him capable of suffering and death. Thus, "one almost sees before one's eyes / The last convulsion of the lingering breath" (lines 10–11). There is beauty in the very human—and male—body of Christ: "'Behold the man!' Robust and frail" (line 12), the speaker says, referencing the words of Pontius Pilate when Christ appeared to the crowd, dressed in purple robes and wearing the crown of thorns (John 19:5). The first body part mentioned is Christ's head, followed by his outstretched arms. Surrounding the head and arms are "Long fluted golden tongues" (line 6), a possible reference to the Holy Spirit. The reader's attention then turns to "That breast" (line 13), linked not only to the breath but also the Sacred Heart and the lips—parts intimately connected to breath and animation: "That breast indeed might throb the Sacred Heart. / And from the lips, so holily dispart, / The dying murmur breaths [*sic*] 'Forgive! Forgive!'" (lines 13–15). The speaker finally rests his eyes on the feet of Christ, along with the attendant wounds, which "Bleed, bleed" in order to "overturn Despair's repose / And urge to Hope and Love, as Faith demands" (lines 22, 20–21). Hope, Love, and Faith are the basis of devotion (1 Corinthians 13:13). The body of Christ and, just as importantly, the act of gazing upon it, furnishes the speaker with substance for his theology. In this way, the crucified body of Christ is a fecund one, like the lovers in the Song of Songs or the male bodies in Solomon's *The Bride, the Bridegroom and the Friend of the*

110 • CHAPTER 4

Bridegroom. As exemplified in the birth imagery associated with the pierced heart and the outpouring of blood and water,[68] Christ's crucified body gives birth to a new religion. We are thus reminded of the medieval depictions of Christ's vulva-like wound in his side.

Gray's depictions of male bodies differ from that of the Song of Songs and other ancient portrayals of rugged masculinity. Gender representation is fluid in renderings of the wounded Christ. The gospel of John subverts Roman imperial, hegemonic manliness and domination by constructing the masculinity of Christ around his bound, beaten, and penetrated body.[69] In Roman understanding of gender, one's position in the hierarchy of manliness was determined by one's autonomy and power over others, especially the power to penetrate, subjugate, and kill.[70] In contrast, Christ's "idealized masculinity" asserts that "true manliness is achieved through the openness and vulnerability motivated by love."[71] The crucified heart is feminized in being penetrated by a Roman lance (19:34) and thus in its fragility and direct link to Christ's love for humanity. Such a heart belongs to a body whose feminization brings Christ into closer alignment, centuries later, with that of a queer, Catholic, and dandy priest than a muscular ideal espoused by high-profile Anglicans such as Charles Kingsley. Sean Gill argues that "Christian male selfhood was multifarious and unstable throughout the second half of the century—a fact that has often been obscured by an over-reliance on stereotypical formulations, such as 'muscular Christianity.'"[72]

The masculinity of a decadent hero or dandy was "confounded by his tendency to androgyny, homosexuality, masochism, mysticism, or neurosis."[73] In contrast, muscular Christianity fed into the combined nationalism, militarism, and imperialism of the second half of the century.[74] To be sure, the muscular Christianity movement also developed "as an antidote to the perceived feminization of the church," especially in light of the encroachment of Catholicism.[75] Catholicism was "central" to the stylistic and thematic interests of the decadents.[76] Unsurprisingly, in Gray's poetry, the hypermasculinized male body of muscular Christianity is unmade or rendered unstable by the crucifixion. The paradox of the crucifixion, as depicted in late medieval Christianity (and later reproduced by Gray), is one of "flesh immortalized, masculinity

---

68. Lee, *Flesh and Glory,* 158–59.
69. Ripley, "Behold the Man," 224.
70. Ripley, "Behold the Man," 226.
71. Ripley, "Behold the Man," 224.
72. Gill, "*Ecce Homo,*" 166.
73. Hanson, *Decadence and Catholicism,* 3.
74. Bradstock et al., introduction to *Masculinity and Spirituality,* 3.
75. Ripley, "Behold the Man," 220.
76. Hanson, *Decadence and Catholicism,* 5.

feminized, and ugliness revered."[77] With the crucifixion, Christ's masculinity is upheld by his body's own subjugation. As Gray says above, "'Behold the man!' Robust and frail." While the word "Robust" might allude to the concept of a valorous and chivalric Christ on the cross, the excessive grotesqueness and abasement of Christ's body in the poem conform more to the decadent interest in the spectacle of martyrdom and hagiography. What we see, then, is the Catholic and Tractarian tendency toward combining male suffering and celibacy. Emulating Christ's example, "queer martyrdom," as Janes calls it, "came to be established as outside normative roles of gender and sexuality in Victorian England. Queer martyrdom, therefore, came to combine Christian witness with aspects of gender and sexual transgression."[78] While the term bears some resemblance to Amanda Paxton's concepts of "sado-erotics" and "masochristianity," it is specific to queer experience.[79]

In Gray's poem, the notion of "masculinity feminized" follows the influence of medieval Catholicism on nineteenth-century homosexual identities, including the concept of marriage to Christ. Asserting "the role of medieval religion in constructing late Victorian homosexual identities," Roden notes that Raffalovich's *Uranisme et Unisexualité* locates Christian same-sex desire within a religious and historical framework: in relation to early Christianity, the mystical tradition, and the development of monasticism.[80] Raffalovich draws a connection between the intensely feeling Christian and the superior invert, going "so far as to speak of uranism as a 'vocation,' rendering it in terms that seem more apostolic than sexual."[81] Raffalovich writes:

> Christianity naturally did not change uranism, but over a very long time it permitted superior inverts to follow enthusiastically and devoutly the principle of Plato. In a world that had witnessed Saturnalia of every kind, debauchery, and scandal, religion greatly attracted superior inverts. Virginity was placed so very high, and the love of one's fellow man turned so sacred and so tender, in the love of its young God *naked and bleeding, disfigured and transfigured, torn and tearing.*[82]

---

77. Wallace, "Bearded Woman, Female Christ," 44.

78. Janes, *Visions of Queer Martyrdom,* 9.

79. Says Paxton, "Whereas by 'sado-erotics' I mean the invocation of eroticized punitive imagery accompanied by an implicit approval, by 'masochristianity' I refer to a Christian tradition of gratifying self-denial, be it in the form of asceticism, self-imposed suffering, or ultimate self-sacrifice." Paxton, *Willful Submission,* 10.

80. Roden, "Medieval Religion, Victorian Homosexualities," 116.

81. Hanson, *Decadence and Catholicism,* 323.

82. Cited in and translated by Roden, "Medieval Religion, Victorian Homosexualities," 117. Emphasis added.

Raffalovich highlights a medieval (or medievalized) image of Christ eroticized in his suffering: "naked and bleeding, disfigured and transfigured, torn and tearing," a body with pierced feet, hands, and heart. In the words of Wilde, "Medievalism, with its saints and martyrs, its love of self-torture, its wild passion for wounding itself, its gashing with knives, and its whipping with rods— Medievalism is real Christianity, and the medieval Christ is the real Christ."[83] Christ's crucified body was disfigured and penetrated but remains virginal, desirable to inverts and saints alike. Such a body provokes one to both adoration and celibacy in the tradition of Song of Songs reception. As Raffalovich says, "The soul of man, made the fiancée of Christ, has expressed over the centuries its desires and its adoration in poetry and prose. Angelus Silesius, Friedrich Spee, Saint John of the Cross, Saint Teresa, and so many graceful and illustrious others have languished in love on the breast of the Divine Lover [Song of Songs 1:13; John 13:23]."[84] In an example of Christian inversion, the feminized body of Christ draws to itself the soul that is described in the feminine, as fiancée.

HORTUS CONCLUSUS AND
CHRIST'S VULVA-LIKE WOUND

Many saints and martyrs have a reputation for holiness, celibacy, and suffering combined. As sources of inspiration to Catholics, their purified bodies reflect the image of Christ. Gray wrote a number of poems after the saints and martyrs, including the most revered saint of all, the Virgin Mary, a figure associated with both nuns and the Song of Songs. Gray shows an affinity with nuns. The illustration facing the first printed poem of *Spiritual Poems,* designed by Charles Ricketts, depicts what looks like an elegant medieval nun, though without a wimple. She is lighting a flame on a wall. Behind her is a vase of flowers, representative of what Janes might call "female material culture."[85] An unpublished poem called "Battledore" employs the well-known image of the enclosed garden (*hortus conclusus*) (Song of Songs 4:12), which for Catholics signifies virginity and the feminine nature of nuns and the Virgin Mary. The first stanza begins thus:

> The sheltered garden sleeps among the tall
> Black poplars which grew round it, next the wall.

---

83. Cited in Roden, "Medieval Religion, Victorian Homosexualities," 129.

84. Cited in and translated by Roden, "Medieval Religion, Victorian Homosexualities," 117.

85. Janes, "Catholic Florist," 79.

The wall is very high, green grown on red.
All is within, white convent, chapel, all. (lines 1–4)

Gray draws our attention to the wall and its potential importance before shifting to the convent and chapel "all . . . within." He emphasizes the bricked wall through the rhymes "tall" and "wall" and by repeating the word "all." Moreover, the red color of the wall serves as a contrast to the whiteness of the convent and chapel. The wall forms a protective enclosure around these sites.

The horticultural and artistic revival of the medieval walled garden in the Victorian era[86] coincided with the emergence of the Pre-Raphaelites and, of course, the Catholic revival. Charles Collins's *Convent Thoughts* (1851) is one of the best-known pictorial examples of a Victorian enclosed garden. Collins was never a formal member of the Pre-Raphaelites, but he was influenced by their interests in medievalism and religion. *Convent Thoughts* depicts a nun inside a walled garden. Standing by a host of flowers, including lilies, she holds a book open at an image of the Virgin Mary. John Everett Millais, a Pre-Raphaelite, designed the painting's frame. Flanked on both sides by lilies, the frame is inscribed at the top with the words "sicut lilium" ("like a lily," from Song of Songs 2:2). The Pre-Raphaelites retained an influence over Decadent artists, including Gray.[87] Indeed, the painterly style of "Battledore," along with the subject matter (nuns) and allusion to the *hortus conclusus,* suggests a possible awareness of Collins's painting or similar depictions. Likewise, the elaborate border around the first poem of Gray's *Spiritual Poems* shows a lily plant, among others, which might be a reference to Collins's frame. Gray's emphasis on flowers in "Battledore" is similarly striking. The poem refers to the lawns that "are foiled with flowers, / Lilies, and ladybell and Marygold" (lines 11–12)—all associated with the Virgin Mary. Marian devotion is a hallmark of fin de siècle Catholicism.[88] In "To the Blessed Virgin" (1896), Gray calls Mary, "flower of earth. / Thornless blossom of salvation," and with the pun on deflowered, "Mother undefloured, / Whiter than the lily is" (lines 4–5, 44–45). As I have explored in the discussion of Augusta Drane, nuns have a close association with the Virgin Mary. Collins's painting depicts a lone novice nun contemplating the passion flower and, by extension, her own sacrifice, leading to celibacy and solitude. "Battledore," however, paints a delightful picture of nuns at play or at pleasurable rest within a religious community. Gray's image is closer to contemporary life, as it depicts an everyday reality for such a community, complete with an asthmatic mother superior. While Collins's nun

---

86. Roe, "Naturally Artificial," 131.

87. Masurel-Murray, "Conversions to Catholicism," 107.

88. Masurel-Murray, "Conversions to Catholicism," 107.

114 • CHAPTER 4

is solitary and somber, walled off from the world and any sense of community, Gray's nuns take delight in each other's company within walls that enable their camaraderie to develop and continue. In the second stanza, the poem references the work necessary to maintain the state of a literal and metaphorical garden (i.e., virginity): the gardening tools, animal feeding, weeding. Despite or because of this labor, there is joy and purpose in religious celibacy within a community of like-minded souls.

The enclosed garden reminds us of another enclosure, which is the wound in Christ's side. The multivalent nature of the walled garden and its symbolic association with the feminine ensures that the enclosure could also be associated with Christ's vulva-like wound, and vice versa. In Song of Songs 4:16, the lover wishes her beloved to enter her (walled) garden, which he obliges in the next chapter (5:1). A walled enclosure provides a sense of safety—the walls are "tall." Similarly, Christ's wound is open to the believer in order to provide sanctuary. Hence, "O precious Wound" is "Thou open door of Grace" (lines 14, 15), remarks the speaker in the poem "To the Stabbed Side of Jesus" (1896), Gray's translation of a piece purportedly by Bernard of Clairvaux. And later, as if the wound had its own agency, "Open thy gates, thou darling Wound, / And let my heart, too bold, / . . . / . . . be consoled" (lines 23–24, 27). The open wound leads to enclosure and thus shelter; in the same poem, Gray writes:

> Conceal me, Wound; within thy cave
> Locked fast, no thing shall harm me;
> There let me nestle close and safe,
> There soothe my soul and warm me. (lines 37–40)

This "cave" is the final resting place:

> When I shall feel death's cold distress,
> And when the hellish beast
> Against my soul and me shall press,
> Then let me, in thy faithfulness,
> Quietly, Saviour, rest. (lines 41–45)

Gray uses the erotic union of saints and martyrs with Christ as examples to which one should aspire. Experiencing a revival in the nineteenth century,[89] Bernard composed numerous well-known sermons on the Song of Songs,

---

89. Bell, "Bibliography of English Translations," 85. For a list of works translated between 1813 and 1891, see pages 101–11.

often written from the perspective of the bride. Gray acknowledges Bernard as the bride of Song of Songs 6:10 in his poem "Hymn to Saint Bernard." The following passage alludes to the bride's spikenard releasing its perfume for the king (Song of Songs 1:12): "When Bernard's soul left earth behind, / The spikenard did yield its smell" to commemorate "Sweet holy Bernard's life undone, / In holy odours deeply graced" (lines 11–12, 15–16). The poem celebrates Bernard's marriage to Christ, like the bride that "hath come from Libanon" (line 17), a reference to Song of Songs 4:8. An image of marital union in Bernard's sermons is that of a bird resting in Christ's wound. In a sermon, Bernard draws a parallel between the wound and a passage from Song of Songs 2:14 ("O my dove, in the clefts of the rock, in the secret places of the cliff"), just as Gray references the wound as "thy cave" above. Bernard says of Christ, "The secret of his heart is laid open through the clefts in his body; that mighty mystery of loving is laid open."[90] Recognizing a relationship between the suffering of the martyr and that of Christ, Bernard acknowledges the suitability of the wound as the martyr's final resting place:

> While gazing on the Lord's wounds he will indeed not feel his own. The martyr remains jubilant and triumphant though his whole body is mangled; even while the steel is gashing his sides he looks around with courage and elation at the holy blood pouring from his flesh. Where then is the soul of the martyr? In a safe place, of course; in the rock, of course; in the heart of Jesus, of course, in wounds open for it to enter.[91]

Like Bernard, John of the Cross illuminates the violent connection between the Song of Songs, martyrdom, and the "safe place" of Christ's wound. G. A. Cevasco believes that Gray was drawn to John of the Cross because both men had experienced the dark night of the soul.[92] The saint's experience included both spiritual tumult and physical torture. Raffalovich was intrigued by John of the Cross and quotes the saint's description of a spiritual person ("of a frail and delicate complexion, and of a nature tender and sensible"), which Hanson argues, "sounds uncannily like the frail and delicate body of the homosexual aesthete as he was immortalized by Wilde and others."[93] The tender sensibility of the queer martyr ensures that he is responsive to suffering. As Raffalovich says in *Uranisme et Unisexualité,*

---

90. Bernard of Clairvaux, *On the Song of Songs,* vol. 3, 144.

91. Bernard of Clairvaux, *On the Song of Songs,* vol. 3, 147.

92. Cevasco, *John Gray,* 91. I discussed the dark night of the soul in relation to Drane in chapter 3.

93. Hanson, *Decadence and Catholicism,* 324.

116 • CHAPTER 4

> Hafiz [the homoerotic Islamic poet] may be compared with the "dark night" of Saint John of the Cross. One could read such poems and ignore what is in the spirit of the man who cries and kisses the feet, the hands, the merciful side, in a way that one does not ignore a lover that Krafft-Ebing places in *Psychopathia Sexualis* as suffering from sadism, masochism, and unisexuality. Only in such moments of sensual and sentimental defiance does the literature of today dare what the poets of divine love have cooed about and moaned over with great delights.[94]

The mention of Richard von Krafft-Ebing's *Psychopathia Sexualis* is significant, as the psychiatrist is known to have popularized the terms "sadism" and "masochism." He also argued that unisexuality, or homosexuality, is part of nature and not an acquired vice. Gray's style of aesthetic sexuality incorporates the spectacle of sadomasochism involving the male body in particular, whether it be Christ or the martyr. Indeed, Byrne holds that sadomasochism "provides an ideal demonstration of sexual aestheticism."[95] In speaking of Swinburne's *Poems and Ballads,* she argues that the subject of perverse decadent sexuality performs an aesthetic appraisal of pain, a phenomenon marked by "the fusion of beauty and grotesquerie."[96]

The preoccupation with redemptive and character-building pain is part of a long tradition inherited by the Victorians. In a letter to Katharine Bradley in 1908, Gray writes, "I have invincible love of S: John of the Cross, because, I suppose, he made a hole in the covering which I had woven about myself to hide me from God."[97] The rending of "a hole in the covering" hints at violence and of the necessary shock that transports the believer into a mystical state. Yet the reward is sanctuary, and the dark night ends with rest. Gray translated John of the Cross's "The Obscure Night of the Soul" (1896), which was influenced by the arcadian landscape of the Song of Songs, along with the anonymity of the protagonists. It depicts a love of exquisite tenderness, apart from a section in which the hand of Christ is both "gentle" and "smiting" (lines 33, 34), sending the speaker into a swoon or mystical state. This juxtaposition of tenderness and violence is again found in Gray's unpublished translation of the saint's "The Living Flame of Love." Referencing the flame of Song of Songs 6:3, he says, "O living flame of love! / O tender wounding wonder, / Wounding my soul in its most secret centre!" and "Tear thou the veil in this sublime encounter" (lines 1–3, 6). In both poems, we are confronted with the combined image of love and violence in the submission of the believer to

---

94. Cited in and translated by Roden, "Medieval Religion, Victorian Homosexualities," 117.

95. Byrne, *Aesthetic Sexuality,* 7.

96. Byrne, *Aesthetic Sexuality,* 15.

97. Cited in McCormack, *John Gray,* 169.

Christ. In "They say, in other days," Gray introduces the reader to a range of characters, but I wish to focus on John of the Cross and his entry into Christ's wounds. We are told that, passing through the door to heaven,

He met the Lover of the Dark Night's tryst;
Saint John was folded in the hands of Christ.
He lay upon their wounds, and wept the whole
Of longing that was in his holy soul. (lines 37–40)

This act of being enfolded in the stigmatic hands foreshadows the ultimate union within Christ's side: "And John was locked within the riven Side, / The Wound said, 'Sleep, beloved, and be calm'" (lines 50–51). And so we find that "John was cradled in the Sacred Heart, / Than which no mansion is more glorious" (lines 59–60). With the visceral and violent language of aesthetic sexuality, we see that the wound in Christ's eternally crucified body allows for the soul to find its rest in the Sacred Heart.

Solomon and Gray lived outside society's charmed circle, whether as queer artists, social pariah, Jew, or celibate Catholic convert to the priesthood. Their attractions to men influenced the depiction of male bodies in their art and their reception of the Song of Songs. I have looked at beautiful effeminate youths or female poets holding hands in Solomon's works, as well as love triangles presaging future unhappiness for one or more of the lovers. For Solomon, the intermixing of the homoerotic with the Hebraic and Hellenistic helped bring legitimacy to same-sex attraction. And what better text to adapt than the Hebrew Bible's major poem about love? In his later years, Solomon would draw his pictures and hum parts of the Song of Songs.[98] It was a text that still resonated, acting like a hymn moving through his mind and body as his hand simultaneously created and touched his work. Gray likewise had a preoccupation with the male body, and, in this chapter, I have focused on the undeniably physical body of a crucified Christ. Gray's ekphrastic poems of the crucifixion, and his use of the waṣf style, contest and invert the masculine ideals of the beloved's body in the Song of Songs. His depiction of Christ's body tells us much about Gray's brand of Catholicism as being one of homosexual desire intermixed with aestheticism, celibacy, and a focus on suffering and martyrdom. For Gray, this combination formed the way to the "riven Side" of the divine bridegroom.

---

98. Kolsteren, "Simeon Solomon," 59.

CHAPTER 5

"Stronger than Death"

Michael Field and the Culture of Death

And for death? When thou art dying
'Twill be love beside thee lying.
—Michael Field, "[Mortal, if thou art beloved]," lines 13–14[1]

Love exists in close proximity to death. It is because of death that love holds enormous power in human imagination, and it is because of love that death can be turned into an opportunity. Elizabeth Barrett Browning concludes the final poem of her volume *The Seraphim and Other Poems* thus:

And e'en that mortal grief shall prove
The immortality of love,
    And lead us nearer Heaven! ("The Name," lines 66–70)[2]

Given the power (or "immortality") accorded to love, death is simply the condition that enables love to reveal its ascendency: the emotion is powerful enough to enable a person entry into the afterlife and reunion with loved ones. As John Donne famously wrote in "Death, be not proud," "One short sleepe past, we liue eternally / And death shalbe no more: Death, thou shalt dye" (lines 13–14).[3] Or, to use a Victorian consolatory euphemism, "Not lost, but gone before." Accordingly, if death robs us of a life, then it is only for a

---

1. Field, *Underneath the Bough*. Future references to poems from *Underneath the Bough* are from this volume.
2. Barrett, *Seraphim and Other Poems*.
3. Donne, *Variorum Edition of the Poetry of John Donne*.

moment: those who remain will eventually be reunited with those who have "gone before."

The passage from death to eternal life, or from separation to reunion with a beloved one, resembles the movement from absence to reconciliation in the Song of Songs (2:14; 5:3; 6:1–3). Mark Gedney believes that "the lovers call out to one another in the expectation that love will prove as strong as the barriers in place against it."[4] Marvin H. Pope argues that love and death are the "twin realities . . . mentioned together toward the end of the Canticle. The asseveration that 'Love is strong as Death' 8:6, must be the climax and immortal message of the Sublime Song."[5] And later, "It has been recognized by many commentators that the setting of Love and Passion in opposition to the power of Death and Hell in 8:6c,d is the climax of the Canticle and the burden of its message: that Love is the only power that can cope with Death."[6]

The reception of the Song of Songs in the nineteenth century was concerned not simply with love but also with death and the link between the two. The era was one in which Victorian men wore black "as never before"[7] and a monarch wore widow's weeds for the remainder of her life following the death of her beloved prince consort. Scholars have explored in rich detail the Victorian cult of death, though few have discussed theology at length and, to my understanding, none have explored death in relation to the Song of Songs.[8] According to Michael Wheeler's wide-ranging *Heaven, Hell, and the Victorians,* a high number of lyric poems, particularly by women poets, addressed themes of dying, death, and grief.[9] The deathbed scene was a familiar convention in narrative poetry, fiction, and biography.[10] Poems concerned with death made their way into anthologies for the bereaved.

Queen Victoria, the era's most famous mourner, relied on the Song of Songs as a text of consolation through its appearance in the queerest elegy of the era. Poems of consolation are found in Victoria's private *Album Consolativum,* compiled after Albert's death in December 1861. In *Album Consolativum,*

---

4. Gedney, "Love as Strong as Death," 65.

5. Pope, *Anchor Bible,* 18.

6. Pope, *Anchor Bible,* 210. See also page 226.

7. Dowling, *Manliness and the Male Novelist,* 14.

8. Mary Elizabeth Hotz argues that death "was at the heart of the Victorian novel" and consequently focuses her attention mostly on the novel in relation to an extensive range of Victorian concerns, such as money and law, architecture and medicine, social planning and nationalism, folklore and religion. Her interest is less in matters of theology than in death's intersection with ostensibly secular themes. The same is apparent in Deborah Lutz's thoughtful study of the Victorians' reverence for the artifacts and personal effects of their deceased loved ones. See Hotz, *Literary Remains,* 1; and Lutz, *Relics of Death.*

9. Wheeler, *Heaven, Hell, and the Victorians,* 28.

10. Wheeler, *Heaven, Hell, and the Victorians,* 28.

120 · CHAPTER 5

she and her household added extracts from Alfred Tennyson's elegy *In Memoriam* (1850). Prompted by the death of Tennyson's close friend Arthur Henry Hallam, *In Memoriam* sold sixty thousand copies within months of publication and went through thirty separate editions during Tennyson's lifetime.[11] After Albert's death, Queen Victoria confided in Tennyson, "Next to the Bible, *In Memoriam* is my comfort."[12] Tennyson's poem is as much about love as it is about grief; Victoria and her contemporaries understood this, even if they also knew it to be about love between two men. Through *In Memoriam* and its central place in Victorian culture, we can understand that the cult of death was the flipside to the cult of love. "Whatever was the immediate prompting of *In Memoriam*," says George Eliot, "whatever the form under which the author represented his aim to himself, the deepest significance of the poem is the sanctification of human love as a religion."[13]

The Song of Songs plays a role in Victoria's chief poem of consolation. The *Album Consolativum* includes excerpts of sections 7 and 8 from *In Memoriam*,[14] which contain echoes of Song of Songs 3 and 5:

Dark house, by which once more I stand
    Here in the long unlovely street,
    Doors, where my heart was used to beat
So quickly, waiting for a hand. (section 7)

And,

So find I every pleasant spot
    In which we two were wont to meet,
    The field, the chamber, and the street,
For all is dark where thou art not. (section 8)[15]

The connection between the Song of Songs and *In Memoriam* has been discussed elsewhere.[16] In brief, the Song of Songs passages found in *In Memoriam* draw readers to the absence or disappearance of the beloved, which sections 7 and 8 emphasize through the sense of darkness, unfriendly urban

---

11. Rosenberg, *Elegy for an Age*, 51.
12. Ross, "Three Faces of *In Memoriam*," 93.
13. Cited in Ricks, *Tennyson*, 209.
14. Queen Victoria, *Album Consolativum*. British Library, Add.MS.62089, fols. 39 and 44.
15. Tennyson, *In Memoriam*. Future references to *In Memoriam* are from this volume.
16. See Dau, *Touching God*, 50–57; and Krasner, "'In Memoriam' 7 and the Song of Solomon," 93–96.

surroundings, the lover's attempts to revisit happier memories, and the futile reaching out for the beloved's hand by a door. As a volume devoted to consolation, however, the *Album Consolativum* includes section 130 from *In Memoriam* (though mislabeled as section 129), in which the speaker is reconciled with the beloved through a metaphysical union with the universe and the divine.[17] Section 130 concludes, "I shall not lose thee tho' I die," as if to imply that "love is strong as death" (Song of Songs 8:6). One can imagine how comforting those words would have been to Victoria, to whom the world seemed to have plunged into darkness after her Albert's death.

I speak of *In Memoriam* as a queer text of consolation, for in this chapter I look at Michael Field to explore the relationship between the Song of Songs and death in the fin de siècle and Edwardian era. Michael Field is the pen name of Katharine Bradley and her niece Edith Cooper, who lived and wrote together, loved as partners, and died within months of each other. When Cooper's mother, Emma, became a permanent invalid following the birth of her second daughter, Amy, in 1864, her sister, Katharine Bradley, then aged eighteen, became Edith Cooper's guardian.[18] Sharon Bickle argues that it is impossible to know when Bradley and Cooper "became more than aunt-and-favored-niece" but holds that it might have been a gradual transition.[19] Emma Donoghue notes that, by the time Bradley was thirty-two (or twice Cooper's age), she and Bradley were already behaving as a couple.[20] The two women were of independent means and were educated in classics and philosophy, which they studied in 1878 at University College in Bristol (Bradley had also attended a summer course at Newnham College, Cambridge, and in 1868 went to the Collège de France in Paris).[21] From early on, Cooper and Bradley wrote together and occasionally separately under several pen names, but mostly under that of Michael Field. Collectively, the women published nine volumes of lyric poetry and twenty-five historical verse dramas.[22] The first volume of plays written under the joint name of Michael Field, *Callirrhoë/Fair Rosamund* (1884), was an immediate success. Nonetheless, biographer Mary Sturgeon believes that their critical reception suffered once it was discovered that Michael Field was not a man but two women.[23] Over the course of their lifetimes, the women cultivated friendships with major literary figures such as

---

17. Queen Victoria, *Album Consolativum*. British Library, Add.MS.62089, fol. 130.

18. Thain, 'Michael Field,' 2–3.

19. Bickle, introduction to *The Fowl and the Pussycat*, xiii.

20. Donoghue, *We Are Michael Field*, 18–19.

21. Thain, 'Michael Field,' 3.

22. Bickle, introduction to *The Fowl and the Pussycat*, xiii.

23. Sturgeon, *Michael Field*, 29.

Robert Browning, Oscar Wilde, and Arthur Symons, sexologist Havelock Ellis, artists Charles Ricketts and Charles Shannon, and art critics John Ruskin, Walter Pater, and Bernard Berenson. In 1906 Cooper and Bradley's beloved dog Whym Chow died, leading the women to a spiritual crisis and in 1907 to the doors of the Roman Catholic Church. Both women succumbed to cancer within months of each other: Cooper on 13 December 1913, Bradley on 26 September 1914. Although Michael Field was first celebrated as a dramatist, the name is best remembered for lyric poetry and a joint—and largely unpublished—twenty-eight-volume diary, *Works and Days*.

In this chapter, I argue for the importance of Song of Songs 8:6, notably the asseveration that love is strong as death, or, rather, for Michael Field, stronger than death. In so doing, I draw extensively on unpublished archival material. Cooper and Bradley presented their lives as "structured around a dichotomy between what they describe as pagan and Christian modes of being."[24] Critics likewise tend to divide Michael Field's poetry into the pre- and postconversion periods. I believe, however, that the Song of Songs is one of the great unexplored texts linking Michael Field's pagan and Catholic periods. The women's conversion did not herald an abrupt end to a hypostasized non-Christian past, for such a past did not exist; Michael Field's singular religious beliefs had always incorporated elements of the Bible including the Song of Songs. In fact, the women's conversion allowed for a continuation of many of their preexisting ideas into a Catholic framework. Michael Field used the Song of Songs in two interrelated ways: first, to understand and articulate passions both romantic and filial (which to them were not mutually exclusive) and, second, to argue that love is stronger than death. These are the two ideas that underpin my discussion, which I divide into three sections exploring the notion of love's ascendancy over death.

The first section looks at the deaths of Emma Cooper and Robert Browning. I introduce readers to Cooper and Bradley's use of the Song of Songs as an attempt to blur the division between the discourses associated with romantic and familial intimacy. It is this slippage between the two kinds of love that enables the deceased Emma Cooper, her daughter, and her sister to become a creative triumvirate and ensure Emma's immortality through artistic creation. The discussion of Whym Chow's death in the second section leads to the exploration of Cooper and Bradley's conversion and suffering for Christ— acts of love signaled by the image of fire—as a means of reuniting with the beloved in heaven. In this section I also posit that the provenance of Whym Chow's designation, "Flame of Love," is the Song of Songs. In the final section,

---

24. Thain, '*Michael Field*,' 4.

I explore Cooper's impending death by focusing on the use of flower imagery from the Song of Songs. Flowers are a reminder of life's brevity and a symbol of Cooper and Bradley's desired aim of becoming eternal spouses of each other and of Christ. In the months leading up to Cooper's death, the poets reveal the increasing importance of flower imagery, in general, and from the Song of Songs, in particular. The subject matter is dolorous, matrimonial, and still largely hopeful of life after death.

STRONGER THAN DEATH:
ARTISTIC INSPIRATION

Edith Cooper did not attend her mother's funeral, for Emma Cooper had left instruction that her daughter was to stay at home on the day. As Emma's sister, Katharine Bradley, explained to Robert Browning in a letter, "Dear Edith will be at home (it is her Mother's wish that thus it should <u>be</u>) in my little blue room, while My Brother, My Amy & I lay in earth that sweet white relic we love so well."[25] The reason for the mother's wish, Emma Donoghue argues, is that "Edith's family all considered her so physically and psychologically delicate that they tried to protect her from trauma."[26] Emma's death, on 19 August 1889, was the first major loss for her daughter, and indeed she felt it keenly, as did Katharine. Cooper and Bradley's joint diary, *Works and Days,* is quiet for the month of September, as it seems they took time off to grieve and recover.

By this time, Cooper and Bradley's religious beliefs were a curious combination of the Christian and pagan, among other things; Bradley told Havelock Ellis, "I am Christian, pagan, pantheist, and other things the name of which I do not know."[27] The year of Emma Cooper's death saw the publication of Michael Field's first volume of poetry, *Long Ago* (1889), which its preface informs us was inspired by Henry Wharton's *Sappho: Memoir, Text, Selected Renderings, and a Literal Translation* (1885). Consisting of sixty-eight numbered poems that refashion Sappho's fragments into lyrics, *Long Ago* has become the source of much critical attention. As Yopie Prins puts it, "How shall we read these poems written by two women writing as a man writing as Sappho?"[28] Michael Field's Sappho, and by extension *Long Ago,* represents Michael Field's pagan mode of being. As defined by Marion Thain, "pagan" is

---

25. Field, Correspondence: 22 August 1889; KB to Robert Browning. British Library, Add. MS.46866, fol. 204v.

26. Donoghue, *We Are Michael Field,* 41.

27. Cited in Donoghue, *We Are Michael Field,* 36.

28. Prins, *Victorian Sappho,* 74.

not simply the Greco-Roman, non-Christian realm and its pantheistic religion; it is also the tenets central to Walter Pater's aestheticism (itself connected to the classical world) and the sexual liberation—including same-sex intimacy—associated with the aesthetes.[29] The preface of *Long Ago* indicates the primacy of love. Cooper and Bradley write that, just as Sappho turned to the goddess of love in the poet's moment of need, so Michael Field turned to Sappho for creative inspiration: "Devoutly as the fiery-bosomed Greek turned in her anguish to Aphrodite, praying her to accomplish her heart's desires, I have turned to the one woman who has dared to speak unfalteringly of the fearful mastery of love."[30] Aphrodite's son, Eros, is likewise invoked at the start of Poem LXVIII: "Thou burnest us; thy torches' flashing spires, / Eros, we hail!" (lines 1–2). The fire of Eros is not incompatible with the biblical flames that I will soon explore. With the discussion of fire and, later, flowers, it will be clear that the theme of love traverses the pagan and Christian elements of Michael Field's faith: Sappho and the Song of Songs are not mutually exclusive, whether in life or at death. Or, as Jill R. Ehnenn remarks, Cooper and Bradley sought to become Catholic poets "by appropriating the formal, including metric, conventions of devotional poetics while also maintaining many of the queer characteristics of their earlier work."[31]

In addition to the Christian, pagan, and pantheistic, Cooper and Bradley's religious beliefs incorporated what Donoghue calls "a cult of the dead."[32] The two women remembered the dead with acts and gifts of love; they spoke to the beloved dead, read poems to them, and put flowers on shrines composed of portraits and relics.[33] Nor could the women think of death without thinking of love—specifically, of love overcoming death. Cooper recounted her mother's death in a letter to her adored mentor, Browning:

> The beloved mother died at four o'clock in the dayspring. She recognised us with looks of travelling love. . . . Her beautiful eyes grew large enough to receive death, but love rose up in them instantly and surmounted their great doom. Those looks will live in me like a second birth. After she became unconscious I went apart to read the grand half-chapter of <u>Corinthians</u> and when I reached the words—'for this mortal must put on immortality'—I cried out 'O mother, mother, come to me, leave that body & come!' She died on the instant and kissed me in her arms—a glorious spirit I felt her round

---

29. Thain, 'Michael Field,' 74.
30. Field, *Long Ago*, i. References to poems from *Long Ago* are from this volume.
31. Ehnenn, "Thy Body Maketh a Solemn Song," 189.
32. Donoghue, *We Are Michael Field*, 41.
33. Donoghue, *We Are Michael Field*, 41.

me and at my lips in an embrace that was like Pentecostal flame—it made
me stronger than death—

    'Soul of my soul! I shall
      Meet her again,
    And with God be the rest.'[34]

In this letter, death meets with love in the same way that Emma embraces her child at the moment of death. Cooper clearly believes in an afterlife and in a soul that outlives the body. It is for these reasons that when she recounts her mother's death she asserts that eternal life is interwoven with love, as if only love can force death into submission. In making her point, she appeals to Corinthians, the Song of Songs, and a slight misquotation from Browning's poem "Prospice," written shortly after Elizabeth Barrett Browning's death in 1861.[35] These religious and secular texts offer Cooper and her family consolation and faith in an afterlife, preventing the living from becoming unstitched by grief and the dying from succumbing to despair. The enduring power of artistic creation is a topic to which I shall return.

The consoling thought for Cooper is that Emma's death allows both mother and daughter to shed an old self and be born anew, which are requirements for future reunion. This language of rebirth and reunion is not only synonymous with the notion of the ascendency of love over death but also foreshadows the role that Emma will play as a creative force in Michael Field's writing. As we shall see, the language prefigures Cooper and Bradley's future conversion after the death of Whym Chow. Emma's dying breath encourages physical tenderness—i.e., the coming together, the embrace, the kiss on the mouth—as well as spiritual intimacy, whereby Emma expels her last breath into her daughter's mouth, as though to instill both a vestige of herself and the Holy Spirit. These intimate physical and spiritual acts allow the mother, as if through the Spirit, to be reborn through her daughter, and vice versa. Similarly, Cooper claims that her mother's looks of love in her final moments "will live in me like a second birth." She feels her mother's death-kiss within "an embrace that was like Pentecostal flame—it made me stronger than death."[36] Pentecost signaled the birth of Christianity, a baptism in which the breath and

---

34. Field, Correspondence: 20 August 1889; EC to Robert Browning. British Library, Add. MS.46866, fols. 199–200v.

35. "Prospice" means to "look forward," and it was among Emma's favorite poems. Field, Correspondence: 20 August 1889; EC to Robert Browning. British Library, Add.MS.46866, fol. 201v.

36. Field, Correspondence: 20 August 1889; EC to Robert Browning. British Library, Add. MS.46866, fol. 200.

flame of the Holy Spirit descended upon the followers of Christ (Acts 2:1–3). Likewise, Cooper commemorates her mother's death as the beginning of new life, for both Emma and herself. Thus, the death heralds a Pentecost of sorts: her mother breathes love and strength into her; love and death comingle, and love proves to be stronger than death. Her mother's passing should therefore have been, at least in theory, a time of joy rather than sorrow. In reality, however, Cooper was devastated by her mother's death. She declared to Browning, "My poet-friend, you will forgive me for writing like this—it is because you are a poet & because I love you that I can talk to you & ease my almost breaking heart sacredly."[37]

Cooper's account of the close intimacy with her dying mother engages the language of the Song of Songs to argue that death is not the end of life. The phrase "it [i.e., her mother's final embrace and kiss] made me stronger than death" recalls Song of Songs 8:6: "Set me as a seal upon thine heart, as a seal upon thine arm: for love is strong as death; jealousy is cruel as the grave: the coals thereof are coals of fire, which hath a most vehement flame." Love's "vehement flame" is like the Pentecostal flame, and Cooper feels it when her mother dies, thereby giving her strength to overcome grief. Cooper's phrase, "stronger than death" (as opposed to "strong as death"), is a common variation on the Song of Songs passage. In fact, we could compare Cooper's letter to Christina Rossetti's poem "Whitsun Day," which recounts the events of Pentecost and makes mention of wind, flame, love, death, and the Holy Spirit. Using the language of romance, Rossetti says that the Holy Spirit is "flesh and blood made spirit and fire" to "woo back a world's desire" (line 4).[38] In their response, the followers of Jesus "Chose love that is strong as death and stronger than death / In the power of the Holy Ghost" (lines 7–8). Similarly, following Emma's death, Bradley speaks of the immense power of love and the ephemeral nature of death in a letter to Browning. By touching Emma's hands and feet (intimate acts), she realizes that "Death is more transitory even than Life; he possesses the body an instant; but the corruption we think [is] his preying work is Love blowing him to the wind."[39] In other words, love is stronger than death.

The evidence so far suggests that it was not inappropriate to use the Song of Songs in order to comprehend and describe relationships beyond that of marriage. Indeed, one could consider close filial and romantic relationships to

---

37. Field, Correspondence: 20 August 1889; EC to Robert Browning. British Library, Add. MS.46866, fols. 201–1v.

38. Rossetti, *Complete Poems of Christina Rossetti*, vol. 2.

39. Field, Correspondence: 22 August 1889; KB to Robert Browning. British Library, Add. MS.46866, fol. 205.

be variations on a continuum, as recent studies of Victorian cousin marriages demonstrate. Talia Schaffer speaks of familiar marriages as being more dispassionate (or "nondesiring") than romantic pairings with outsiders because erotic desire in the first set of relationships is secondary to maintaining family networks.[40] Yet, for someone like Cooper, filial love, while not usually erotic, was far from dispassionate and in fact could be understood through texts associated with erotic attachment, such as the Song of Songs. One wonders if the love that Cooper developed for those in her adult life, such as Bradley (for whom filial and romantic loves were combined), a father figure such as Browning, and her future animal companion, Whym Chow, was built upon her love for her mother. Certainly, all these loves were of such immense importance that Cooper employed the language of the Song of Songs in celebrating them or grieving over their loss. For example, upon hearing of Browning's death from a newspaper dated 13 December 1889, she writes, "I love him as I love my Mother. It was my anticipation to have shown to him her lovely mortal face— God has shown her to him; they have met."[41] Browning was Cooper and Bradley's "poet Father,"[42] their literary mentor and hero, such that in a diary entry for 12 December, the day of Browning's death (but unbeknown to Cooper and Bradley, who at the time only knew him to be gravely ill), Cooper references the previously quoted passage from Song of Songs 8:6, as well as 8:7: "Many waters cannot quench love, neither can floods drown it; if a man would give all the substance of his house for love, it would be utterly contemned."[43] By again invoking love's capacity to surmount obstacles, she compares her love for Browning to a force of nature that eliminates objects in its path: "Reserve with me must be as utterly broken as the rock by the stream, when I love indeed and am close to the beloved one."[44]

The connection drawn above between the biological mother and the "poet Father" enables us to understand an unexplored aspect of Michael Field's thinking: the creative link between Emma Cooper and Michael Field. This link between the three women originates from Cooper and Bradley's desire to demonstrate that the deceased progenitors, Emma Cooper and Robert Browning, could endure through art. For Cooper and Bradley, it is Browning's writing that makes him immortal, stronger than death. Bradley says, "He has given them [i.e., the English people] access to the spiritual world, quite apart from Revelation—he has shown them the deep things of Revelation as

---

40. Schaffer, *Romance's Rival*, ix.

41. Field, Diaries: 13 December 1889. British Library, Add.MS.46777, fol. 121.

42. Field, *Works and Days*, 7.

43. Field, *Works and Days*, 35.

44. Field, *Works and Days*, 36.

128 • CHAPTER 5

in *Karshish* but he has found new pathways to God."[45] The poem that Bradley mentions, "An Epistle Containing the Strange Medical Experience of Karshish, the Arab Physician" (1855), is a meditation on the incarnation, resurrection, and the preeminence of love. By understanding the extent of the love-death connection, Browning has revealed hidden truths and "found new pathways to God." Thus, he is assured a place in the presence of the Divinity. A clipping about him in *Works and Days* includes the lines (written in Bradley's hand) "He passed, fresh as Apollo's bay, / Into God's hand."[46] By his association with Apollo, the god of the arts and leader of the muses, Browning remains eternally "fresh."

After her death, Emma Cooper becomes a progenitor like Browning. The belief that love is stronger than death is what enables Cooper and Bradley to claim that Emma has come to assist them in giving birth to Michael Field's creative works. Indeed, in emphasizing the notion of art as progeny, Cooper calls her own artistic creation "the children of my brain."[47] In a letter to Browning, written after Emma's death, Bradley says,

> We will work for her—her hand closes over the first copy of the faun scene, & <u>Brutus Ulton</u>. Henceforth she will be with us, not as our reader only— [but] intimately in the shaping of our work. Ah, how good to have one's dear ones not outside one anymore; but with & of one, as ones [*sic*] art & life![48]

Emma is a genetic link between Cooper and Bradley, yet after her death her daughter and sister feel a closer connection to her, imagining that she now offers a creative "hand." Emma's newfound role draws the three women into a tighter embrace as co-creators of the one work: she is "not outside one anymore." Here, co-creation is an act by which the authors write each other into the text as memorial. Thus, a work can become an artifact of love. Together, aunt, niece, and sister-mother form a creative triumvirate that scholars have largely ignored in favor of the later trinity of aunt, niece, and Whym Chow. Moreover, this death-love-creation link has undeniable religious undertones. Adam's inspiration (Genesis 2:7) was the source of the Second Adam's expiration (Mark 15:37). This one breath was transmitted through the kiss between God and Adam, between Cooper and her dying mother, and between the

---

45. Field, *Works and Days*, 36.

46. Field, Diaries: 13 December 1889. British Library, Add.MS.46777, fol. 123.

47. Field, Correspondence: 13 June [? 1885]; EC to "Beloved Cousin Fanny." British Library, Add.MS.4686, fol. 215.

48. Field, Correspondence: 22 August 1889; KB to Robert Browning. British Library, Add. MS.46866, fols. 205–5v.

lovers of Song of Songs 1:2: "Let him kiss me with the kisses of his mouth." Furthermore, this kiss of life-death-love is the one continuous breath of the Holy Spirit, which, as we have seen, was imparted at Pentecost to create the world anew. In an artistic sense, Emma's final exhalation into Cooper's mouth became a source of creation for Cooper and the other woman in her life, Bradley.

STRONGER THAN DEATH:
FLAME OF LOVE

The flame of which Cooper spoke in the previous section would burn brightest with the life and death of the flame-colored dog, Whym Chow, who died on 28 January 1906. The two women essentially deified the dog, who was gifted to Cooper as an early birthday present eight years earlier, shortly after the death of her father in the Swiss Alps. In "My loved One is away from me," a poem from *Whym Chow: Flame of Love* (1914), the animal companion is likened to the Egyptian god Anubis (line 44), a psychopomp who is represented in the form of a dog or as a human with a dog's head.[49] In the same volume, "Trinity" compares Whym Chow to the Holy Spirit (lines 5–8). Whym Chow's death—the most devastating—played a significant role in Cooper and Bradley's conversion and in shaping their views of death and the afterlife. Upon his death, Cooper wrote, "Sunday—how terrible Sundays are! Milestones of doom to us as a family. Today I have had the worst loss of my life—yes, worse than that of beloved Mother or the tragic father.—My Whym Chow, my little Chow—Chow, my Flame of Love is dead."[50] And soon after: "Michael [Bradley's nickname] & I love Chow as we have loved no human being—for central & to us was is his Love—our Flame of Love."[51] Their overwhelming grief spans many pages of their diary. Shortly after Whym Chow's death, Cooper observed, "Our grief is blind, is potent . . . we scarcely touch food."[52] Indeed, Bradley continued to speak of loss a month later, this time in relation to Adam and Eve's expulsion from Eden: "O perfect, realised dream of a garden Paradise! And now we are driven forth from it—and it is well. The pain is [what] we have been reaping, & now we must go forth to sow."[53] Whym Chow's death left such an indelible absence that a year after his death Cooper wrote of "the

---

49. Field, *Whym Chow*. Future references to poems from *Whym Chow* are from this volume.

50. Field, Diaries: 28 January 1906. British Library, Add.MS.46795, fol. 14v.

51. Field, Diaries: January[?] 1906. British Library, Add.MS.46795, fol. 25v.

52. Field, Diaries: January[?] 1906. British Library, Add.MS.46795, fol. 18.

53. Field, Diaries: 18 May 1906. British Library, Add.MS.46795, fol. 87.

utter agony of loneliness."[54] The women's grief over Whym Chow confirms that the dog was "the most important being on earth" for the two poets.[55]

The women's intense pain at the loss of Whym Chow reveals the passionate nature of their relationship with him, one which garnered the language of matrimony, family, and the Song of Songs to describe it. Whereas Cooper and Bradley had been passionate in their mourning for Emma and Browning, their devotion to Whym Chow, especially after his death, scaled new heights, culminating in the volume of poetry printed for friends, *Whym Chow: Flame of Love* (1914). Certainly, a good deal of the grief originated from the fact that he was the one who had made their home complete; as Bradley would write in a letter to fellow convert and priest John Gray, "a house without dogs is a house without solicitude—& cannot be a house."[56] The existence of a third, a dog, completed their simultaneously holy and queer family unit. Dog love and same-sex love united in an interspecies trinity through the language of mystical union in which Whym Chow acted as a "symbol of our perfect union" ("Trinity," line 17). Alice Kuzniar says of the poets, "The intensity and purity of [Cooper and Bradley's] love for their dog allegorises the innocence, even sacredness of their love for each other."[57] Indeed, Whym Chow was a "creature of Love's flame" ("Trinity," line 10), a product of love, not from wombs but from hearts and from the union of aunt and niece. As a result, aunt, niece, and dog were each other's "fellow," one definition of which, according to the *OED*, is "consort, spouse, husband or wife." In a letter to Gray, written at some point after Whym Chow's death, Bradley claims that the dog "is my little Fellow, as Henry [Cooper's nickname] is my Fellow."[58]

The closeness—indeed, fellowship—between Cooper, Bradley, and Whym Chow points to a Trinitarian marriage that after the dog's death was reconfigured as Catholic, queer, and inspired by the Song of Songs. Frederick Roden argues that, for Michael Field,

> love of and devotion to an animal enabled the two women to avoid the standard heteroerotic trope of bridal mysticism. Although united together in love, they could not conventionally marry. Instead, Bradley and Cooper joined together in the devotion to their "son," a progeny who was not bio-

54. Field, Diaries: 20 January 1907. British Library, Add.MS.46796, fol. 15v.

55. Thain, *'Michael Field,'* 6.

56. Field, Correspondence: KB to John Gray. National Library of Scotland, Dep. 372, no. 19, fol. 8v.

57. Kuzniar, "I Married My Dog," 209.

58. Field, Correspondence: KB to John Gray. National Library of Scotland, Dep. 372, no. 19, fol. 9v. Moreover, Bradley and Cooper referred to each other as "My dear fellow." Sturgeon, *Michael Field*, 37.

logically procreated: Whym Chow. Thus the two women could come to God not as brides of Christ but as mothers and lovers of their dog.[59]

Roden's argument appeals to the language of mystical marriage drawn most often in Catholic discourse from the Song of Songs, just as Thain argues that John of the Cross appealed to Michael Field "because he wrote mystic love poetry as sensuous as the 'Song of Songs.'"[60] I would add that the saint's writing displays the sensuousness of the Song of Songs *because* it was influenced by it; in *The Living Flame of Love,* John of the Cross's commentary of his titular poem alludes to the flame of Song of Songs 8:6.[61] Roden and Thain believe that the subtitle of *Whym Chow: Flame of Love* refers to this very text by John of the Cross.[62] I argue differently. As we have seen, Whym Chow was already known as "Flame of Love" by the time of his death. Bradley first met Gray (who was influenced by the saint) only days before Whym Chow's death. Hence, either Cooper and Bradley had already known of *The Living Flame of Love* before their friendship with Gray, which is unlikely since their letters to Gray suggest that it was he who introduced them to the saint's work,[63] or there is another source for the designation. This source, I argue, is Song of Songs 8:6, which Cooper quoted at the deaths of her mother and Browning. Equally, Song of Songs 8:6 played a part in the subtitle of *Whym Chow* in order to assert that love is stronger than death. The flame burns away the ephemeral to uncover the eternal; the epigraph of *Whym Chow* originates from Browning's poem "Rabbi Ben Ezra," which declares the following: "Leave the fire ashes, what survives is gold" (line 87).[64]

Whym Chow's demise initiated the spiritual crisis that led Cooper and Bradley into the embrace of Rome. In their conversion experience, the "Flame of Love" became one with the Pentecostal flame, thereby heralding the possibility of reunion with Whym Chow in heaven. The speaker utters in "Introit," a poem from *Whym Chow,* "Our dead comes back again, the dead, our dead, / The dead comes back again, the dead, our dead" and "O Chow, my little

---

59. Roden, *Same-Sex Desire,* 194.

60. Thain, '*Michael Field,*' 193. For more on the influence of Spanish mysticism, see Barrera-Medrano, "St. Theresa, I Call on You to Help," 210–29.

61. John of the Cross, *Living Flame of Love,* 60, 63. The Song of Songs is referenced throughout the commentary.

62. Roden, *Same-Sex Desire,* 200; and Thain, '*Michael Field,*' 193.

63. Bradley wrote in an undated letter to Gray, "How I thank God for you—first of all that you made me a Catholic & then the good method—St. John of the Cross. When, & how did you first draw him into my life? How bitter he was to me!" Field, Correspondence: KB to John Gray. National Library of Scotland, Dep. 372, no. 20, fol. 28.

64. Browning, *Robert Browning's Selected Poems.*

132 • CHAPTER 5

Love, thou art come home. / O Chow, my little Love, thou art come home"
(lines 21–22, 28–29). Multifaceted in nature, the flame of love inflicts wounds
of pleasure and pain. It sears as it purifies in order to redeem. John of the
Cross's poem "The Living Flame of Love," which John Gray translated but did
not publish, begins,

> O living flame of love!
> O tender wounding wonder,
> Wounding my soul in its most secret centre! (lines 1–3)[65]

The pain of love is a theme to which John of the Cross returns in *The Spiritual
Canticle*, a rewriting of the Song of Songs in miniature. This is another text
with which Cooper and Bradley were familiar, having requested from Gray a
copy along with *The Living Flame of Love*.[66] Once smitten—i.e., struck by love
as if by lightning—the speaker in *The Spiritual Canticle* begins her journey
toward healing and reunion with her beloved. Such love imprints and inflicts
a necessary, purgative pain. In the previous chapter, I spoke of the preoccupation with redemptive and character-building pain inherited by the Victorians.
Attesting to the love-death connection, the loss of Whym Chow inflicted the
pain[67] that led Cooper and Bradley into the arms of the church and on the
journey toward a longed-for reunion with Whym Chow.

Conversion led the women into a relationship with Christ that was based
on a mutual admixture of love and suffering, leading ultimately to life ever-
lasting. The language of the Song of Songs plays a part in Michael Field's
depiction of pain as a necessary means to an end. The spiritual pain that one
feels is likened to a longed-for experience of handling fire. Thus, in "Viaticum," published in *Poems of Adoration* (1912), the speaker claims that "When
I behold His sign, / And touch His Offering Hand[,]" Christ "Is felt by me
as Fire" (lines 44–45, 50).[68] Clearly, Christ is another "Flame of Love." When
it comes to Christ's pain, however, Cooper and Bradley play with the visual
slippage between wounds, lips, and labia. In short, the sacred wounds have
a connection to the joyous marital and oral delights expressed in the Song
of Songs. They use these images to celebrate the victory of life over earthly

---

65. Gray, Spiritual Poems (MS). National Library of Scotland, Dep. 372/52, n.p.

66. Field, Correspondence: KB to John Gray. National Library of Scotland, Dep. 372, no.
17, unmarked letter.

67. See the opening lines of "Requiescat," the first poem in *Whym Chow*, "I call along the
Halls of Suffering / Hark! Down each aisle reverberated cries / Out of deep wounds, out of each
fiery spring / Of nerve, or piteous anguish of surprise" (lines 1–4).

68. Field, *Poems of Adoration*. Future references to poems from *Poems of Adoration* are
from this volume.

suffering and death. In highly eroticized language, the two women begin a poem from *Mystic Trees* (1913) like so: "We love Thy ruddy Wounds, / We love them pout by pout" ("The Captain Jewel," lines 1–2).[69] Here, the wounds resemble inflamed—and possibly feminized—lips, ripe for the kissing.

In the same way that "The blood is the life" (Deuteronomy 12:23), the Song of Songs is the life at Easter. Bradley writes in an undated letter to Gray, "We have been learning the Miserere by heart, with pain, & in . . . penance—repeating it every morn: we shall repeat it every Friday morn—On Easter Day I throw it off for the Song of Songs."[70] Just as Christ's suffering and death made way for the resurrection, so the Miserere (Psalm 51), pain, and penance make way for pleasure, for the Song of Songs at Easter. Cooper and Bradley's devotion to Christ's wounds and their attention to his suffering explain why the two women forwent opiates during their own cancers. In this way, some kind of pleasure—the experience of penance and the subsequent feeling of closeness to Christ—might be extracted from suffering and ultimately lead Michael Field to a heavenly marriage with Christ.

STRONGER THAN DEATH:
FLOWERS AND BRIDES OF CHRIST

In this final section, I explore Cooper's impending death in relation to the Song of Songs. Anyone who reads through the original diary entries will note the gradual decline in her handwriting in the months leading up to her demise. One will also note an increasing attention to flowers in her diary entries, particularly to lilies and roses, which are the two most common flowers in Christian iconography and literature. The two flowers feature in the Song of Songs (at least in the King James Version regarding the rose of Sharon). Moreover, the text's bride is called, among other things, *šošanah* (lily), "attributing to the central persona of the story the name of a flower."[71] Hence the flower has a central place in this text on love. As we shall see, in addition to the image of flame, Cooper and Bradley use the image of flowers to draw on a common trope in sapphic literature, connect their pagan and Christian poetry, and represent love's preeminence over death.[72]

---

69. Field, *Mystic Trees*. Future references to poems from *Mystic Trees* are from this volume.

70. Field, Correspondence: KB to John Gray, KB to John Gray, National Library of Scotland, Dep. 372, no. 18, unmarked letter.

71. Lacocque and Ricoeur, *Thinking Biblically*, 236.

72. Floral imagery was common in sapphic writing. See Vanita, *Sappho and the Virgin Mary*, 120.

134 • CHAPTER 5

By the Victorian era, flowers held both pagan and Roman Catholic connotations and were thus wholly suited to Michael Field's religious and poetic iconography. In *The Culture of Flowers*, anthropologist Jack Goody notes that flowers had been used in pagan worship and were therefore a subject of controversy in the early church. Even so, popular enthusiasm and a new fascination with ancient Rome led to the widespread use of flowers and floral imagery in medieval rituals and churches. Likewise, the symbolism of flowers was revived and Christianized in literature, such that the red rose now took on a different meaning and was associated with Christ's suffering and death rather than the earthly love to which the early Church Fathers objected.[73] Through much of the first half of the nineteenth century, the use of flowers in churches was associated with Roman Catholicism, as Dominic Janes has explored. It was only with the rise of the Oxford Movement in the 1830s that "renewed Catholicity of practice within a part of the Church of England led to the increasing reintroduction of blooms to ecclesiastical interiors."[74] Roman Catholicism's association with flowers is an important reason as to why Cooper and Bradley spoke abundantly of flowers in their Catholic period; it also complemented their enduring fondness for things pagan. It is therefore instructive to read the pre- and postconversion volumes side by side, as adjacent and fenceless "fields" in the Michael Field oeuvre.

Flowers exemplify Michael Field's fascination with love, death, and the connection between the two: flowers bloom and then they wither. Two months before Cooper's death, Michael Field composed an untitled poem, later published in *The Wattlefold* (1930), which begins, "Lo,' my love is dying, and the call / Is come that I must die" (lines 1–2).[75] The next lines introduce images of autumn:

All the leaves are dying, all
Dying, drifting by.
Every leaf is lonely in its fall,
Every flower has its speck and stain. (lines 3–6)

It is difficult to imagine just how deeply Bradley would have been affected by the knowledge that Cooper was dying and that she herself would soon follow as a result of a cancer diagnosis that she kept a secret from Cooper. For Bradley, loving Cooper even before the cancer diagnosis produced its own kind of pangs. In a letter to Gray, she declared poignantly, "She makes my heart

---

73. Goody, *Culture of Flowers*, 120–29.
74. Janes, "Catholic Florist," 78.
75. All poems from *The Wattlefold* are from Field, *Michael Field, the Poet*.

"STRONGER THAN DEATH" · 135

like that china that is all cracks."[76] For most of their adulthood, their collaboration—their "coming together"—was a site of "shared intimacy and intellectual *jouissance*."[77] Among many other things, Bradley called Cooper "O my chosen, my delight" and herself "Your own spouse-friend."[78] Both women were bound by blood and emotional bonds and were thus doubly close. Cooper signed off a letter by declaring Bradley "my dearly loved sister-friend,"[79] suggesting not simply their familial ties but also the "sister" bride of Song of Songs 5:1. She proclaimed in a letter five years later, "I have given myself to you as your spouse forever."[80] Accordingly, when one's life companion is ailing, the world seems to fade along with her: "All the leaves are dying" and "Every flower has its speck and stain." Physical beauty is ephemeral and death inevitable.

The two women demonstrated the increasing importance of flower imagery, in general, and from the Song of Songs, in particular, in the months leading up to Cooper's death. The subject matter concerns the mournful, the matrimonial, and the afterlife. Following the diagnosis of terminal cancer in February 1911, Cooper attempted to treat herself with violets mixed in water from Lourdes, "a suitable mixture of the floral and the mystical," says Donoghue.[81] Cooper started the 1912 diary with a burst of images from the Song of Songs, both with and without flower imagery. Two of the four epigraphs at the start of the volume are from the biblical text. The first is the Latin from 2:3: "Sub umbra illius quem desideraveram sedi et fructus ejus dulcis gutturi meo" ("I sat down under his shadow with great delight, and his fruit was sweet to my taste").[82] The second is from the next verse, 2:4, though mistakenly attributed to Isaiah 11:4: "And his banner over me was love."[83] For Cooper, these are pronouncements of God's love and protection: in the first reference, the speaker sits "under" the beloved's shadow, whereas in the second the beloved's flag is "over" her. On 3 January, the day she writes of "my Solemn Vow of Chastity,"[84] Cooper again alludes to the Song of Songs. In referring to the lilies for the shrine in the sunroom, she notes the following: "So the crucifix is 'inter lilia,' as the Beloved is among the spouses in Paradise; & 'inter lilia' in

---

76. Field, Correspondence: KB to John Gray. National Library of Scotland, Dep. 372, no. 20, fol. 28.

77. Ehnenn, *Women's Literary Collaboration,* 2.

78. Letter from KB to EC, 12 August [1882], in Field, *Fowl and the Pussycat,* 63.

79. Letter from EC to KB, [12–14 September 1880], in Field, *Fowl and the Pussycat,* 39.

80. Letter from EC to KB, [October 1885], in Field, *Fowl and the Pussycat,* 155.

81. Donoghue, *We Are Michael Field,* 116.

82. Field, Diaries: [January] 1912. British Library, Add.MS.46802, fol. 2v.

83. Field, Diaries: [January] 1912. British Library, Add.MS.46802, fol. 3.

84. Field, Diaries: [January] 1912. British Library, Add.MS.46802, fol. 4v.

136 • CHAPTER 5

His real earthly Presence, as the Holy Host, He will rest when he comes to our Home."[85] The Latin words "inter lilia" refer to the phrase "among the lilies," from Song of Songs 2:16 and 6:3. In this diary entry, Cooper starts by using the biblical reference to denote the lilies on the shrine, only to progress to the moment's rich, theological significance about the incarnation and human union with the divine in "Paradise"—a word denoting both a garden and the afterlife.

The image of the beloved among the lilies recurs in *Poems of Adoration,* a volume published later that year and written mostly by Cooper but published under the joint name. The poem "Garden of Lazarus" begins with an affecting focus on the Virgin Mary's pain at the realization that her son is soon to die. At sunset, the birds sing a farewell song, while the flowers are aflame with the golden light. When Mary finds peace with her insight, the landscape suddenly unveils its purpose:

Song of Songs the birds now chaunt
And the lilies vaunt
How among them, white, He feeds,
Who but now hath left her—fair and white,
As the lover of the Sumanite. (lines 36–40)

Christ's fate is not to remain at Mary's side but to die and be resurrected as the lover among the lilies, his eternal brides.

Nearing death, Cooper saw herself and Bradley as one of these lilies or spouses of Christ. On 12 January 1912, she noted that, in the early hours of the morning, they lit candles on Mary's shrine and, "in one another's arms," said prayers to Mary and Christ. "What joy & thanks that we are together in our little home, unscathed by the presence of a nurse, blessed by the marvellous union of being both Spouses of the Beloved."[86] It is only fitting that the two converts and "Spouses of the Beloved" prayed to Mary, the Second Eve to Christ's Second Adam. The shrine to Mary was often graced with lilies, as suggested by a diary entry for 2 July 1907, the Feast of the Visitation: "We cut heads of my noble lilies—flame—ruddy & cinder-spotted pale gold ones to wh: we add more than one handful of white lilies, & take them to our Lady's altar, this day when the Voice of the Turtle-dove was heard in the land as a Magnificat.[87] One can imagine the white lilies (like Christ, like Mary) amid

85. Field, Diaries: [January] 1912. British Library, Add.MS.46802, fol. 5.
86. Field, Diaries: 12 January 1912. British Library, Add.MS.46802, fol. 12v.
87. Field, Diaries: 2 July 1907. British Library, Add.MS.46796, fols. 154–54v.

their red and gold counterparts. In fact, the diary entry, like the quoted scene of birds and flowers from "Garden of Lazarus," aspires to a Catholic interpretation of Song of Songs 2:12: "The flowers appear on the earth; the time of the singing of birds is come, and the voice of the turtle[dove] is heard in our land." Life, art, and religious experience thus converge for Michael Field. The lilies on the shrines are more than merely ornamental: they are imparted with theological significance originating from Michael Field's reception of the Song of Songs. In July 1907, when they placed these lilies on the altar, Cooper and Bradley were celebrating both summer and their recent conversion. Perhaps, for the first time since Whym Chow's death, life seemed truly joyous and revivified. In 1912 death loomed again; Cooper and Bradley were experiencing the final months of their lives together. They were at once still very much in love and looking forward to their future as "spouses in Paradise": spouses of each other and of Christ, or, in the words of a poem later published in *The Wattlefold,* "Lovers in Christ" ("Lovers," line 2).

The rose is another important flower to Michael Field, as it is connected to the Song of Songs and the belief that love is stronger than death. Roses are found in "Garden of Lazarus" and throughout *Poems of Adoration.* The risen Christ, for instance, is depicted as a rose in the poem "Ascension":

Pass to the East,
New-born our priest—
The East,
And where the rose is born! (lines 6–9)

The poem "Relics" alludes to the rose of Sharon from the Song of Songs and turns its attention to the relics stored away by the newly deceased Mary Magdalene, the patron saint of converts, penitent sinners, hairdressers, perfume, and women (among other things). These relics are, first, the curls of her hair that allegedly washed and anointed the feet of Christ with perfume (Luke 7:37–38) and, second, the dirt onto which Christ's blood fell from the cross at Golgotha. Crushed together and hardened by an oil-based perfume, the curls are "Knotted as rose of Sharon, when the winds / Sweep it along the desert" (lines 52–53). The sacred relics are placed alongside the corpse of Mary Magdalene in an alabaster coffin decorated with "Transparent rose, / Translucent white" (lines 13–14), a kind of reliquary for her body. The poem speaks of the importance vested in objects of the dead, quite often taken from the body itself (particularly hair) and which the Victorians held close to their hearts, sometimes literally, as Deborah Lutz explores in *Relics of Death in Victorian*

138 • CHAPTER 5

Literature and Culture. Lutz explains that the relic, from the Latin plural *reliquiae,* which means "remains," became increasingly significant in Victorian death culture as the century wore on:

> Granting the corpse and its oddments a place in living narrative is a means to recognize the singularity and irreplaceability of all individuals, their incommensurable otherness. . . . As commodities became ever more symbolic by the middle of the nineteenth century, as the object lost its quality as the "thing itself" and became increasingly mediated by its role as a market "good," the death memento held onto its immediacy. Corporal keepsakes, having no "use value," kept the thing as thing enchanted. A lively memento culture respects the object's magic.[88]

When bodies and body parts are granted personal and religious significance, they are invested with a certain desirable and special quality or "magic," despite, or rather because of, the fact that they are relics: they remind us of the singular qualities of that person because they are of that person. How else could "A clod of bloodied soil" ("Relics," line 85), and thus a thing doubly abject, have meaning otherwise? Likewise, the gnarled and windswept rose of Sharon is a flower that Christian interpreters over the centuries have identified with Christ or the Virgin Mary and therefore endowed with special meaning. For Catholics, however, religious relics are significant because they ultimately reference the power and person of Christ: Mary Magdalene's hair is precious partly because it is from her body but largely because of its alleged role in anointing Christ's feet.

Golgotha appears again in "Gardens Enclosed," the title of which alludes to Song of Songs 4:12 and therefore draws an explicit link between the biblical book and Christ's death. The first garden in the poem is that of his Passion, the second is of his death. In the first garden, where there is "blood and strife divine," red flowers grow (line 5). "Relic" and "Gardens Enclosed" mention neither the resurrection nor heaven, although "Relic" closes with a reference to Judgment Day in the final line. While the resurrection and eternal life are unspoken elements in the background, the lack of explicit references to Christ's resurrection in "Gardens Enclosed" and to the certainty of eternal life for a famed penitent such as Mary Magdalene seem significant. Indeed, the absence of reassurance foregrounds the horror of death and perhaps hints at an understandable wavering of faith as the end was drawing nearer for Cooper.

---

88. Lutz, *Relics of Death,* 3–4.

The diaries record that Cooper received Viaticum on 22 May 1912, though—and the women could not have known it at the time—she was to linger on in pain until her death on 13 December the following year. On that day in May, Bradley brought Cooper prematurely blossoming roses, "a bowl of roses that belong to mid-June."[89] The younger woman reflected on them thus:

> Very frail, illusive are these premature flowers like children of 7 months, their beauty is a fortune made and lost too quickly. Their rich, marvellous blossoming fades as a very dream. They lean on the bowl with exquisiteness almost aerial but no crispness of substance. Lovely, unnatural roses of May, wonders I have never seen before![90]

Compare these "unnatural roses of May" with roses from more than twenty years earlier. On 4 May 1889, just before penning a poem called "A Crown of Praise," Bradley wrote, "Sappho loves the Rose & always crowns it with some praise, likening beautiful maidens to it she likens it also to the arms of the graces, when she describes their elbows bare."[91] Roses might be likened to Sappho's beautiful maidens, and Cooper was described as beautiful, particularly in her youth. One suspects that, in reflecting on the bowl of "premature flowers" and seeing in them the relics that they would soon become, Cooper was also meditating on her own premature demise. She was to die at the age of fifty-one.

Michael Field's reception of the Song of Songs is rich in detail about love, death, and the link between the two. Cooper and Bradley used the Song of Songs to understand and articulate their romantic and filial relationships and to assert that love is stronger than death. As I have demonstrated, Michael Field's poetry and life-writing attest to the importance of Song of Songs 8:6. Cooper and Bradley's closest relationships were of such immense importance that the women employed the language of the Song of Songs to celebrate the lives and grieve the losses of their beloveds. The biblical text entered Cooper and Bradley's letters, diaries, and poems at the deaths of Emma Cooper, Robert Browning, and Whym Chow, and at Cooper's impending demise, enabling the women to make sense of death and to deliver hope for an afterlife. The epigraph to this chapter announces, "And for death? When thou art dying / 'Twill be love beside thee lying." Following the invocation to Apollo, the poem from which the epigraph originates, "[Mortal, if thou art beloved]," is the first to appear in *Underneath the Bough* (1893). While love is manifest throughout the

---

89. Field, Diaries: May 1912. British Library, Add MS.46802, fol. 51.
90. Field, Diaries: May 1912. British Library, Add MS.46802, fol. 51v.
91. Field, Diaries: 4 May 1889. British Library, Add.MS.46777, fol. 4.

volume, so, too, is death—a pattern that recurs in Michael Field's writing. Certainly, there is a five-line poem in the volume called "A Death-Bed," in which a husband keeps watch by the side of his dying wife. Like the husband, love in the first poem of the volume lies alongside the dying, for only love could help Michael Field make meaning out of death. The two most common images from the Song of Songs in Michael Field's iconography are flames and flowers, and both are deployed to assert that love is stronger than death. Searching for that which is greater than the inevitable loss of the body, Cooper and Bradley's secession to Rome was not so much an obliteration of their pagan mode of being but, like the transfiguration of Christ's body after his resurrection, a passage into another phase of life and, ultimately, life beyond death.

CODA

> Queer Theology is then a sexual theology with a differ-
> ence: a passion for the marginalized. That passion is compas-
> sion but also a commitment to social justice, because there is
> a wider understanding of human relationships involved.
>
> —Marcella Althaus-Reid and Lisa Isherwood,
> "Thinking Theology and Queer Theory"[1]

> Any articulation of nineteenth-century religion is never just a work
> of the past, a relic we study objectively from a distance: our own
> scholarly inquiries also actively construct religion, engaging in a
> dynamic activity by which our disciplinary assumptions, and indeed
> personal and lived investments, necessarily shape what we find
> in a 'religious' novel, poem, sermon, artwork, event, or activity.
>
> —Joshua King and Winter Jade Werner, introduction
> to *Constructing Nineteenth-Century Religion*[2]

This book began as a postdoctoral research project around ten years ago. Over the past decade, my positionality as a bisexual and feminist scholar-activist has strengthened and solidified. Indeed, I have become more of an *activist-scholar*, with my work in recent years shifting toward social and applied research. Despite the challenges and changes that have altered the trajectory of my career ambitions, this book has remained the project I have been unable to let go. I want to ensure that the project has a chance to contribute to the fields of queer and feminist theology and literature. When faced with the suffering of another, one whose experiences make them seem like kin, I feel there is no choice but to commit to social justice. I ask that this project on Song of Songs reception be received as "a passion for the marginalized," to use the words of Marcella Althaus-Reid and Lisa Isherwood. In echoing the sentiments of Joshua King and Winter Jade Werner, the works I have discussed are "never just a work of the past, a relic we study objectively from a distance."

Having said that, I readily admit that there are limitations in this study. I have focused on writers and artists who were born or died in comfortable circumstances. In short, I have focused largely on middle-class or upper-middle-class writers and artists, or who, like John Gray, were upwardly mobile. Hence,

---

1. Althaus-Reid and Isherwood, "Thinking Theology and Queer Theory," 308.
2. King and Werner, introduction to *Constructing Nineteenth-Century Religion*, 2.

142 • CODA

this book does not participate in the burgeoning field of working-class literature, though it would be instructive to explore the reception of the Song of
Songs in writing or art for working-class Victorians. A genre of writing that
the working class would have had ready access to is hymns, such as "Rock of
Ages," which alludes to the Song of Songs. Composed as a poem in 1776 by
Anglican clergyman Augustus Montague Toplady, the poem was altered and
condensed in 1815 by Thomas Cotterill and published as a hymn in *Psalms
and Hymns*. Set to its now-familiar tune in 1830 by Thomas Hasting, the hymn
quickly became popular and was reprinted in hymn books throughout the rest
of the century; David R. Breed lists it among the top four hymns of the nineteenth century.[3] The hymn opens and concludes with these two lines: "Rock
of Ages, cleft for me, / Let me hide myself in thee!" Victorian commentators
from across denominations associated the "cleft" with the "clefts of the rock"
in which the dove finds shelter (Song of Songs 2:14). Hence, the influential and
prolific Baptist preacher Charles Spurgeon combines the hymn with the Song
of Songs in his assertion, "The clefts of the Rock of Ages are safe abodes."[4]
Toplady's hymn closes by addressing the speaker's fate, future death, and hope
for eternal life:

> While I draw this fleeting breath,
> When mine eyes shall close in death,
> When I soar to worlds unknown,
> See Thee on Thy judgement throne,
> Rock of Ages, cleft for me,
> Let me hide myself in Thee.[5]

The hymn addresses Christ as the "cleft" from the Song of Songs, offering a
hopeful vision of atonement and the afterlife. As one of the most poetic and
versatile texts in the Bible—used at both weddings and funerals—the Song
of Songs proclaims a love as strong as death. We have seen throughout this
book that this message resonated strongly with Victorian readers. Nonetheless, there is much more that could be explored about death, including the use
of the Song of Songs at funerals. For instance, at the British Library I came
across a funeral sermon (1829) for a widow based on Song of Songs 8:5: "Who
is this that cometh up from the wilderness, leaning upon her beloved?"[6]

---

3. Breed, *History and Use of Hymns*, 85.

4. Spurgeon, *Devotional Classics of C. H. Spurgeon*, 336. See also Leaper, *Song of Solomon
Compared*, 78–80; Marsh, *Bride of Christ*, 43; and Stuart, *Song of Songs*, 230–33.

5. Anonymous, *Last Hours of His Royal Highness*, 8.

6. Anonymous, *Funeral Sermon*.

In addition to hymns and (funeral) sermons, other genres would be worth exploring. Apart from a mention in my introduction of August Renan's dramatization, one genre that I have neglected is the dramatization of the Song of Songs. These adaptations aim to provide a stronger narrative- and character-driven structure to the biblical text, much like the panels of Traquair's decorated piano. Arthur Malet's *The Marriage of Solomon with the Daughter of Pharaoh* (1876) includes an extract of a review from the 23 July 1876 edition of *Church Bells*. This review draws our attention to the accessibility of Malet's dramatization: "We venture to think that many readers of the English Bible will obtain from it a much more accurate and more vivid impression of the nature and structure of the book than they possessed before."[7] The reviewer is convinced the play's purpose is educational, with the specific aim of improving a reader's understanding of the Song of Songs. Indeed, the preface offers a signpost of the action to come: "The drama represents the meeting of Solomon and the Bride on the frontier of the Egyptian and Israelite territories, the journey to Jerusalem, the entry into the King's palace, and the commencement of their wedded life."[8]

Even so, the play is not what one would call a walk in the park; it retains a lot of the literary qualities of the source material. The entire play is composed in verse inspired by events and descriptions from the Song of Songs. The Bride and Solomon likewise speak to each other in verse. The play includes a chorus and a semichorus, while the list of characters is not scant: the Bride's attendants, the guards, queens and ladies of the court, the populace, and friends. The language approaches that of the King James Bible. The bride speaks first, after receiving the kiss of welcome:

> Sweet odours thee surrounding,
> > Like frankincense thy fame:
> Therefore with love abounding
> > The virgins praise thy name. (act 1, scene 1)[9]

As with Renan's dramatization, some of the figurative and erotic language of the source text is retained:

> Thy bosom like two roes,
> > Twins that their dam doth heed,

---

7. Malet, *Marriage of Solomon,* n.p.
8. Malet, *Marriage of Solomon,* n.p.
9. Malet, *Marriage of Solomon,* 1.

Each with the other goes
   To the lilies where they feed. (act 3, scene 2)[10]

At the same time, the God-given might of Solomon is emphasized in a way that is not present in the biblical text. The chorus sings:

O king of ours, than other men more fair,
   Grace on thy lips, God's blessing on thy head,
Gird on thy sword mighty beyond compare,
   With majesty and glory oer [*sic*] thee shed. (act 4, scene 2)[11]

Malet's dramatization, then, appears to shift the balance of power away from the bride toward the monarch.

The political dimensions or possibilities of the Song of Songs is not a topic that I have explored in any detail, yet it is ripe with potential. I did not have the opportunity to discuss a fascinating half-length portrait of King Edward VII by Jewish artist Shlomo Yakov Feifeh (1911).[12] Composed entirely of micrographic Hebrew writing from Ruth, Esther, and the Song of Songs—all female-centered texts—the portrait is somewhat of a mystery. These three biblical texts feature kings and are from the five Megiloth, or books that are annually read in the synagogues: the Song of Songs on the Feast of Passover, Ruth on Pentecost, Lamentations on the Ninth of Ab, Ecclesiastes on Tabernacles, and Esther on Purim.[13] Interestingly, Edward VII's face, hair, and beard are made up of waṣf descriptions for both the bride and the bridegroom as well as the dream sequence wherein the bride is beaten by the watchmen. The climax of the Song of Songs (8:5–7) runs along his right shoulder, while Ruth begins on his left shoulder. Edward VII died in 1910, and hence this work was created a year after his death, potentially to commemorate the length of his reign. While Edward VII is known to have had wealthy Jewish friends at a time of mounting anti-Semitism in Europe,[14] the intended purpose of the portrait is a matter of speculation. While I discuss Simeon Solomon in chapter 4, I believe that further research on the Song of Songs in the Victorian era should be able to illuminate some of the sociopolitical and Jewish influences of the Song of Songs in art and literature.

---

10. Malet, *Marriage of Solomon*, 10.
11. Malet, *Marriage of Solomon*, 16.
12. Feifeh, *King Edward VII*.
13. Ginsburg, *Song of Songs and Coheleth*, 2.
14. See Allfrey, *Edward VII and his Jewish Court*.

Finally, Victorians understood there to be something decidedly erotic and "exotic" about the Song of Songs. Act 1 of Renan's dramatization of the Song of Songs describes Solomon in the midst of his seraglio. It is not the Shulamite but a woman of the harem who voices the famous line, "Let him kiss me with a kiss of his mouth!" (act 1, scene 1).[15] The women in the harem utter in unison to Solomon: "Thy caresses are sweeter than wine when they mingle with the odor of thy exquisite perfumes; thy name is as oil poured out; and therefore the maidens love thee" (act 1, scene 1).[16] Brought in by force, The Shulamite addresses her absent lover thus: "Draw me after thee; let us run together. The King has made me enter his harem" (act 1, scene 1).[17] Hinting at an erotic tale set in a foreign land, translator Havelock Ellis informs the reader that the story is a "secular" rather than an allegorical one.[18] In each chapter of this study, I have touched on the religio-erotic elements, while in the introduction, I noted that Unitarian minister William Maccall denounced the biblical text as "the chief stench in the Bible."[19] But much more remains to be written of adaptations found in the "stench." Research questions that I would ask myself if I were starting the project now include: Did gothic novels and lewd anti-Catholic propaganda allude to the Song of Songs? And what about pornography?

While my research on Victorian pornography has not yielded any obvious allusions,[20] the elements of orality and sweetness in pornography are two things that seem promising for future research. Inspired by Matthew Kaiser's remarkable article "Pater's Mouth,"[21] I discussed the nature of the mouth, sweetness, and sugar in relation to Christina Rossetti and pornography in chapter 3. Yet I have only touched on what is likely a larger subject. The Holy Grail for a study of the Song of Songs in Victorian pornography would be a text that recreates the Song of Songs as a hardcore pornographic text, much like contemporary theologian Roland Boer's chapter, "Night Sprinkle(s): Pornography and the Song of Songs," in *Knockin' on Heaven's Door: The Bible in Popular Culture.*[22] Between discussing the political dimensions of pornography and explicating the pornographic nature of the Song of Songs, Boer creates his own pornographic storyline of the biblical text. Anyone who has read

---

15. Renan, *Song of Songs as a Drama*, 3.
16. Renan, *Song of Songs as a Drama*, 3.
17. Renan, *Song of Songs as a Drama*, 3.
18. Renan, *Song of Songs as a Drama*, xi.
19. Maccall, *Song of Songs*, 3.
20. See Dau, "Governess, Her Body."
21. Kaiser, "Pater's Mouth," 47–64.
22. Boer, *Knockin' on Heaven's Door*, 53–70.

hardcore Victorian pornography would know that such a text might indeed exist. After all, Swinburne himself wrote pornography. The most surprising rendering of the text I have discovered so far is in some classical nude and seminude illustrations by Herbert Granville Fell.[23] Accompanying a verbatim arrangement of the text, the main images and illustrated capital initials reveal the Shulamite in various stages of dress and undress—sometimes sensual.

The Song of Songs is a rich text that has lent itself to debate and diverse interpretations over the centuries. In the Victorian era, it was still heavily discussed, debated, and featured in literature and art. This book offers only a small selection of all the relevant works that are to be found from the period. I have no doubt that the topic will continue to invite readers to enter its garden and eat its pleasant fruits.

---

23. Fell, *Song of Solomon.*

BIBLIOGRAPHY

Ahmed, Sara. *The Cultural Politics of Emotion.* 2nd ed. Edinburgh: Edinburgh University Press, 2014.

Aldrich, Robert. *The Seduction of the Mediterranean: Writing, Art and Homosexual Fantasy.* London: Routledge, 1993.

Allfrey, Anthony. *Edward VII and His Jewish Court.* London: Weidenfeld and Nicolson, 1991.

Althaus-Reid, Marcella, and Lisa Isherwood. "Thinking Theology and Queer Theory." *Feminist Theology* 15, no. 3 (2007): 302–14.

Anonymous. *A Funeral Sermon, Preached in Wingfield Church on Sunday, August the 23rd, 1829; Bearing Testimony to the Gracious Life and Peaceful Death, of a Widow, and Published by the Particular Desire of the Deceased's Religious Friends: And for the Benefit of the Fatherless and Motherless Surviving Children.* 1829.

———. *The Last Hours of His Royal Highness Prince Albert, of Blessed Memory.* London: John Snow, 1864.

———. "'[There Was a Young Lady of Rheims].'" *The Pearl: A Journal of Facetiae and Voluptuous Reading.* No. 2, August 1879: 31.

———. "'[There Was a Young Lady of Troy].'" *The Pearl: A Journal of Facetiae and Voluptuous Reading.* No. 1, July 1879: 31.

———. "Professor Ruskin on Burne-Jones and the 'Mythic School.'" *The Art Journal* (1883): 224.

Apuleius. *The Golden Ass: Or Metamorphoses.* Translated by E. J. Kenney. London: Penguin Books, 2004.

Aristotle. *De Anima (On the Soul).* Translated by Hugh Lawson-Tancred. London: Penguin Books, 1986.

Arscott, Caroline. "Edward Burne-Jones (1833–1898)." In *The Cambridge Companion to the Pre-Raphaelites,* edited by Elizabeth Prettejohn, 223–35. Cambridge, UK: Cambridge University Press, 2012.

148 · BIBLIOGRAPHY

Arseneau, Mary. *Recovering Christina Rossetti: Female Community and Incarnational Poetics.* Houndmills: Palgrave, 2004.

Barfoot, C. C. "'In This Strang Labourinth How Shall I Turne?': Erotic Symmetry in Four Female Sonnet Sequences." In *'And Never Know the Joy': Sex and the Erotic in English Poetry,* edited by C. C. Barfoot, 223–46. Amsterdam: Rodopi, 2006.

Barrera-Medrano, Leire. "'St. Theresa, I Call on You to Help': Michael Field and Spanish Mysticism." In *Michael Field: Decadent Moderns,* edited by Sarah Parker and Ana Parejo Vadillo, 210–29. Athens: Ohio University Press, 2019.

Barrett Browning, Elizabeth. *Aurora Leigh.* Edited by Margaret Reynolds. Athens: Ohio University Press, 1992.

———. Vol. 1 of *The Works of Elizabeth Barrett Browning.* Edited by Marjorie Stone and Beverly Taylor. London: Pickering and Chatto, 2010.

Barrett, Elizabeth B. *The Seraphim and Other Poems.* London: Saunders and Otley, 1838.

Beach, Joseph Warren. *The Method of Henry James.* London: Yale University Press, 1918.

Begiato, Joanne. "Beyond the Rule of Thumb: The Materiality of Marital Violence in England c. 1700–1857." *Cultural and Social History* 15, no. 1 (2018): 39–59.

Bell, David N. "A Bibliography of English Translations of Works by and Attributed to St. Bernard of Clairvaux." *Caiteaux: Commentarii Cistercienses* 48 (1997): 83–129.

Bernard of Clairvaux. Vol. 3 of *On the Song of Songs.* Translated by Killian Walsh and Irene Edmonds. Kalamazoo: Cistercian Publications, 1979.

Bickle, Sharon. Introduction to *The Fowl and the Pussycat: Love Letters of Michael Field, 1876–1909,* edited by Sharon Bickle, xiii–xxxii. Charlottesville: University of Virginia Press, 2008.

Black, Fiona C., and J. Cheryl Exum. "Semiotics in Stained Glass: Edward Burne-Jones's Song of Songs." In *Biblical Studies/Cultural Studies: The Third Sheffield Colloquium,* edited by J. Cheryl Exum and Stephen D. Moore, 315–42. Sheffield: Sheffield Academic Press, 1998.

Blair, Kirstie. *Form and Faith in Victorian Poetry and Religion.* Oxford, UK: Oxford University Press, 2012.

Bloch, Chana, and Ariel Bloch. *The Song of Songs: Translated, with an Introduction and Commentary, by Chana Bloch and Ariel Bloch.* New York: The Modern Library, 2006.

Bloom, Harold. *Charlotte Brontë's Jane Eyre.* New York: Chelsea House, 1987.

Boer, Roland. *The Earthy Nature of the Bible: Fleshly Readings of Sex, Masculinity, and Carnality.* New York: Palgrave Macmillan, 2012.

———. *Knockin' on Heaven's Door: The Bible and Popular Culture.* London: Routledge, 1999.

Bonar, Horatius. Introduction to *The Song of Songs Arranged in Twelve Canticles and Rendered into English Blank Verse,* edited by B. S. Clarke, 1–24. London: James Nisbet, 1881.

Bourke, Joanna. "Sexual Violence, Marital Guidance, and Victorian Bodies: An Aesthesiology." *Victorian Studies* 50, no. 3 (2008): 419–36.

Bowe, Nicola Gordon, and Elizabeth Cumming. *The Arts and Crafts Movements in Dublin and Edinburgh: 1885–1925.* Dublin: Irish Academic Press, 1998.

Bowers, R. H. "The Canceled 'Song of Solomon' Passage in Reade's 'Hard Cash.'" *Ninteenth-Century Fiction* 6, no. 4 (1952): 225–33.

Boyarin, Daniel. *Unheroic Conduct: The Rise of Heterosexuality and the Invention of the Jewish Man.* Berkeley: University of California Press, 1997.

Bradstock, Andrew, Sean Gill, Anne Hogan, and Sue Morgan. Introduction to *Masculinity and Spirituality in Victorian Culture,* edited by Andrew Bradstock, Sean Gill, Anne Hogan, and Sue Morgan, 1–9. Basingstoke: Macmillan, 2000.

Brady, Sean. *Masculinity and Male Homosexuality in Britain, 1861–1913.* Houndmills: Palgrave Macmillan, 2005.

Breed, David R. *The History and Use of Hymns and Hymn-Tunes.* New York: Fleming H. Revell, 1934.

Brenner, Athalya. "On Feminist Criticism of the Song of Songs." In *A Feminist Companion to the Song of Songs,* edited by Athalya Brenner, 28–37. Sheffield: Sheffield Academic Press, 1993.

Brontë, Charlotte. *Jane Eyre.* Edited by Margaret Smith. Oxford, UK: Oxford University Press, 2000.

———. Vol. 1 of *The Letters of Charlotte Brontë: With a Selection of Letters by Family and Friends.* Edited by Margaret Smith. Oxford, UK: Clarendon Press, 1995.

———. *The Poems of Charlotte Brontë.* Edited by Tom Winnifrith. Oxford, UK: Basil Blackwell, 1984.

———. *Villette.* Edited by Margaret Smith and Herbert Rosengarten. Oxford, UK: Oxford University Press, 2000.

Browning, Robert. *Robert Browning's Selected Poems.* Edited by Charlotte Porter and Helen A. Clarke. New York: Thomas Y. Crowell, 1896.

Buckton, Oliver S. "'An Unnatural State': Gender, 'Perversion,' and Newman's *Apologia Pro Vita Sua.*" *Victorian Studies* 35, no. 4 (1992): 359–83.

Bullough, Kathy M. "Serpent, Angels and Virgins: The Virgin Mary as 'Second Eve' in the Art of Edward Burne-Jones." *Religion and the Arts* 4, no. 4 (2000): 463–90.

Burdett, Carolyn. "The New Woman." In *Thomas Hardy in Context,* edited by Phillip Mallett, 363–73. Cambridge, UK: Cambridge University Press, 2013.

Burgan, Mary. "Heroines at the Piano: Women and Music in Nineteenth-Century Fiction." *Victorian Studies* 30, no. 1 (1986): 51–76.

Burne-Jones, Edward. *The Secret Book of Designs.* Cat. no. 140. 1899-7-13-390. British Museum. 1885.

———. *Sketchbook.* Accession no. 1971.1. Call no. B3 031 A09. The Morgan Library and Museum. [18??].

Burne-Jones, Georgiana. *Memorials of Edward Burne-Jones.* 2 vols. London: Macmillan, 1904.

Byrne, Romana. *Aesthetic Sexuality: A Literary History of Sadomasochism.* London: Bloomsbury, 2014.

Capuano, Peter J. *Changing Hands: Industry, Evolution, and the Reconfiguration of the Victorian Body.* Ann Arbor: University of Michigan Press, 2015.

Cevasco, G. A. *John Gray.* Boston: Twayne Publishers, 1982.

Chase, Karen, and Michael Levenson. *The Spectacle of Intimacy: A Public Life for the Victorian Family.* Princeton, NJ: Princeton University Press, 2009.

Clarke, B. S. *The Song of Songs Arranged in Twelve Canticles and Rendered into English Blank Verse.* London: James Nisbet, 1881.

Claybaugh, Amanda. "*Jude the Obscure*: The Irrelevance of Marriage Law." In *Subversion and Sympathy: Gender, Law, and the British Novel,* edited by Alison L. LaCroix and Martha C. Nussbaum, 48–64. Oxford, UK: Oxford University Press, 2013.

Colligan, Colette, and Margaret Linley. "Introduction: The Nineteenth-Century Invention of Media." In *Media, Technology, and Literature in the Nineteenth Century: Image, Sound, Touch,* edited by Colette Colligan and Margaret Linley, 1–19. Farnham: Ashgate, 2011.

Coluzzi, Federica. "Illuminating the *Vita Nuova*: Phoebe Anna Traquair, Evelyn Paul, and Medievalist Practices of Visual Mediation." *Italian Studies* 77, no. 2 (2022): 190–201.

150 · BIBLIOGRAPHY

Cooper, Suzanne Fagence. "The Liquefaction of Desire: Music, Water and Femininity in Victorian Aestheticism." *Women: A Cultural Review* 20, no. 2 (2009): 186–201.

Corbett, Mary Jean. *Family Likeness: Sex, Marriage, and Incest from Jane Austen to Virginia Woolf.* Ithaca, NY: Cornell University Press, 2008.

Cox, Kimberly. *Touch, Sexuality, and Hands in British Literature, 1740–1901.* Milton: Routledge, 2021.

Craft, Christopher. *Another Kind of Love: Male Homosexual Desire in English Discourse, 1850–1920.* Berkeley: University of California Press, 1994.

Crawford, Alan. "Burne-Jones as a Decorative Artist." In *Edward Burne-Jones: Victorian Artist-Dreamer,* edited by Stephen Wildman and John Christian, 5–23. New York: The Metropolitan Museum of Art, New York, 1998.

Cruise, Colin, Roberto C. Ferrari, Debra N. Mancoff, Elizabeth Prettejohn, Gayle M. Seymour, Frank C. Sharp, and Victoria Osborne. *Love Revealed: Simeon Solomon and the Pre-Raphaelites.* London: Merrell and Birmingham Museums and Art Gallery, 2005.

Cumming, Elizabeth. "Patterns of Life: The Art and Design of Phoebe Anna Traquair and Mary Seton Watts." In *Women Artists and the Decorative Arts, 1880–1935: The Gender of Ornament,* edited by Bridget Elliott and Janice Helland, 15–34. Aldershot: Ashgate, 2002.

——. *Phoebe Anna Traquair: 1852–1936.* Edinburgh: National Galleries of Scotland, 2011.

Cumming, Elizabeth, and Wendy Kaplan. *The Arts and Crafts Movement.* London: Thames and Hudson, 1991.

D'Amico, Diane. *Christina Rossetti: Faith, Gender, and Time.* Baton Rouge: Louisiana State University Press, 1999.

D'Cruze, Shani. *Crimes of Outrage: Sex, Violence and Victorian Working Women.* London: UCL Press, 1998.

da Sousa Correa, Delia. "'The Music Vibrating in Her Still': Music and Memory in George Eliot's *The Mill on the Floss* and *Daniel Deronda.*" *Nineteenth-Century Contexts* 21, no. 4 (2000): 541–63.

Dakers, Caroline. "Yours Affectionately, Angelo: The Letters of Edward Burne-Jones (1833–98) and Frances Horner (1858–1940)." *The British Art Journal* 2, no. 3 (2001): 16–21.

Daleski, H. M. *Thomas Hardy and Paradoxes of Love.* Columbia: University of Missouri Press, 1997.

Dalziel, Pamela. "The Gospel According to Hardy." In *Thomas Hardy Reappraised: Essays in Honour of Michael Millgate,* edited by Keith Wilson, 3–19. Toronto: University of Toronto Press, 2006.

Dau, Duc. "The Governess, Her Body, and Thresholds in *The Romance of Lust.*" *Victorian Literature and Culture* 42, no. 2 (2014): 281–302.

——. "Perfect Chastity: Celibacy and Virgin Marriage in Tractarian Poetry." *Victorian Poetry* 44, no. 1 (2006): 77–92.

——. "Reception." In *The Routledge Companion to Literature and Religion,* edited by Mark Knight, 113–23. New York: Routledge, 2016.

——. "The Song of Songs for Difficult Queers: Simeon Solomon, Neil Bartlett, and *A Vision of Love Revealed in Sleep.*" In *Queer Difficulty in Art and Poetry: Rethinking the Sexed Body in Verse and Visual Culture,* edited by Jongwoo Jeremy Kim and Christopher Reed, 34–47. New York: Routledge, 2017.

——. *Touching God: Hopkins and Love.* London: Anthem Press, 2012.

DeJean, Joan. *Fictions of Sappho, 1546–1937.* Chicago: University of Chicago Press, 1989.

Dellamora, Richard. *Masculine Desire: The Sexual Politics of Victorian Aestheticism.* Chapel Hill: University of North Carolina Press, 1990.

Denisoff, Dennis. *Decadent Ecology in British Literature and Art, 1860–1910: Decay, Desire, and the Pagan Revival.* Cambridge, UK: Cambridge University Press, 2021.

Dickinson, Colby, and Meghan Toomey. "The Continuing Relevance of 'Queer' Theology for the Rest of the Field." *Theology and Sexuality* 23, no. 1–2 (2017): 1–16.

Dijkstra, Bram. *Idols of Perversity: Fantasies of Feminine Evil in Fin-De-Siècle Culture.* New York: Oxford University Press, 1986.

Donne, John. *The Variorum Edition of the Poetry of John Donne, Volume 7, Part 1: The Holy Sonnets.* Edited by Gary A. Stringer and Paul A. Parrish. Bloomington: Indiana University Press, 2005.

Donoghue, Emma. *We Are Michael Field.* Bath: Absolute Press, 1988.

Dowling, Andrew. *Manliness and the Male Novelist in Victorian Literature.* Aldershot: Ashgate, 2001.

Dowling, Linda. *Hellenism and Homosexuality in Victorian Oxford.* Ithaca, NY: Cornell University Press, 1994.

Drane, Augusta Theodosia. Flores Sanctorum. n.d. (Stone Dominican Sisters).

———. G/Frd/Ii/1a Album. n.d. (Stone Dominican Sisters).

———. G/Frd/Ii/1b "Examen" Notebook. n.d. (Stone Dominican Sisters).

———. G/Frd/Ii/1c the Imitation of Christ: Text and Notes. n.d. (Stone Dominican Sisters).

———. Vol. 1 of *The History of St. Catherine of Siena and Her Companions.* 2nd ed. London: Burns and Oates, 1887.

———. *The History of St. Dominic: Founder of the Friars Preachers.* London: Longmans, Green, 1891.

———. *The Knights of St. John: With the Battle of Lepanto and Siege of Vienna.* London: Burnes and Oates, 1858.

———. *A Memoir of Mother Francis Raphael, O.S.D.* Edited by Bertrand Wilberforce. 2nd ed. London: Longmans, Green, 1897.

———. *Songs in the Night and Other Poems.* 2nd ed. London: Burns and Oates, 1887.

Ehnenn, Jill R. "'Thy Body Maketh a Solemn Song': Desire and Disability in Michael Field's 'Catholic Poems.'" In *Michael Field: Decadent Moderns,* edited by Sarah Parker and Ana Parejo Vadillo, 188–209. Athens: Ohio University Press, 2019.

———. *Women's Literary Collaboration, Queerness, and Late-Victorian Culture.* Aldershot: Ashgate, 2008.

Ekeh, Ono. "Newman's Account of Ambrose St. John's Death." *Newman Studies Journal* 2, no. 2 (2011): 5–18.

Eliot, George. *The Mill on the Floss.* Edited by Gordon S. Haight. Oxford, UK: Oxford University Press, 1996.

Ellis, Havelock. "Concerning *Jude the Obscure.*" *Savoy* October, no. 6 (1896): 35–49.

Engelhardt, Carol. "The Paradigmatic Angel in the House: The Virgin Mary and Victorian Anglicans." In *Women of Faith in Victorian Culture: Reassessing the Angel in the House,* edited by Anne Hogan and Andrew Bradstock, 159–71. London: Palgrave Macmillan UK, 1998.

———. "The Revival of the Religious Life: The Sisterhoods." In *The Oxford Handbook of the Oxford Movement,* edited by Stewart J. Brown, Peter Nockles and James Pereiro, 387–97. Oxford, UK: Oxford University Press, 2017.

152 • BIBLIOGRAPHY

Engelhardt Herringer, Carol. *Victorians and the Virgin Mary: Religion and Gender in England, 1830–85.* Manchester: Manchester University Press, 2008.

Exum, J. Cheryl. "Song of Songs." In *The Oxford Handbook of English Literature and Theology,* edited by Andrew W. Hass, David Jasper, and Elisabeth Jay, 259–73. Oxford, UK: Oxford University Press, 2009.

Faber, Frederick William. *The Life and Letters of Frederick William Faber, D.D.* Edited by John Edward Bowden. London: Thomas Richardson and Son, 1869.

Faxon, Alicia Craig. "The Pre-Raphaelites and the Mythic Image: Iconographies of Women." *Visual Resources* 27, no. 1 (2011): 77–89.

Feifeh, Shlomo Yakov. "King Edward VII." Object no. c 1978.4.24.5. London: Jewish Museum, 1911.

Fell, H. Granville. *The Song of Solomon.* London: Chapman and Hall, 1897.

Field, Michael. Correspondence: 13 June [? 1885]; EC to "Beloved Cousin Fanny." British Library, Add.MS.4686.

———. Correspondence: 20 August 1889; EC to Robert Browning. British Library, Add.MS.46866.

———. Correspondence: 22 August 1889; KB to Robert Browning. British Library, Add.MS.46866.

———. Correspondence: KB to John Gray, National Library of Scotland, Dep. 372, No. 18.

———. Correspondence: KB to John Gray. National Library of Scotland, Dep. 372, No. 20.

———. Correspondence: KB to John Gray. National Library of Scotland, Dep. 372, No. 17.

———. Correspondence: KB to John Gray. National Library of Scotland, Dep. 372, No. 19.

———. Correspondence: KB to John Gray. National Library of Scotland, Dep. 372, No. 20.

———. Diaries: 2 July 1907. British Library, Add.MS.46796.

———. Diaries: 4 May 1889. British Library, Add.MS.46777.

———. Diaries: 12 January 1912. British Library, Add.MS.46802.

———. Diaries: 13 December 1889. British Library, Add.MS.46777.

———. Diaries: 18 May 1906. British Library, Add.MS.46795.

———. Diaries: 20 January 1907. British Library, Add.MS.46796.

———. Diaries: 28 January 1906. British Library, Add.MS.46795.

———. Diaries: [January] 1912. British Library, Add.MS.46802.

———. Diaries: January[?] 1906. British Library, Add.MS.46795.

———. Diaries: May 1912. British Library, Add MS.46802.

———. *The Fowl and the Pussycat: Love Letters of Michael Field, 1876–1909.* Edited by Sharon Bickle. Charlottesville: University of Virginia Press, 2008.

———. *Long Ago.* London: G. Bell and Sons, 1889.

———. *Michael Field, the Poet: Published and Manuscript Materials.* Edited by Marion Thain and Ana Parejo Vadillo. Buffalo, NY: Broadview Press, 2009.

———. *Mystic Trees.* London: Everleigh Nash, 1913.

———. *Poems of Adoration.* London: Sands, 1912.

———. *Underneath the Bough.* London: George Bell and Sons, 1893.

———. *Whym Chow: Flame of Love.* London: Eragny Press, 1914.

———. *Works and Days: From the Journal of Michael Field.* Edited by T. Sturge Moore and D. C. Sturge Moore. London: J. Murray, 1933.

Franklin, J. Jeffrey. "The Merging of Spiritualities: Jane Eyre as Missionary of Love." *Nineteenth-Century Literature* 49, no. 4 (1995): 456–82.

Gagné, Ann. *Embodying the Tactile in Victorian Literature: Touching Bodies/Bodies Touching.* Lanham: Lexington Books, 2021.

Gaskell, Elizabeth. *The Life of Charlotte Brontë.* Edinburgh: J. Grant, 1924.

Gedney, Mark. "A Love as Strong as Death: Ricoeur's Reading of the Song of Songs." In *Transforming Philosophy and Religion: Love's Wisdom,* edited by Norman Wirzba and Bruce Ellis Benson, 63–72. Bloomington: Indiana University Press, 2008.

Gill, Sean. "*Ecce Homo*: Representations of Christ as the Model of Masculinity in Victorian Art and Lives of Jesus." In *Masculinity and Spirituality in Victorian Culture,* edited by Andrew Bradstock, Sean Gill, Anne Hogan, and Sue Morgan, 164–78. Houndmills: Macmillan, 2000.

Gilman, Sander L. "AIDS and Syphilis: The Iconography of Disease." *October* 43 (1987): 87–107.

Ginsburg, Christian D. *The Song of Songs and Coheleth (Commonly Called the Book of Ecclesiastes) Translated from the Original Hebrew, with a Commentary, Historical and Critical.* New York: Ktav, 1970.

Goddard, Arabella. "How to Play the Piano." *Girl's Own Paper* 1 (1880): 164–66.

Goody, Jack. *The Culture of Flowers.* Cambridge, UK: Cambridge University Press, 1993.

Gray, Erik. "Come Be My Love: The Song of Songs, *Paradise Lost,* and the Tradition of the Invitation Poem." *PMLA* 128, no. 2 (2013): 370–85.

Gray, F. Elizabeth. *Christian and Lyric Tradition in Victorian Women's Poetry.* London: Routledge, 2010.

Gray, John. *The Poems of John Gray.* Edited by Ian Fletcher. Greensboro, NC: ELT Press, 1988.

———. Spiritual Poems (MS). National Library of Scotland, Dep. 372/52.

Graybill, Rhiannon. *Texts after Terror: Rape, Sexual Violence, and the Hebrew Bible.* New York: Oxford University Press, 2021.

Hands, Timothy. *Thomas Hardy: Distracted Preacher? Hardy's Religious Biography and Its Influence on His Novels.* Basingstoke: Macmillan, 1989.

Hanson, Ellis. *Decadence and Catholicism.* Cambridge, MA: Harvard Universe Press, 1997.

Hardy, Florence Emily. Vol. 1 of *The Life of Thomas Hardy.* London: Macmillan, 1933.

Hardy, Thomas. Vol. 2 of *The Collected Letters of Thomas Hardy.* Edited by Richard Little Purdy and Michael Millgate. Oxford, UK: Clarendon Press, 1980.

———. Vol. 1 of *The Complete Poetical Works of Thomas Hardy.* Edited by Samuel Hynes. Oxford, UK: Clarendon Press, 1982.

———. Vol. 2 of *The Complete Poetical Works of Thomas Hardy.* Edited by Samuel Hynes. Oxford, UK: Clarendon Press, 1984.

———. *Far from the Madding Crowd.* Edited by Suzanne B. Falck-Yi. Oxford, UK: Oxford University Press, 2002.

———. *Jude the Obscure.* Edited by Patricia Ingham. Oxford, UK: Oxford University Press, 1985.

Healy, Philip. "Man Apart: Priesthood and Homosexuality at the End of the Nineteenth Century." In *Masculinity and Spirituality in Victorian Culture,* edited by Andrew Bradstock, Sean Gill, Anne Hogan, and Sue Morgan, 100–115. Houndmills: Macmillan Press, 2000.

Heeney, Brian. *The Women's Movement in the Church of England, 1850–1930.* Oxford, UK: Clarendon Press, 1988.

Heilmann, Ann. "Marriage." In *Thomas Hardy in Context,* edited by Phillip Mallett, 351–62. Cambridge, UK: Cambridge University Press, 2013.

Henson, Eithne. *Landscape and Gender in the Novels of Charlotte Brontë, George Eliot, and Thomas Hardy: The Body of Nature.* London: Routledge, 2016.

Hill, Marylu. "'Eat Me, Drink Me, Love Me': Eucharist and the Erotic Body in Christina Rossetti's *Goblin Market.*" *Victorian Poetry* 43, no. 4 (2005): 455–72.

Hotz, Mary Elizabeth. *Literary Remains: Representations of Death and Burial in Victorian England.* Albany: State University of New York Press, 2009.

Huxtable, Sally-Anne. "'The Drama of the Soul': Time, Eternity and Evolution in the Designs of Phoebe Anna Traquair." In *Design, History and Time: New Temporalities in a Digital Age,* edited by Zoë Hendon and Anne Massey, 23–34. London: Bloomsbury, 2019.

Jane, Thomas. "In Defence of Emma Hardy." *The Hardy Society Journal* 9, no. 2 (2013): 39–59.

Janes, Dominic. "'The Catholic Florist': Flowers and Deviance in the Mid-Nineteenth-Century Church of England." *Visual Culture in Britain* 12, no. 1 (2011): 77–96.

———. "Seeing and Tasting the Divine: Simeon Solomon's Homoerotic Sacrament." In *Art, History and the Senses: 1830 to the Present,* edited by Patrizia di Bello and Gabriel Koureas, 35–50. Burlington: Ashgate, 2010.

———. *Visions of Queer Martyrdom from John Henry Newman to Derek Jarman.* Chicago: Chicago University Press, 2015.

Jiménez, Nilda. *The Bible and the Poetry of Christina Rossetti: A Concordance.* Westport, CT: Greenwood Press, 1979.

John of the Cross. *The Complete Works of Saint John of the Cross.* Translated by David Lewis. Edited by the Oblate Fathers of Saint Charles. 2 vols. London: Longman, Green, Longman, Roberts, and Green, 1864.

———. *Dark Night of the Soul.* Translated by E. Allison Peers. New York: Image Books, 1990.

———. *The Living Flame of Love.* Translated by David Lewis. London: Thomas Baker, 1919.

Kaiser, Matthew. "Pater's Mouth." *Victorian Literature and Culture* 39, no. 1 (2011): 47–64.

Kaye, W. J. "Outrages on Women." *North British Review* 25, no. 49 (1856).

King, Joshua, and Winter Jade Werner. Introduction to *Constructing Nineteenth-Century Religion: Literary, Historical, and Religious Studies in Dialogue,* edited by Joshua King and Winter Jade Werner, 1–21. Columbus: The Ohio State University Press, 2019.

Knight, Mark. "Wilde's Uses of Religion." In *Constructing Nineteenth-Century Religion: Literary, Historical, and Religious Studies in Dialogue,* edited by Joshua King and Winter Jade Werner, 206–21. Columbus: The Ohio State University Press, 2019.

Knight, Mark, and Emma Mason. *Nineteenth-Century Religion and Literature: An Introduction.* Oxford, UK: Oxford University Press, 2006.

Kolsteren, Steven. "Simeon Solomon and the Song of Songs." *Journal of Jewish Art* 6 (1985): 47–59.

Kooistra, Lorraine Janzen. *Christina Rossetti and Illustration: A Publishing History.* Athens: Ohio University Press, 2002.

———. "*Goblin Market* as a Cross-Audienced Poem: Children's Fairy Tale, Adult Erotic Fantasy." *Children's Literature* 25, no. 1 (1997): 181–204.

Krasner, James. "'In Memoriam' 7 and the Song of Solomon." *Victorian Poetry* 29 (1991): 93–96.

Kreilkamp, Ivan. "Pitying the Sheep in *Far from the Madding Crowd.*" *Novel* 42, no. 3 (2009): 474–81.

Kuzniar, Alice. "'I Married My Dog': On Queer Canine Literature." In *Queering the Non/Human,* edited by Noreen Giffney and Myrna Hird, 205–26. Aldershot: Ashgate Press, 2008.

Lacocque, André, and Paul Ricoeur. *Thinking Biblically: Exegetical and Hermeneutical Studies.* Translated by David Pellauer. Chicago: University of Chicago Press, 1998.

Landow, George P. *Victorian Types, Victorian Shadows: Biblical Typology in Victorian Literature, Art, and Thought.* Boston: Routledge, 1980.

LaPorte, Charles. *Victorian Poets and the Changing Bible*. Charlottesville: University of Virginia Press, 2011.

Larsen, Timothy. *A People of One Book: The Bible and the Victorians*. Oxford, UK: Oxford University Press, 2011.

Lawson, Kate, and Lynn Shakinovsky. *The Marked Body: Domestic Violence in Mid-Nineteenth-Century Literature*. Albany: State University of New York Press, 2002.

Leaper, Adelaide Newton. *The Song of Solomon Compared with Other Parts of Scripture*. New York: Robert Carter and Brothers, 1864.

Lee, Dorothy. *Flesh and Glory: Symbolism, Gender and Theology in the Gospel of John*. New York: Crossroad, 2002.

Leighton, Angela. *Victorian Woman Poets: Writing against the Heart*. New York: Harvester Wheatsheaf, 1992.

Littledale, Richard Frederick. *A Commentary on the Song of Songs. From Ancient and Medieval Sources*. London: Joseph Masters, 1869.

Ludlow, Elizabeth. *Christina Rossetti and the Bible: Waiting with the Saints*. London: Bloomsbury Academic, 2014.

Lutz, Deborah. *Relics of Death in Victorian Literature and Culture*. New York: Cambridge University Press, 2015.

Lysack, Krista. "Goblin Markets: Victorian Women Shoppers at Liberty's Oriental Bazaar." *Nineteenth-Century Contexts* 27, no. 2 (2005): 139–65.

Maccall, William. *The Song of Songs. A Lecture Delivered at the Hall of Science, City Road, London, on Sunday, Feb. 16, 1862*. London: J. B. Bebbington, 1862.

MacCarthy, Fiona. *The Last Pre-Raphaelite: Edward Burne-Jones and the Victorian Imagination*. London: Faber and Faber, 2011.

Mahoney, Kristin Mary. *Queer Kinship after Wilde: Transnational Decadence and the Family*. Cambridge, UK: Cambridge University Press, 2022.

Malet, Arthur. *The Marriage of Solomon with the Daughter of Pharaoh: A Drama, Rendered into English Verse from the Song of Songs, by A. Malet*. Bridgwater: Ashcott, 1880.

Marcus, Sharon. *Between Women: Friendship, Desire, and Marriage in Victorian England*. Princeton, NJ: Princeton University Press, 2007.

Marsh, Catherine M. *The Bride of Christ; or, Explanatory Notes on the Song of Solomon*. London: Seeley, Jackson, and Halliday, 1861.

Marzials, Theo, and Walter Crane. *Pan Pipes: A Book of Old Songs*. London: George Routledge and Sons, 1883.

Mason, Emma. "Christina Rossetti and the Doctrine of Reserve." *Journal of Victorian Culture* 7, no. 2 (2002): 196–219.

Masurel-Murray, Claire. "Conversions to Catholicism among Fin de Siècle Writers: A Spiritual and Literary Genealogy." *Cahiers Victoriens & Édouardiens,* no. 76 (2012): 105–25.

Matthews, Susan. *Blake, Sexuality and Bourgeois Politeness*. Cambridge, UK: Cambridge University Press, 2011.

McAdam, Gloria. "Willing Women and the Rise of Convents in Nineteenth-Century England." *Women's History Review* 8, no. 3 (1999): 411–41.

McCormack, Jerusha Hull. *John Gray: Poet, Dandy, and Priest*. Waltham, MA: Brandeis University Press, 1991.

McSweeney, Kerry. *Supreme Attachments: Studies in Victorian Love Poetry*. Brookfield: Ashgate, 1998.

156 · BIBLIOGRAPHY

Meyers, Carol. *Discovering Eve: Ancient Israelite Women in Context.* Oxford, UK: Oxford University Press, 1988.

Michie, Elsie B. *The Vulgar Question of Money: Heiresses, Materialism, and the Novel of Manners from Jane Austen to Henry James.* Baltimore, MD: Johns Hopkins University Press, 2011.

Millgate, Michael. *Thomas Hardy: A Biography Revisited.* Oxford, UK: Oxford University Press, 2004.

———. "Thomas Hardy's Library at Max Gate: Catalogue of an Attempted Reconstruction." University of Toronto Library, last updated 4 October 2021. http://hardy.library.utoronto.ca/.

Mintz, Sidney. *Sweetness and Power: The Place of Sugar in Modern History.* New York: Penguin Books, 1986.

Monkhouse, Cosmo. "Edward Burne-Jones." *Scribner's Magazine,* February 1894, 135–53.

Moon, Jina. "Domestic Violence in Victorian and Edwardian Fiction." PhD diss., University of Tulsa, 2015.

Moore, Stephen D. *God's Beauty Parlor: And Other Queer Spaces in and Around the Bible.* Stanford: Stanford University Press, 2001.

Moran, Maureen. *Catholic Sensationalism and Victorian Literature.* Liverpool: Liverpool University Press, 2007.

Morgan, Thaïs E. "Perverse Male Bodies: Simeon Solomon and Algernon Charles Swinburne." In *Outlooks: Lesbian and Gay Sexualities and Visual Cultures,* edited by Peter Horne and Reina Lewis, 61–85. London: Routledge, 1996.

Moro Tornese, Sebastian Francisco. "Philosophy of Music in the Neoplatonic Tradition: Theories of Music and Harmony on Proclus' Commentaries on Plato's *Timaeus* and *Republic.*" PhD diss., University of London, 2010.

Morris, A. F. "Versatile Art Worker: Mrs. Traquair." *The Studio: An Illustrated Magazine of Fine and Applied Art,* 1905, 339–43.

Mosse, George L. "Nationalism and Respectability: Normal and Abnormal Sexuality in the Nineteenth Century." *Journal of Contemporary History* 17, no. 2 (1982): 221–46.

Mumm, Susan. *Stolen Daughters, Virgin Mothers: Anglican Sisterhoods in Victorian Britain.* London: Leicester University Press, 1999.

Newman, John Henry. *Lectures on the Present Position of Catholics in England: Addressed to the Brothers of the Oratory in the Summer of 1851.* London: Longmans, Green, 1908.

Nixon, Jude. "'Kill[ing] Our Souls with Literalism': Reading *Essays and Reviews.*" *Religion and the Arts* 5 (2001): 34–64.

Norcia, Megan A. "'Come Buy, Come Buy': Christina Rossetti's 'Goblin Market' and the Cries of London." *Journal of Victorian Culture* 17, no. 1 (2012): 24–45.

Nunokawa, Jeff, and Amy Sickels. *Oscar Wilde.* Philadelphia: Chelsea House Publishers, 2005.

Nussey, Ellen. "School Days at Roe Head." *Brontë Studies* 41, no. 2 (2016): 99–105.

Oliphant, Margaret. "The Anti-Marriage League." *Blackwood's Edinburgh Magazine.* January (1896): 135–49.

Page, Norman. *Thomas Hardy.* Abingdon: Routledge, 2011.

Palazzo, Lynda. *Christina Rossetti's Feminist Theology.* Houndmills: Palgrave Macmillan, 2002.

Paxton, Amanda. *Willful Submission: Sado-Erotics and Heavenly Marriage in Victorian Religious Poetry.* Charlottesville: University of Virginia Press, 2017.

Pease, Allison. *Modernism, Mass Culture, and the Aesthetics of Obscenity.* Cambridge, UK: Cambridge University Press, 2000.

Peschier, Diana. *Nineteenth-Century Anti-Catholic Discourses: The Case of Charlotte Brontë.* New York: Palgrave Macmillan, 2005.

Peters, John G. "'We Stood at God's Feet, Equal': Equality, Subversion, and Religion in *Jane Eyre*." *Brontë Studies* 29, no. 1 (2004): 53–64.

Peterson, Linda H. *Traditions of Victorian Women's Autobiography: The Poetics and Politics of Life Writing.* Charlottesville: University Press of Virginia, 1999.

Picker, John M. *Victorian Soundscapes.* Oxford, UK: Oxford University Press, 2003.

Polhemus, Robert M. *Erotic Faith: Being in Love from Jane Austen to D. H. Lawrence.* Chicago: University of Chicago Press, 1990.

Pope, Marvin H. *The Anchor Bible: Song of Songs.* Garden City, NY: Doubleday, 1977.

Prettejohn, Elizabeth. "Solomon, Swinburne, Sappho." *Victorian Review* 34, no. 2 (2008): 103–28.

Prins, Yopie. *Victorian Sappho.* Princeton, NJ: Princeton University Press, 1999.

Purcell, Kathleen. "The Design of Grand Pianos." In *The House and Its Equipment,* edited by Lawrence Weaver, 61–66. London: Country Life, 1912.

Pyper, Hugh S. *The Unchained Bible: Cultural Appropriations of Biblical Texts.* London: T and T Clark, 2012.

Queen Victoria. *Album Consolativum.* British Library, Add.MS.62089.

Rager, Andrea Wolk. "'Smite This Sleeping World Awake': Edward Burne-Jones and *The Legend of the Briar Rose*." *Victorian Studies* 51, no. 3 (2009): 438–50.

Raykoff, Ivan. "Piano, Telegraph, Typewriter: Listening to the Language of Touch." In *Media, Technology, and Literature in the Nineteenth Century: Image, Sound, Touch,* edited by Colette Colligan and Margaret Linley, 159–86. Farnham: Ashgate, 2011.

Renan, Ernest. *The Song of Songs as a Drama.* Translated by Havelock Ellis. Berkeley Heights: Oriole Press, 1932.

———. *The Song of Songs Translated from the Hebrew. With a Study of the Plan, the Age, and the Character of the Poem.* Translated by William M. Thomson. London: W. M. Thomson, 1895.

Réville, Albert. *The Song of Songs, Commonly Called the Song of Solomon, or, the Canticle.* London: Williams and Norgate, 1873.

Richards, Fiona. "The Goat-God in England: A Musical Context for Lawrence's Fascination with Pan." *The D. H. Lawrence Review* 40, no. 1 (2015): 90–106.

Rimmer, Mary. "'My Scripture Manner': Reading Hardy's Biblical and Liturgical Allusion." In *Thomas Hardy Reappraised: Essays in Honour of Michael Millgate,* edited by Keith Wilson, 21–37. Toronto: University of Toronto Press, 2006.

Ripley, Jason J. "'Behold the Man'? Subverting Imperial Masculinity in the Gospel of John." *Journal of the Bible and its Reception* 2, no. 2 (2015): 219–39.

Roden, Frederick S. "Medieval Religion, Victorian Homosexualities." *Prose Studies: History, Theory, Criticism* 23, no. 2 (2000): 115–30.

———. "Michael Field, John Gray, and Marc-Andre Raffavolich: Reinventing Romantic Friendship in Modernity." In *Catholic Figures, Queer Narratives,* edited by Lowell Gallager, Frederick S. Roden, and Patricia Juliana Smith, 57–68. Houndmills: Palgrave Macmillan, 2006.

———. *Same-Sex Desire in Victorian Religious Culture.* Basingstoke: Palgrave, 2003.

———. "Sisterhood Is Powerful: Christina Rosetti's *Maude*." In *Women of Faith in Victorian Culture: Reassessing the Angel in the House,* edited by Anne Hogan and Andrew Bradstock, 63–77. London: Palgrave Macmillan, 1998.

Roe, Dinah. "Naturally Artificial: The Pre-Raphaelite Garden Enclosed." *Victorian Poetry* 57, no. 1 (2019): 131–53.

Rosenberg, John D. *Elegy for an Age: The Presence of the Past in Victorian Literature.* London: Anthem Press, 2005.

Ross, Robert H. "The Three Faces of *In Memoriam.*" In *In Memoriam: An Authoritative Text, Backgrounds and Sources of Criticism,* edited by Robert H. Ross, 93–97. New York: Norton, 1973.

Rossetti, Christina. Vol. 1 of *The Complete Poems of Christina Rossetti.* Edited by R. W. Crump. Baton Rouge: Louisiana State University Press, 1979.

———. Vol. 2 of *The Complete Poems of Christina Rossetti.* Edited by R. W. Crump. Baton Rouge: Louisiana State University Press, 1986.

Rubin, Gayle S. "Thinking Sex: Notes for a Radical Theory of the Politics of Sexuality." In *Pleasure and Danger: Exploring Female Sexuality,* edited by Carole S. Vance, 267–319. Boston: Routledge and Kegan Paul, 1984.

Rudy, Jason R. *Electric Meters: Victorian Physiological Poetics.* Athens: Ohio University Press, 2009.

Ruskin, John. *Fors Clavigera: Letters to the Workmen and Labourers of Great Britain.* Edited by E. T. Cook. London: George Allen, 1902.

Sanders, Valerie. *The Brother-Sister Culture in Nineteenth-Century Literature: From Austen to Woolf.* Houndmills: Palgrave, 2002.

Schaffer, Talia. *Romance's Rival: Familiar Marriage in Victorian Fiction.* New York: Oxford University Press, 2016.

Scholl, Lesa. *Hunger, Poetry and the Oxford Movement: The Tractarian Social Vision.* London: Bloomsbury Academic, 2020.

Seymour, Gayle M. "Simeon Solomon and the Biblical Construction of Marginal Identity in Victorian England." *Journal of Homosexuality* 33, no. 3–4 (1997): 97–119.

Shanley, Mary Lyndon. *Feminism, Marriage, and the Law in Victorian England.* Princeton, NJ: Princeton University Press, 1989.

Sherwood, Yvonne. *Biblical Blaspheming: Trials of the Sacred for a Secular Age.* Cambridge, UK: Cambridge University Press, 2012.

Skelly, Julia. "The Paradox of Excess: Oscar Wilde, Caricature, and Consumption." In *The Uses of Excess in Visual and Material Culture, 1600–2010,* edited by Julia Skelly, 137–60. Abingdon: Routledge, 2016.

Solie, Ruth A. *Music in Other Words: Victorian Conversations.* Berkeley: University of California Press, 2004.

Spurgeon, Charles Haddon. *The Devotional Classics of C. H. Spurgeon: Morning and Evening I & II.* Lafayette: Sovereign Grace Publishers, 1990.

Strauss, David Friedrich. Vol. 1 of *A New Life of Jesus.* 2nd ed. London: Williams and Norgate, 1879.

Strømmen, Hannah M. "Animal Poetics: Marianne Moore, Ted Hughes and the Song of Songs." *Literature and Theology* 31, no. 4 (2017): 405–19.

Stuart, A. Moody. *The Song of Songs: An Exposition of the Song of Solomon.* 2nd ed. London: Nisbet, 1860.

Sturgeon, Mary C. *Michael Field.* London: George G. Harrap, 1922.

Styler, Rebecca. *Literary Theology by Women Writers of the Nineteenth Century.* Farnham: Ashgate, 2010.

Sulivan, Henry. *The Song of Songs: A Sermon Preached on Sunday, 17th May, 1857.* London: Hatchards, 1857.

Surridge, Lisa. *Bleak Houses: Marital Violence in Victorian Fiction.* Athens: Ohio University Press, 2005.

Tate, Rosemary. "The Aesthetics of Sugar: Concepts of Sweetness in the Nineteenth Century." PhD diss., University of Oxford, 2010.

Tennyson, Alfred Lord. *In Memoriam: An Authoritative Text, Backgrounds and Sources of Criticism.* Edited by Robert H. Ross. New York: Norton, 1973.

Terdiman, Richard. *Discourse/Counter-Discourse: The Theory and Practice of Symbolic Resistance in Nineteenth-Century France.* Cornell University Press, 1985.

Thain, Marion. "'Damnable Aestheticism' and the Turn to Rome: John Gray, Michael Field, and a Poetics of Conversion." In *The Fin-de-Siècle Poem: English Literary Culture and the 1890s,* edited by Joseph Bristow, 311–36. Athens: Ohio University Press, 2005.

———. *'Michael Field': Poetry, Aestheticism and the Fin de Siècle.* Cambridge, UK: Cambridge University Press, 2007.

Thormählen, Marianne. *The Brontës and Religion.* Cambridge, UK: Cambridge University Press, 1999.

Tkacz, Catherine Brown "The Bible in *Jane Eyre*." *Christianity and Literature* 44 (1994): 3–27.

Tookey, Helen. "'The Fiend That Smites with a Look': The Monstrous/Menstruous Woman and the Danger of the Gaze in Oscar Wilde's *Salomé*." *Literature and Theology* 18, no. 1 (2004): 23–37.

Tosh, John. *A Man's Place: Masculinity and the Middle-Class Home in Victorian England.* New Haven, CT: Yale University Press, 1999.

Tucker, Herbert F. "Rossetti's Goblin Marketing: Sweet to Tongue and Sound to Eye." *Representations* 82, no. 1 (2003): 117–33.

Vance, Norman. "Thomas Hardy: The Church or Christianity." In *Bible and Novel: Narrative Authority and the Death of God.* Oxford, UK: Oxford University Press, 2013.

Vanita, Ruth. *Sappho and the Virgin Mary: Same-Sex Love and the English Literary Imagination.* New York: Columbia University Press, 1996.

Wallace, Lewis. "Bearded Woman, Female Christ: Gendered Transformations in the Legends and Cult of Saint Wilgefortis." *Journal of Feminist Studies in Religion* 30, no. 1 (2014): 43–63.

Wang, Lisa. "Uses of Theological Discourse in the Novels of the Brontë Sisters." PhD diss., Birkbeck College, 1998.

West, M. L. *The Orphic Poems.* Oxford, UK: Oxford University Press, 1983.

Wheeler, Michael. *Heaven, Hell, and the Victorians.* Cambridge, UK: Cambridge University Press, 1994.

———. *The Old Enemies: Catholic and Protestant in Ninteenth-Century English Culture.* Cambridge, UK: Cambridge University Press, 2006.

Wilde, Oscar. *Salomé: A Tragedy in One Act.* London: John Lane, 1907.

Wildman, Stephen, and John Christian. "The Seven 'Blissfullest Years.'" In *Edward Burne-Jones: Victorian Artist-Dreamer,* edited by Stephen Wildman and John Christian, 141–90. New York: The Metropolitan Museum of Art, 1998.

Williams, Rowland. "Bunsen's Biblical Researches." In *Essays and Reviews,* 50–93. London: John W. Parker and Son, 1860.

Willis, Ika. *Reception.* London: Routledge, 2018.

Wright, T. R. *Hardy and the Erotic.* Basingstoke: Macmillan, 1989.

INDEX

aesthetic sexuality, 107–8, 116, 117

animals, 22, 33, 81; and human nature, 33–34; sheep, 33, 34, 35, 58. *See also* shepherds; teeth; Whym Chow

anti-Catholicism, 10, 11–12, 66, 145. *See also* deviance

Aphrodite, 35, 97, 99, 124

Arts and Crafts movement, 17, 54, 56

Aurora Leigh (Barrett Browning), 15–17, 21, 33

Barrett Browning, Elizabeth, 10, 15–17, 21, 33, 55, 62, 118, 125. See also *Aurora Leigh*

Bernard of Clairvaux, 114–15

Bible, 1–2, 4–5, 6–8, 9, 13–14, 22, 23, 24–25, 26, 33, 41, 42, 49, 53, 81, 93, 95, 98–99, 120, 122, 142. *See also* Eden; rape; Song of Songs; typological interpretation; unchained Bible; violence

Birth of Venus (Botticelli), 35

bisexuality, 19, 93, 96, 99, 101, 141

bitterness, 9, 66, 85, 90, 131n63; and bitter-sweetness, 99, 100, 101

bodies, 94, 101, 108–11, 112, 115, 137–38. *See also* crucifix; hands; masculinity

Bradley, Katharine: becoming Edith's guardian, 121; becoming Edith's lover, 121; cancer, 122, 133, 134; university studies, 121. *See also* Cooper, Edith; Field, Michael; Whym Chow

Briar Rose, The (Burne-Jones), 45

Brontë, Charlotte, 25–27, 30–32; early life, 22; knowledge of Bible, 22; and pleasure in nature, 28–29; poems, 29; and religious hypocrisy, 22–23. See also *Jane Eyre*

Browning, Robert, 15, 19, 35, 121–22, 123, 124–25, 126, 127–28, 130, 131

Burne-Jones, Edward, 42, 45–48, 52–54: ambition to enter the church, 44; and Dante Gabriel Rossetti, 44; early life, 43–44; and the Song of Songs, 49–50, 51; versatility and prolific output, 44; and William Morris, 44. See also *Briar Rose, The*; *King Cophetua and the Beggar Maid*; medievalism; pianos; stained glass

Burne-Jones, Georgiana, 44, 45, 46

Catherine of Siena, 67, 78; Dominican Congregation of St., 70

celibacy, 10, 11, 12, 13, 72, 88, 104–5, 111, 112, 113, 114, 117; allowing career advancement

161

162 • INDEX

and freedom from maternity, 40; association with the Virgin Mary, 65; and creative freedoms, 64; and freedom from marriage, 65, 68; and the queer priest, 106–7; and religious manliness, 74; and religious sisterhoods, 66–70, 87. *See also* anti-Catholicism; deviance; nuns; sisterhoods; virginity

Church of England, 14, 22, 66, 69, 106, 136. *See also* Tractarianism

convents, 11, 30, 69, 72, 112–14. *See also* nuns; sisterhoods

conversion, 26, 66, 70, 75, 103, 105–6, 107, 122, 125, 129, 131, 132, 137; and decadent movement, 107; outside the charmed circle, 117; as "perversion," 11

Cooper, Edith: cancer, 122, 133, 135; and Emma Cooper, 121, 122, 123, 124–26, 127–29. *See also* Bradley, Katharine; Field, Michael; Whym Chow

counter-discourse, 6

coverture, 37–38, 46

crucifix, 19, 93, 108, 109–11, 135–36

Dante Alighieri, 55, 96

dark night of the soul, 18, 65, 77–80, 115–17

death, 9, 19–20, 30, 46, 74, 85, 100–101, 118–40, 142; ascendency of love over, 9, 108, 109; deathbed scenes, 15, 119; love is strong as (Song of Songs 8:6) or love is stronger than, 19, 36, 37, 38, 49, 89, 90, 91, 119, 121, 122, 126, 127, 128, 131, 137, 139; of spouses, 24, 28. *See also* mourning

deviance, 10–12, 94–95. *See also* anti-Catholicism; celibacy; queer

Donne, John, 118

Drane, Augusta Theodosia, 18, 64–65, 66–68, 74–75; and courtship and marriage, 72; early life, 70; and military orders, 73; poetry, 71–72, 73, 76–80. *See also* celibacy; convents; dark night of the soul; friendship; John of the Cross; masculinity; nuns

eating, 65, 68, 81n77, 82–83, 87, 89–90. *See also* bitterness; Eucharist; pornography; sex; sweetness

Eden, 50, 87, 90, 129. *See also* gardens

Ellis, Havelock, 12, 37, 122, 123, 145

Eliot, George, 3, 61, 120

Eros, 57, 58, 62–63, 124. *See also* Psyche

Eucharist, 75, 90. *See also* bitterness; eating

Far from the Madding Crowd (Hardy), 17, 23, 24, 33–37, 41

feminist theology, 9, 81, 141

Field, Michael, 55, 62, 105–6, 118, 121–40. *See also* Bradley, Katharine; conversion; Cooper, Edith; John of the Cross; Whym Chow

flame, 20, 90, 116, 122, 124–26, 129–32

flowers, 20, 29, 30, 57, 67, 72, 103, 112, 113, 123, 124, 133n72, 133–34, 135; association with paganism and Catholicism, 134; lily, 108, 133, 136–37; rose, 133, 139. *See also* fruit; gardens

friendship, 89, 96, 100, 101–4, 120, 135; "Catholic homosexual," 103, 105; in Christ, 74–75; and companionate marriage, 31, 36; of David and Jonathan "passing the love of women," 95; literary and intellectual, 55, 96–97, 105–6, 121–22; as redirection of sexual desires, 106

fruit, 50, 67–68, 70, 84–86, 87, 89–90, 135, 146; and consumption of, 65, 81–83. *See also* eating; flowers; gardens; sweetness

gardens, 83, 89–90, 96, 97, 99, 129, 136–37, 138; and *hortus conclusus* (enclosed garden) of Song of Songs 4:12, 30, 40, 49, 50, 68, 72, 98, 112–14. *See also* Eden; flowers; fruit; virginity

"Goblin Market" (Rossetti), 18, 64, 65, 81–91. *See also* fruit; pornography; sweetness

Gray, John, 19, 92, 93, 103, 105–17, 130, 131, 131n63, 132, 141; early life, 104. *See also* celibacy; Field, Michael; friendship; John of the Cross; queer; Raffalovich, Marc-André; Wilde, Oscar

hands, 19, 53–54, 59, 61, 92–96, 99, 100, 101, 102–3, 112, 116–17, 120–21, 132; and creativity, 60, 128

Hard Cash (Reade), 3

Hardy, Emma, 24, 33, 34, 35, 37, 38

Hardy, Thomas, 17, 23, 32–41; ambition to enter the church, 24; influence of higher criticism, 3–4, 23; and marriage, 21,

INDEX · 163

23–24, 37, 39; and religion, 23, 24–25. *See also* animals; *Far from the Madding Crowd*; *Jude the Obscure*; marriage

healing, 90, 132

Hellenism, 19, 93, 96–97, 102, 106

higher criticism, 3, 4–5, 37

Holy Spirit, 68, 109, 125–26, 129

In Memoriam (Tennyson), 94, 120–21. *See also* Queen Victoria

Jane Eyre (Brontë), 13, 17, 21–32, 41; number of scriptural allusions in, 26. *See also* flowers; pastoral

Jesus Christ, 18–19, 20, 43, 58, 64, 66, 68, 78, 80, 88, 89, 132; as betrothed or spouse, 25, 26, 27–28, 65, 67, 74, 75–76, 107, 112, 136, 137; body of, 90, 93, 108–12, 137; wounds of, 114, 115, 117, 133. *See also* celibacy; crucifix; dark night of the soul; friendship; marriage; sisterhoods

John of the Cross, 18, 20, 65, 76–80, 81, 93, 112, 115–17, 131, 131n63, 132. *See also* Drane, Augusta Theodosia; Field, Michael; Gray, John

Jude the Obscure (Hardy), 1–3, 5–6, 17, 21, 23–24, 32–33, 36, 37, 38–39, 41; and alternatives to marriage, 40. *See also* flowers; higher criticism; marriage; New Woman

King Cophetua and the Beggar Maid (Burne-Jones), 45–46, 49–50

Kingsley, Charles, 11, 110

kissing, 7–9, 65, 84, 89–90, 95, 98, 100, 102, 116, 124–25, 128–29, 133, 143, 145

love. *See* death; friendship; marriage; mourning; Song of Songs

marriage, 32, 74, 87, 88, 89, 100, 105, 111, 126–27, 143; companionate, 17, 21, 31, 35, 38, 41; and divorce, 38, 46–47; and equality, 31; ideal, 25, 35–36; mutual affection in, 36; and social norms, 12, 68–69; spiritual, 78, 115, 130–31, 133; unhappy, 37, 41; and women's property law, 38, 46. *See also* celibacy; Jesus Christ; rape; violence

Mary Magdalene, 12, 137, 138

masculinity, 72–73, 96; and androgyny, 102, 110; and effeminacy, 102, 104–5; feminized, 9, 81n77, 110–11; muscular Christianity, 19, 93, 110; rugged, 110. *See also* nuns

medievalism, 2, 48, 49, 55, 112, 113

Mill, J. S., 31–32, 48

Mill on the Floss (Eliot), 61

mourning, 12, 119, 130; and grief, 24, 74, 118, 119, 120, 125, 126, 129–30. *See also* death

nationalism, 10–11, 110, 119n8

New Woman, 39, 40

Newman, John Henry, 11–12, 44, 50, 66, 74, 75, 76

nudity, 57, 101, 102, 146

nuns, 12, 67–68, 88, 106, 112–14; and loneliness of religious life, 74; as lovers and spouses of Christ, 72, 74, 75, 78; and manliness, 72, 74; as warrior nuns, 18, 72–73; working, 65, 69, 71. *See also* celibacy; convents; friendship; Jesus Christ; marriage; virginity

Oliphant, Margaret, 38

pain, 19, 20, 24, 30, 39, 70, 71, 85, 93, 109, 111, 115–16, 117, 129–30, 132n67, 132–33, 134, 139. *See also* aesthetic sexuality; queer; violence

Pan, 18, 43, 57, 62–63

pastoral, 22, 30, 33–37, 39, 62, 73, 77n61. *See also* shepherds

Pater, Walter, 35, 55, 96, 122, 124, 145

patriarchal power, 7, 54

Pearl, The (anonymous), 18, 82, 85–86

pianos, 17–18, 43, 44, 46, 56–63

poetry: ekphrastic, 93, 105, 108–9, 117; waṣf, 19, 93, 108–9, 117, 144

pornography, 18, 65–66, 82, 85–86, 145–46. See also *Pearl, The*

Pride and Prejudice (Austen), 36

priests, 19, 93, 101, 104, 106–7, 110, 137. *See also* celibacy; marriage; Roman Catholicism; virginity

Psyche, 18, 57, 58, 62–63. *See also* Eros

164 · INDEX

Queen Victoria, 119–20, 121

queer, 7–9, 19, 92–112, 115–17, 121, 123–24, 130–31, 132–33, 135, 139, 141; inverts, 106, 107, 111, 112; martyrdom, 111, 115; outside the charmed circle, 117. *See also* friendship; hands; kissing

queer theology, 6, 7, 9n45, 141

Raffalovich, Marc-André, 103, 104, 105–6, 107, 111–12, 115–16. *See also* celibacy; friendship; Gray, John; queer

rape, 47–48, 51, 53, 54; rape culture, 17, 53. *See also* violence

reception, 2, 4–5, 7–10, 19, 24, 112, 119, 139, 142. *See also* Bible; feminist theology; higher criticism; queer theology; Song of Songs; typological interpretation

religion, 13, 113; association of love with, 23, 120; constructed by scholarly inquiry, 141; and construction of Victorian homosexual identity, 111; and the crucifixion, 10; feminist depictions of, 31, 81; literature as means for women to contribute to, 15; and role of poetry, 15; as vital part of Victorian culture, 14. *See also* Bible; Church of England; Roman Catholicism; Tractarianism

respectability, 10–12

Roman Catholicism, 4, 14, 112; and decadent movement, 93, 107–8, 110; and First Vatican Council, 66; foreign status and marginalization of, 11, 107; nineteenth-century revival, 66; and reestablishment of the Catholic hierarchy, 66; and religious relics, 137–38; and Roman Catholic Relief Act 1829, 66. *See also* anti-Catholicism; celibacy; flowers; nuns; priests; religion

romance, 12, 16, 126; ideals of, 23, 25, 35–36. *See also* marriage

Rossetti, Christina, 7, 18, 64–66, 80–91, 126, 145. *See also* celibacy; "Goblin Market"; sisterhoods; virginity

Rossetti, Dante Gabriel, 44, 49, 55, 57

Ruskin, John, 28, 35, 44, 48–49, 54–55, 56, 122

Salomé (Wilde), 8–9

Sappho, 19, 92–93, 95, 96–99, 123–24, 139

sex, 6, 7, 10, 11, 12, 25, 36, 43, 62, 76, 81n77, 82, 87, 103, 106, 111, 124. *See also* marriage; pornography

shepherds, 33, 34–35, 57, 58, 59, 62. *See also* animals; pastoral; Shulamite

Shulamite, 36, 40, 42, 49, 50–51, 57–59, 61–62, 75, 88, 99, 145, 146. *See also* rape; shepherds; stained glass; Song of Songs; violence

sisterhoods, 18, 64, 83, 91; and domestic settings, 65, 87–91; and religious communities, 10, 12, 65–69. *See also* convents; nuns

Solomon, Simeon, 19, 92–93, 95–103, 104, 106, 109–10, 117, 144. *See also* hands; Hellenism; queer

Song of Songs, 6–8, 12–13, 15–20, 142–46; and allegorical interpretation, 2–3, 4–5, 9n45, 40, 48, 57–58, 145; as "the chief stench in the Bible," 5; female speaker, 21; and magnetic attraction, 61; queerness of, in the biblical canon, 8; relation to Ephesians, 26–27, 28; relation to Genesis, 26, 27–28, 50, 128–29; relation to Revelation, 26–28, 30, 68, 108. *See also* Bible; death; Eden; feminist theology; flowers; fruit; gardens; higher criticism; pastoral; queer; queer theology; reception; shepherds; Shulamite; teeth; typological interpretation; unchained Bible; Virgin Mary

stained glass, 17, 42, 43, 44, 47, 51–54

Strauss, David Friedrich, 3, 5–6

sweetness, 18, 65–66, 67, 71, 73, 76, 79, 81–83, 84–86, 90; and sugar, 82. *See also* eating; fruit; pornography

Swinburne, Algernon Charles, 82, 85, 96–97, 98, 116, 146

teeth, 33, 81n77; "are like a flock of sheep" (Song of Songs 4:2), 33, 35

Tractarianism, 4, 44, 49, 51, 64, 65, 66, 68–69, 70, 74, 87, 105, 111, 134; and reserve, 64. *See also* celibacy; convents; Church of England

Traquair, Phoebe Anna, 17–18, 43, 54–63, 143; early life, 55; reputation, 55–56. *See also* Arts and Crafts movement; Ruskin, John

typological interpretation, 2–3, 4, 26–28, 32, 50, 88, 90

unchained Bible, 2, 6–7. *See also* Bible

Victorian studies: privileging poetry of religious doubt, 13–14; secularization of, 13

violence, 17, 42, 44, 53, 54, 115–16, 117; biblical, 50–51, 53; marital, 42–43, 46–48, 52, 54; and physiognomy, 52; against the Shulamite, 41, 51–53. *See also* aesthetic sexuality; pain; rape; stained glass

Virgin Mary, 12, 50, 138; associated with nuns and the Song of Songs, 112; devotion to, as hallmark of fin de siècle Catholicism, 113; as figure of dispute between Catholics and Protestants, 67; and the Immaculate Conception, 66–67; as Madonna, 35, 67; and Tractarians, 66. *See also* anti-Catholicism; flowers; gardens; Roman Catholicism; virginity

virginity, 18, 40, 50, 67, 71–72, 87, 88, 91, 111, 112, 114. *See also* celibacy; deviance; gardens; sisterhoods; Virgin Mary

Whym Chow, 20, 122, 125, 127, 128, 129–32, 137, 139. *See also* Field, Michael; flame; mourning

Wilde, Oscar, 7–8. See also *Salomé*

LITERATURE, RELIGION, AND POSTSECULAR STUDIES
LORI BRANCH, SERIES EDITOR

Literature, Religion, and Postsecular Studies publishes scholarship on the influence of religion on literature and of literature on religion from the sixteenth century onward. Books in the series include studies of religious rhetoric or allegory; of the secularization of religion, ritual, and religious life; and of the emerging identity of postsecular studies and literary criticism.

Sex, Celibacy, and Deviance: The Victorians and the Song of Songs
Duc Dau

American Exceptionalism as Religion: Postmodern Discontent
Jordan Carson

Missionary Cosmopolitanism in Nineteenth-Century British Literature
Winter Jade Werner

Constructing Nineteenth-Century Religion: Literary, Historical, and Religious Studies in Dialogue
Edited by Joshua King and Winter Jade Werner

Good Words: Evangelicalism and the Victorian Novel
Mark Knight

Enlightened Individualism: Buddhism and Hinduism in American Literature from the Beats to the Present
Kyle Garton-Gundling

A Theology of Sense: John Updike, Embodiment, and Late Twentieth-Century American Literature
Scott Dill

Walker Percy, Fyodor Dostoevsky, and the Search for Influence
Jessica Hooten Wilson

The Religion of Empire: Political Theology in Blake's Prophetic Symbolism
G. A. Rosso

Clashing Convictions: Science and Religion in American Fiction
Albert H. Tricomi

Female Piety and the Invention of American Puritanism
Bryce Traister

Secular Scriptures: Modern Theological Poetics in the Wake of Dante
William Franke

Imagined Spiritual Communities in Britain's Age of Print
Joshua King

Conspicuous Bodies: Provincial Belief and the Making of Joyce and Rushdie
Jean Kane

Victorian Sacrifice: Ethics and Economics in Mid-Century Novels
Ilana M. Blumberg

Lake Methodism: Polite Literature and Popular Religion in England, 1780–1830
Jasper Cragwall

Hard Sayings: The Rhetoric of Christian Orthodoxy in Late Modern Fiction
THOMAS F. HADDOX

Preaching and the Rise of the American Novel
DAWN COLEMAN

Victorian Women Writers, Radical Grandmothers, and the Gendering of God
GAIL TURLEY HOUSTON

Apocalypse South: Judgment, Cataclysm, and Resistance in the Regional Imaginary
ANTHONY DYER HOEFER